Now Tigers!

The Early Years of Hull City
by Nicholas Turner

Introduction

Writing his account of the origins of Hull City a few years after its genesis, Ernest Morison – one of the original promoters of the club and owner of a successful advertising agency – subtitled the piece 'A romance of daring, pluck and luck'.

There was perhaps no one better placed to recount the story. Morison, a confident, energetic and accomplished publisher of local leisure periodicals, was also a long time sports enthusiast and active director of the club. Not only had he been privy to details of the earliest events in the club's story, but he also had a vested interest in publicising them in the most positive light possible. His account, featured in this book, must be considered the definitive version of the events leading to the club's formation and admission to the second division of the Football League (or the Second League as it was often known then) just over a year later.

The club's birth was seemingly inevitable, as football swept through the land capturing the imagination in towns and cities in the late Victorian era and into the Edwardian period. West and East Yorkshire were comparatively late starters in the round ball game as rugby held sway in the county, but aided by sympathetic assistance from the Football League, football took hold in the region's cities.

The club soon established a place for itself in the sporting landscape in the city – and experienced for itself the latent resistance from the vested interests of the Northern Union, as rugby league was known at that time. Despite a three-year tenancy agreement at Hull FC's Boulevard ground, the agreement started to fray after barely six months, and the club acted promptly to find alternative accommodation.

Unfortunately almost none of these dramatic and momentous early events were captured by photographers or bioscope operators, and only the words of journalists in their contemporary accounts chronicle the story. However, two men emerged from the dozens of local photographers to capture the images of the early years of the club, its players and its supporters – Robert 'Bob' Watson and then William 'Billy' Duncan. Both were in business near the city's Paragon railway station, and living very close to the Boulevard and the Anlaby Road grounds where the Tigers played their earliest games. The energetic activities of these two men have ensured that a rich visual archive exists, albeit scattered worldwide in the form of photographic postcards depicting packed terraces, optimistic team groups and individual players. It seems unlikely that the total number of Hull City-related photographs taken by Billy Duncan will ever be known – but it seems not unreasonable to calculate that the figure would be in excess of a thousand.

The vast majority of postcard images in this book were published by Duncan from his studio shop at 15 Anlaby Road, from where on match-days he would have observed the large crowds travelling down to the ground by the 'A' tram or walking from the station. The club's Grosvenor Hotel headquarters were a short walk in the other direction in Carr Lane. Duncan came to be appointed as the club's official photographer, advertising the fact in the club's match-day programme (edited and published, of course, by Ernest Morison's advertising agency).

Duncan's annual team group images provide the best photographic record of the Hull City players of the early twentieth century – some of whom only feature for one year – and that image is almost certainly the only visual evidence of their time with the club. Other players were already established locally and enjoyed a national reputation, but were still photographed in his Anlaby Road studio in their black and amber striped shirts, along with hopeful young players and lesser lights. Duncan himself would have been known to the club's directors who sometimes appeared on his team photographs. Most were not unlike Duncan himself – local businessmen, from a variety of trades and professions. These directors brought their capital, their influence, their enthusiasm and their skills into the service of the club. Inevitably in an era of rigid social hierarchy, some of the original founders of the club, whose enthusiasm outweighed their wealth or social status, found themselves slowly but surely ousted from the heart of the club and its management.

If the club appeared at times to possess a solid middle class aspect, with its cricket club connections and well-to-do senior directors, most of its support came from local city-dwellers who made their way to Anlaby Road after a Saturday morning spent in offices, factories, shops or schools. These are the people depicted in the crowd-scene postcards that Billy Duncan took and then quickly sold from his shop.

If Duncan provided the images, the local press chronicled not just the goals and the victories, but also the songs, the trips, the grievances, the catch phrases, the nicknames, the quirky minutiae, the poems and the enthusiasm of the early supporters of the club. Cartoonists plied their trade immortalising the notable players and portraying events that photographers could not – and journalists dare not. In the years before moving images and recorded sound, this rich mixture of written word, cartoon and photograph was absorbed by supporters to reinforce their preferences or, in some cases, prejudices.

The founders of the club gave themselves the target of establishing 'class football' in Hull. They achieved that in little over a year, and the next goal became promotion to the First League – a prospect that seemed invitingly within reach, yet proved out of the club's grasp.

Both supporters and directors would have been aware of the success of other Yorkshire clubs in getting promotion and winning the FA Cup (or 'English Cup' as it was more usually known), which would only have increased their exasperation and frustration that the club could continually unearth rich talent, yet fall at the last hurdle. Despite this disappointment, the continued healthy final league positions and the stirring Cup ties ensured that optimism continued to rise each September at Anlaby Road as Billy Duncan produced his annual team photograph.

The growing awareness of the scale and nature of the conflict in France and Flanders in late 1914 displaced most non-essential peace-time concerns and activities of national life, but the directors ensured that the club and its supporters would be more than ready to resume their quest when the hostilities had ceased.

© Nicholas Turner • Hull • September 2012

Frontispiece • An expectant Tigers crowd photographed by local photographer William 'Billy' Duncan.

This page • Another early Duncan photograph.

Page 3 • Billy McDonald.

Back cover • Jack Houghton.

ISBN 978-0-9568385-3-7

Typesetting, design and publishing by Paul Gibson at
www.paul-gibson.com
Printed by Dolman Scott Books
www.dolman-scott.com

1904 – 05

On the 24th June 1904, the Hull Daily Mail carried a report, tucked away among other accounts of topical local events, of the previous evening's AGM of the East Riding of Yorkshire Football Association. This genial midsummer event was held at the Manchester Hotel in George Street, Hull, and one topic in particular at the gathering was deemed worthy of prominence in the reporting of the article, which was headed:

"ASSOCIATION GAME
Annual meeting of E.R.Y.F.A.
The Hopes of a Second League Team

A most gratifying announcement was made by the East Riding of Yorkshire Football Association at the annual general meeting held in the Manchester Hotel, Hull, last evening. It was in connection with the running of better class 'Soccer' and went far to justify an assertion made during the winter that the probabilities pointed to there being a 'class' team in the city before the end of next season. In local 'Soccer' circles Mr Spring is recognised as one who knows the requirements of the district and his statement that the Association had never been nearer in their lives to having a first class team may be taken as significant. Certain gentlemen, whose names he did not consider polite to mention, had been in communication with the Association with the result that practically in a few minutes £600 or £700 was subscribed. Certain difficulties, however, cropped up, and the matter had been dropped, but only for the time being. The gentlemen concerned, added the president, were quite convinced that the time had arrived when Hull should have a good team and he did not think they would have to wait long. They had thought of running a Midland League team, but had come to the conclusion that the public of Hull would be satisfied with nothing short of a first-class eleven. From £2,500 to £3,000 was the amount estimated as necessary and he believed gentlemen would be forthcoming, willing to take the scheme in hand and carry it through towards the back end of the season.

A new rule was subsequently carried, that the rules of the Football Association Ltd, and the laws of the game be embedded in the rules of the local Association, and clubs, officials, players, and spectators should be deemed to have knowledge of them. Mr. Spring explained that this was essential if they had to deal with professional players.

One great difficulty in the way is that of procuring a ground, for the Association's experience of the enclosure at Dairycoates has not been a very favourable one, and it is not deemed suitable as the headquarters of a 'class' team. At the same time, the writer has been assured by two prominent officials of the Association that there is a good prospect of the project coming off, and that the aim is to have a second division team. At all events a good many promises of support have been received towards this end. Another item that was not on the agenda, and which came as a genuine surprise to the president, was the presentation to Mr Spring of a gold inscribed medal bearing the City arms in enamel. Unconscious of the reason, he, in fact, suggested to Mr Bielby (the treasurer), when he asked to be allowed to interrupt the business for a few moments, that he would be out of order. The recognition came from the members of the Council, and Mr. J. F. Haller (the honorary secretary), in handing the medal over, described it as the most pleasant task in his football experience.

All, he remarked, must realise what Mr. Spring had done in promoting Association Football in Hull, for he had been connected with the ruling body since its inception. The present position of the Association was due to the tact and energy shown by the president, which had spurred other members of the Council to do their share of the work. What the players think of him is best illustrated by a conversation Mr Haller overheard between two budding footballers. Said one: 'Well, you will have to go before Spring, and he'll slate you but he'll do it like a gentleman' – laughter and applause – Mr Spring who was completely taken by surprise, replied that he only held office by virtue of an accident, and what he had said or done was at the instigation of the council."

As late as 8th August the club were still uncertain where they would be playing their home games, and the search for a suitable venue had been a difficult one. The promoters of the club (as the local press referred to them) sought somewhere fairly central and convenient, and had been negotiating for some time for the venue of their choice.

Received opinion on the success of the new venture was that a winning team was crucial and that local tastes of 'soccer' supporters favoured a "light brigade with a few tricky players."

The extent of the lack of knowledge of the local sporting public was reflected in the fact that it was deemed a good idea to include the chief points of the game on the back of any programme showing the teams, as newly-elected Bradford had done the year before. "The innovation has proved most instructive to spectators who made a first acquaintance with the game."

An unattributed article in the Hull Daily Mail declared that:

"From the first the promoters have recognised that their only hope lay in securing the Boulevard ground, and in arranging their fixtures so as not to clash with those of the Hull Rugbyites. Not that they despised the opposition of the Rovers, but the possession of such a fine ground and good stand accommodation is a great factor towards success."

The same article also noted that:

"... the Rugby and Soccer sections are interested in the deal. Many of the former are doubtful as to the advisability of fostering what may become a serious rival. There is plenty of logic in their arguments which, however, are not quite sound. Whilst admitting that the Boulevard is a great help to the success of the new scheme, I do not think it was absolutely necessary. Another season when the new club enters the Second Division of the League, they will undoubtedly prove strong opponents to Rugby and the Hull Rugby Club have taken care that they are not the club to suffer from the opposition, however much Kingston Rovers may be damaged."

WHAT WE MAY EXPECT.

ASSOCIATION FINDING A WAY TO DRAW THE £ s. d. OF PUBLIC SUPPORT.

The financial implications for the city's rugby teams – particularly Hull – were a favourite topic of cartoonists.

A newspaper article a few weeks later revealed details of the players who had been recruited to represent the new team:

"The last two that have been signed on are Leiper, a well known full back from Motherwell, a Scottish League team like St. Mirren, from whence comes 'Jimmie' Whitehouse, the one-time Grimsby idol. The other acquisition is Martin, of Millwall. The team up to the present is composed of:-
Whitehouse, of St.Mirren, who will be in goal
Leiper, of Motherwell, a full back
Jones, of Belfast Celtic, a left full back
Raisbeck, brother of the International of Liverpool, who will be seen at centre half
Geordie Spence, Southampton inside right forward
Wilkinson, Manchester United, outside right forward
Peter Howe, Reading, centre forward
Martin, Millwall, right half
Scott, Newcastle, left half.

All these men have signed on to play right through the season, and we are informed that there is no possibility of the Hull City Club losing them. The question of paying transfer fees will, of course, arise when the matter of entering a League comes up at the end of next season."

WILL IT COME TO THIS?

Master Association may take up premier place in the Hull bed, and Hull and Rovers must "move up." Holbeck was "converted" to "Soccer" last night, and the Leeds City A.F.C. established. Bradford, Leeds, and Hull, all Rugby "strongholds," have now Association "Class" teams.

A prospectus was issued by the Hull City Association Football Club Company. In it the capital of the club was revealed as £2,000, divided into 4,000 shares of 10 shillings each, it noted the shares were:

"... payable as follows:- 2s 6d per share on application, 2s 6d per share on allotment, and the remaining 5s per share as and when the directors may determine, but with not less than one month's notice."

The prospectus contained the following statement:

"Unquestionably, 'Association' football is the game of the present and of the future. It is rapidly gaining in popular favour by leaps and bounds – even in localities which in the past have been regarded as Rugby strongholds.

Arrangements have been entered into with the Hull (Rugby) Football Club, Limited, for the use of their well-known ground, 'The Boulevard,' on alternate Saturdays and for any mid-week or holiday occasion when they have no match, and accordingly this company has already fixed up twenty-three matches to be played on the 'Boulevard' during the approaching season. The ground has been taken for a period of three years on terms which the directors consider very advantageous to the company."

The Boulevard stadium was Hull's most developed sporting venue. In their prospectus in late 1889, The Hull Athletic Ground Company had outlined their plans to create a venue for sporting activity in the city. This had in part been precipitated because the cycling and running track in the Botanic Gardens would no longer be available for use, as had previously been the case. The perceived gap in the city's facilities when compared to similarly sized towns and cities, and Victorian entrepreneurial zeal may also have played a part in speeding up the process of constructing a suitable sports ground.

"The opinion has for some considerable time been expressed that Hull and the immediate neighbourhood fails signally in its accommodation and provision of a suitable ground for Athletic Recreation, where sports and Out-door Entertainments generally can be advantageously pursued. Having this opinion in view, the Directors have conceived the idea of forming this Company with the object of attracting to one large recreation ground the whole of the Athletic population of the town and neighbourhood, whether attached to clubs or unattached, where Football, Cricket, Cycling, Tennis, and other games can be enjoyed. The Directors will spare no endeavours to make the proposed ground as perfect as possible, and on a par with any Recreation and Sports ground in the United Kingdom."

A sports ground was planned in which a central grass playing area (width 81 yards) was surrounded by an oval track (width 20 feet). The maximum length of the grass oval was 200 yards. On the western side of the ground a small spectating stand which only ran for a fraction of the length of the side of the track was positioned to the northern half. This side of the ground was the site of what became known as the Threepenny Stand. Over on the eastern side of the track there were two similar stands, one located to the north and one to the south. The changing rooms were positioned at the most northerly point of the curve at the Airlie Street end of the ground. The main entrance for the public was via Airlie Street. The prospectus gave further details of the proposed venue:

"The track will measure about 3 ½ laps to the mile.
There will be a straight run of 130 yards.
There will be a cinder track and also a grass track, the one alongside the other for cycling and foot racing.
The Grand Stands will be well and substantially built, affording spectators comfort and freedom from wind and rain.
The Dressing Rooms will be comfortable and complete; suitable baths, and other requirements for Athletes will be supplied.
Attention will also be paid to the erection of Refreshment Rooms and licences when necessary, will be applied for.
It is also proposed to erect a Band Stand."

The promoters of the scheme were Edward Robson, Sheriff of Hull; Frederick Blackburn, captain of Hull Tricycle Club; R. Simpson of Coltman Street; George Shaw, captain of Hull Bicycle Club; James Simpson, Hull Tricycle Club; Archibald Campbell, vice president Hull Grosvenor Cycle Club; James Jesse Fowler of the Hull Athletic Club; George Scaum of the Hull Athletic Club, and Charles Merrikin of the Hull Harriers.

On August 24th, the Hull Daily Mail carried a small article in which it stated that "The Hull City team, we are informed, have decided to play in black and amber vertically striped shirts." It also advised that any local player wishing to train with the team, or to practise, could get the necessary permission by applying at 29 Washington Street or 11 Brook Street. These were the homes of Ben Crompton and Fred Levitt respectively. Crompton worked as a secretary and Levitt was a furnisher and decorator. Both were active players associated with the founding of the club but whose involvement with City was not destined to be long-term, and their names soon cease to appear in reports of club events. Crompton had played for Hull Comet from 1899 until 1901. His colleague Fred Levitt had kept goal in the same team, as well as its successors Hull Association FC (1901-02) and a prototype Hull City (1902-03).

The first game – a hastily-arranged practice match – was played on Thursday 29th August at the Boulevard, as City played a local representative District team. City's team consisted of Pearce in goal, fullbacks Wilkinson and Alston, half-backs Wolfe, Raisbeck and Martin, with the forwards comprising Wilkinson, Rushton, Howe, Spence and Burke. This was the publicised line-up, although goalkeeper Whitehouse along with full-backs Leiper (who arrived just as the game was ending) and Jones "at the time of commencing, had failed to put in an appearance." As a result, the defence was somewhat makeshift and goalkeeper Pearce, of a side referred to as 'C.H.G. Old Boys', took Whitehouse's place behind full-backs Wilkinson of Nelson and Alston from Lincoln.

By kick-off well over 1,000 curious spectators many of them Rugby followers had made their way into the Boulevard Stadium. This augured well for the first game proper the following Thursday – at short notice a game had been arranged for a team with no support, and the public had turned out in good numbers. Pearce excelled in goal, saving a stinging penalty from one of the founders of Hull City, Mark Andrews of the District side (which also included fellow Association pioneers Ben Frost and William Hay). City went ahead very early in the game through speedy winger (Henry) Wilkinson, and then four more goals were added for the City XI after the interval (Howe (2), Wolfe and Spence) as their superior fitness and technique prevailed. This encouraging start by the players would have boosted their morale as they went about their daily practice on the Boulevard in preparation for the challenges ahead. The modest threat posed by the District XI would soon be eclipsed by a variety of experienced League teams.

City's directors had already contacted most of the leading clubs about the possibility of playing matches, ideally at the Boulevard. The requests were reportedly well received and undertook to give the fledgling club every assistance. The full first team rather than the reserve XI was promised by a number of clubs in response to the Tigers' request, Aston Villa being specifically mentioned. It was envisaged that there would be "a match on most Saturdays, as well as on several Thursday afternoons and two attractive holiday engagements are Newcastle (during Hull Fair week) and Middlesbrough on Good Friday."

The enthusiastic idealism of the founders transmitted itself to some local journalists who were happy to carry uncritically these lively plans and ambitious programmes. This favourable and evangelistic reporting continued up to the opening game at the Boulevard against Notts County on 1st September. The game was played at 5pm to maximise the crowd numbers and enable workers to attend without taking time off. The Lord Mayor, Alderman Jarman, had been prevailed upon to kick off – a sign that the new club had influence within the city and understood the value of publicity.

All those involved with the club must have been anxious to see how large a crowd turned up at the Victorian stadium so as to try to gauge the popularity of this new sporting enterprise, in which they had invested considerable amounts of hard work and money. Curious rugby fans with season tickets gained admission free of charge and some may have come to scorn, but others may have become converts or sympathisers to the new game. On the eve of the match the Hull area had incessant rain, which must have worried the directors as they contemplated the fixture next day. Although rain threatened menacingly in the morning, the skies remained clear in the afternoon to boost the gate.

At the start of the game it was estimated that some 4,000 people were on the Boulevard to see the kick-off. Both teams had received a cordial welcome as they took the field, as did the Mayor, who having kicked-off, lingered in midfield before a friendly call brought him off the field to safety. Some Rugby fans were assisted by prominent notices around the ground explaining the important rules, and programmes containing the points of the game were also given away.

Gate receipts were some £80 which did not include the Rugby pass-holders, and the Boulevard grandstand alone took over £25 – this was deemed a very encouraging success. The timing of the game meant that some spectators arrived after the start and this steady trickle of fans took the total attendance to some 6,000. City fielded an XI which contained many of the players who would form the backbone of their team for the following season. In goal Whitehouse, full-backs were Leiper and Jones, half-backs Wolfe, Raisbeck, and Martin, forwards Wilkinson, Rushton, Howe, Spence and McKiernan. George Rushton had the honour of scoring the first ever goal for Hull City as he put them in the lead early in the first half "amidst tremendous applause." Rushton scored a second after the break before the City team were pegged back by a penalty goal midway through the second half – the visitors equalising at the very end of the game.

The outcome was satisfactory for all concerned – an eventful scoring draw, no losers and a healthy crowd went home thoroughly entertained. Just as importantly for the City directors, their hopes of a favourable reaction from Hull's sporting public had been fulfilled. It was not quite a triumph but it was good enough to encourage all involved that there was a future for their new club. The Hull Daily Mail's 'Athleo' concluded his review of the game with an account of a brief conversation he had had with a "Notts official" after the game, as the visitors prepared to rush back to Paragon Station to catch the eight o' clock train back to Nottingham.

"I waited till the rubbing down process was over and approached one of the Notts officials who had travelled down with the team. 'What do you think of our new City team?' I asked

Local photographer Robert Thomas Watson captured that first Hull City team, and a group of the men who had helped create the club. The photograph is taken outside the changing room at the Boulevard shortly before kick-off. Aside from capturing a historic occasion in its history, it is probably the first ever photograph of the club and one that features several of the younger founders, whose association with the club was not destined to last in any recognised capacity. Pictured in this historic image were Ben Frost, Ernest Morison, Alf Spring, Bill Leach, Fred Levitt, Joe Leiper, Jack Bielby, Jimmy Whitehouse, James Ramster, Alderman W. Jarman JP (mayor), William Gilyott (chairman), Tom Jones, James Barraclough, Billy Martin, Marcus Andrews, E. Rodgerson (mayor's beadle). Middle row: Dr George W. Lilley (vice chairman), Frank Wolfe, George Rushton, George Spence, Peter Howe, McKiernan, Ben Crompton. Front row: Andy Raisbeck, Henry Wilkinson. Some of the original founders are missing from this group, but 11 out of the original 16 are present – the absentees being Messrs Emmerson, Hay, Hobbs, Shaw and Wrightson.

Full-back Tom Jones

Forward Peter Howe

Goal-keeper Jimmy Whitehouse

Full-back Harry Davies

'Good! Very good!' he replied.

'Are there any improvements required in the XI, that is so far as you can judge?'

'No, not really,' he said; 'but you will require some good reserves in the back division in case of accidents.'

'Is this really a representative Notts County team?' I ventured to ask.

'Most decidedly,' he said emphatically. 'The team you have seen play to-day with the exception of Iremonger will meet Everton on Saturday and Sunderland on Monday; so if we happen to come out on the right side you can congratulate your City XI.'

'Do you think the Association game should take in this city?'

'Rather!' he replied; 'look at the enthusiastic crowd, and the attendance for an evening match. Oh yes! The prospects look bright.'

'What do you think to …' but he was off. I would have liked a few more words with him, but his train time was near at hand."

The club was up and running.

On September 17th another notable first was achieved as the club played its first game in the English Cup (or the FA Cup, as it would become more commonly known) against Stockton – their first ever away fixture. The game was in fact a preliminary qualifying round and City ceded ground advantage to their Teesside opponents because of Hull FC's need of the Boulevard on that day. It was reported that:

"… Hull City set off on the 8.35 train this morning … Trainer Leach had the team in perfect trim, and they entered the special saloon amid many expressions of good luck. A number of the officials and

City supporters who had a keen desire to see the 'mill' accompanied the team, the train being due to run into Stockton about 12 o'clock. The men consequently had plenty of time to pull themselves together, after the shaking up of the railway journey before the match (which was not timed to commence before four o'clock) on the Victoria ground in Mill-lane.

A number of Hull excursionists for Darlington travelled by the same train as far as York, from whence they went on to Darlington. Here, by taking advantage of the local service of trains – Darlington and Stockton being near neighbours – they were able to see the game, and many left Hull with the idea of getting to their destination by this in and out, but inexpensive way."

The game was drawn and the replay was also played in Stockton, this time the Tigers being eliminated. This brief presence was enough to capture the imagination of the city's more adventurous and enthusiastic football followers, and the report of their travelling in support of the new club heralded a new local trend which was to take root in the coming years. The games then began to come thick and fast as the promoters – as they were frequently referred to in the local press – sought to build up a following for the game in Hull and persuade local sports enthusiasts to pay their money into the club's coffers. Gates were not large at first – sometimes under 5,000 – but superior quality opponents with respectable credentials would draw the crowds. Everton 'A' and Derby County drew 6,000 and 6,500 respectively. Middlesbrough Reserves and Burton United could both only pull in 2,000 to the Boulevard. This in spite of local press encouragement such as:

"... the (Burton) fixture should prove a most attractive one.
The City officials want me to point out that the whole of the west side (including stand) will be thrown open for sixpence. The kick-off is at three o'clock and Thursday men should rally round like Britons – No, we are not downhearted!"

ILLUSTRATED HULL.

A Football Cartoon by our Football Artist.

Hull City at Home – A very early collection of caricatures drawn by R.W. Lawson. Clockwise from top: Henry Wilkinson, Marcus Andrews, Tom Jones, Bill Leach, George Spence, George Rushton and Jimmy Whitehouse.

Some of the opposition invited to Hull were not renowned names and served to fill the gaps when more attractive opposition could not be found.
The games against league clubs and their reserve sides seemed to thin out around springtime.
In this category teams such as Wellingborough (gate 2,500), the Army Service Corps gate 2,000), the Coldstream Guards (gate 4,000) and Scarborough (gate only 400) could be found. This last game was played at Dairycoates as the club was forced to utilise a venue far from the city centre. The intermittent availability of the Boulevard, then the counter attraction of Hull Kingston Rovers' home games and the difficulty of arranging suitable opposition on the most convenient dates, combined to make the fixture list appear chaotic and haphazard. Leeds City were played (and beaten) three times, and the Military in the form of the Prince of Wales Hussars and the York Garrison occasionally stepped in to fill vacant dates in the calendar. Of a total of 44 friendlies, some 30 were played in Hull, often making use of the Boulevard on Thursday afternoons to tempt the workers who only worked a half day. The bigger names attracted the larger crowds while the smaller ones kept the players ticking over and provided a steady trickle of revenue.

The hitherto latent conflict with the handling code, occasionally alluded to in the local press and usually avoided by the directors of the clubs, was starting to develop into something more tangible. The rivalry between sports came to a head on December 10th – the day City had arranged a friendly game against Glossop at the Boulevard.

HULL CITY ASSOCIATION FOOTBALL CLUB.

Below we give the fixtures arranged:—
1904.

Sept. 1.—Notts County	....	home
Sept. 3.—		away
Sept. 5.—Blackburn Rovers	....	home
Sept. 10.—Everton (Combination)	....	home
Sept. 17.—English Cup Preliminary Round	....	
Sept. 19.—Leicester Fosse	....	home
Sept. 24.—Darlington	....	home
Oct. 1.—English Cup Qualifying Round.	....	
Oct. 8.—Sheffield	....	home
Oct. 12.—Middlesbrough Res.	....	home
Oct. 13.—Derby County	....	home
Oct. 15.—English Cup 2nd Qualifying Round	....	
Oct. 20.—Lincoln City	....	home
Oct. 22.—		away
Oct. 29.—English Cup 3rd Qualifying Round	....	
Nov. 5.—		away
Nov. 12.—Bradford City	....	home
Nov. 17.—Burslem Port Vale	....	home
Nov. 19.—		away
Nov. 26.—Grimsby Town	....	home
Dec. 3.—		away
Dec. 10.—Glossop	....	home
Dec. 17.—		away
Dec. 22.—Wellingborough	....	home
Dec. 24.—		home
Dec. 31.—Middlesbrough Reserves	....	away
1905.		
Jan. 2.—Stockton	....	home
Jan. 3.—Darlington	....	away
Jan. 7.—Scarborough	....	away
Jan. 14.—Barnsley	....	home
Jan. 28.—Chesterfield Town	....	home
Feb. 4.—Doncaster Rovers	....	home
Feb. 18.—Luton	....	home
Feb. 25.—Sheffield	....	away
Mar. 4.—Darlington St Aug.	....	home
Mar. 18.—Scarborough	....	home
April 8.—Barnsley	....	home
April 15.—Sheffield United Res.	....	home
April 21.—Grimsby Town (Good Friday)	...	away
April 24.—Liverpool (Easter Monday)	......	home
April 29.—Gainsborough Trinity	....	home

Negotiations are in progress with Aston Villa, Manchester United, Newcastle United, West Bromwich Albion, and other class clubs.

City's first fixture list – incomplete and a constant work in progress in 1904/5.

The directors would have expected a healthy attendance for this game, having the city to themselves, but events elsewhere had conspired to test the resolve of the newly formed outfit and its supporters.

Hull Kingston Rovers, before City's formation, had become used to alternating with Hull FC for the custom of the sporting public. If hard-core fans of either club would not watch their rivals, floating spectators would. Rovers quickly began to feel short-changed by Hull's agreement with City which pitted the football club against them for every home game. This was in effect indirect economic aggression. Rovers' grievance was with Hull, whom they saw as having broken an unwritten agreement.

Rovers sought the opinions of their sporting legislators, the Northern Union, who were acutely aware of the threat posed not only by City to Rovers, but by football to rugby in general. Leeds City had formed that very year, and Manningham Rugby Club had converted to the Association game the year before (and been admitted immediately to the Football League without ever having played a match) such was the League's

desire to make inroads into West Yorkshire's rugby heartland. These incursions into rugby strongholds could not be accepted without some form of self-defence against the invader. Rovers' dispute with their city rivals was used by the NU as a form of attack on football itself.

The Northern Union decreed that Rovers and Hull, who were both without a game that day, should play each other at Rovers' ground in Craven Street on the same day as City's game – the assumption being that City would have a reduced gate, and Rovers would have a bumper one. The rugby game was advertised intensely in the city like none before, to the irritation of City, who felt that they were being bullied by the NU and in effect their landlords Hull FC. The rugby teams had also attempted to sway the floating spectators by offering a brass band and a boys' match before the kick-off. City, in retaliation, offered the appearance of Miss Ada Reeve, the nationally-known music hall and vaudeville star, to kick off the game.

Below: A crowd on the popular side at the Boulevard.

The day of the games saw dismal weather, incessant rain following overnight frost. The projected boys' rugby match was therefore cancelled, and attendances were lower than had been hoped at both events. At Craven Street a modest crowd assembled and Hull's entrance onto the pitch was made to 'the accompaniment of silence – quite a contrast to olden times,' the attendance being approximately 4,000.

City on the other hand managed to draw some 5,000 or so fans – a small but significant victory. Local junior football clubs rallied round them to boost the gate and one Hull season pass-holder (who therefore had free admission to City games) declared in a letter to the local press that he would be PAYING to see the new local football team, so unsporting did he consider the treatment meted out by the NU to the fledgling Association team – and he urged others to do so.

Fans at the City game massed in the covered popular stand – out of the rain – in what was also known locally as the Three-penny Stand, and would have been delighted to see Ada Reeve, who was wearing 'a smart tailor made blue costume, made with a basque, and was warmly attired in ermine furs' walking gaily onto the field accompanied by two City directors Mr Cyd Smurthwaite and Mr Glossop. The star walked to centre with a smile, greeted the referee and then shook hands with the City captain, George Spence. Having spun the coin, she spiritedly kicked the ball to a City player before running off, just managing to evade a Glossop player and causing the 5,000 or so fans to cheer noisily.

Not having a brass band to entertain them, some enterprising cornet-playing City fan (reportedly 'a Mr S. of Witty Street') provided the musical fare at the interval when he and his miniature band struck up a selection of popular favourites in the covered stand that included "Won't you come home, Bill Bailey?" and "Farewell, my little Yosan" – accompanied by the enthusiastic singing of appreciative spectators.

City won the game 2-1 amid general satisfaction with the occasion, and a recognition of the significance of the events that day. A local journalist, in reviewing the aftermath, noted "It is more than ever evident that the swing of the pendulum has set in towards 'soccer', and that is a fact Rugby managers have to face, whether they like it or not."

As the end of 1904 loomed, City found themselves playing yet another Friendly at Preston North End on December 27th and the Lancashire side included most of their first team as they narrowly beat their Yorkshire visitors 3-2, in front of 2,000 spectators on an icy, sand-covered pitch, which was a better gate than Glasgow Rangers had attracted to Deepdale the previous Saturday. City's spirited display won them some sympathy in front of watching players and officials of Manchester City and Bolton Wanderers. Manchester United's representatives also made it known to

City officials that they would have willingly visited the Boulevard had the date been vacant. Games such as these provided valuable meetings with important league clubs and their officials – ideal for publicising the Tigers' cause and gaining friends and influence amongst established senior clubs in the game. City's complement of directors attending the game would have introduced themselves to their Preston counterparts in an attempt to gain their support and establish good relations, and no doubt compared notes on the railway trip home about their impressions. The Preston defeat was only the fourth in the 22 games played thus far (the Stockton cup defeat, Bradford and Port Vale being the only other losses) – a very solid start and a suitable reward for the all the hard work and countless hours put in by the directors and promoters of the club.

Their constant efforts in publicising the game in Hull, in finding a steady stream of opponents, overcoming setbacks and obstacles (such as against Glossop and the Northern Union) and seeking new capital and backers, were starting to bear fruit.

At least that's probably how the directors and players could have consoled themselves as they were stranded at Goole station at eleven o'clock that wintry night. The fire in the waiting room was getting very low and the tired and hungry party roamed the streets of "Sleepy Hollow" (as Goole was described) in search of warmth and sustenance. Some of the players found some 'fried fish' and other members of the group located a 'coffee and bun' refreshment house. At one o'clock, the train for Hull finally left Goole and on arrival at Paragon, a group of fans awaited them. No doubt the bonds forged that night between players and directors (who included Messrs Shaw, Smurthwaite, Glossop, Morison and Stringer) strengthened the collective resolve and sense of mission.

Two days after a hard-fought victory at Leeds City in their third encounter of the season on March 4th, the Hull Daily Mail's 'Athleo' reflected on the team name in a short article (see left); this significant article is transcribed here for clarity:

THIRD BEATING OF THE SEASON

HULL CITY TRIUMPH OVER RIVALS

WHY NOT "THE TIGERS?"
(BY "ATHLEO.")

The City colours were once again on Saturday carried to victory, and once more was the Leeds pot upset. Watching the Hull men's performance on the Holbeck ground, and finding the atmosphere of the district hardly fit to use, it occurred to me that Hull City should have a battle cry. We have our "All Blacks" and our "Robins," so why should not the wearers of the yellow and black stripes be the "Tigers?" A lusty chorus of "Played, Tigers!" would have suited the occasion when the Hull men went thundering down the field. The "Wolves" we all know, is a very popular name with the supporters of one League club.

athleo

"WHY NOT 'THE TIGERS'?

The City colours were once again carried to victory, and once more was the Leeds pot upset. Watching the Hull men's performance on the Holbeck ground, and finding the atmosphere of the district hardly fit to use, it occurred to me that Hull City should have a battle cry. We have our 'All Blacks' and our 'Robins' so why should not the wearers of the yellow and black stripes be the 'Tigers'? A lusty chorus of 'Played, Tigers!' would have suited the occasion when the Hull men went thundering down the field."

Hitherto Hull City AFC, when not referred to as City or Hull, had enjoyed several nicknames. These included the Citizens – sometimes abbreviated to the Cits, the Third Porters (in recognition of Hull's maritime commercial importance and in keeping with the then contemporary habit of linking a football team's nickname to the local industry or traditions) and more descriptively, the Amber and Blacks – even on occasion the Gold and Blacks. All accurate and correct, but they were hardly inspiring or likely to generate enthusiasm. The Tigers, however, soon proved to be a success, aided by the local press' usage in reports and articles. The tiger proved to be a godsend for the local sports cartoonists in their regular drawings depicting the club's triumphs or disappointments, a raging beast or meek creature depending on situation or context. Soon the first cartoons would be printed showing the fortunes of the City tiger.

The City directors continued their ceaseless activities behind the scenes, seeking to arrange as many matches as possible, maintain the gathering momentum of the club and keep the coffers full. Opposition varied greatly in terms of quality. The visit of Second Division pacesetters Liverpool on February 18th resulted in a 2-6 defeat but produced a record crowd of 8,000; this was followed by a 5-1 victory against the Army Service Corps the following Thursday afternoon (it was a stated policy of the club to develop the Thursday afternoon supporters, representing as they did a section of would-be fans who had to work on Saturday afternoons) in front of a more modest gate of 2,000. Games often had to be arranged at short notice and as always had to be fitted around Hull FC's use of the Boulevard,

If City's match against Glossop on December 10th had been a triumph against the hostile intent of rugby's Northern Union, a bigger and more decisive battle awaited the club, the consequences of which were to be far more profound and lasting.

Hull FC's cup tie at the Boulevard against Hunslet on March 11th ended amid stormy scenes of brawling involving spectators and visiting players. The official enquiry into this by the NU resulted in Hull being punished by having their home ground closed for the rest of the season (in effect the final two home games). City's directorate acted quickly on this news

and must have been delighted to get the consent of FA cup holders Manchester City to play at the vacant Boulevard on March 25th. The NU had other ideas however and an extraordinary dispute ensued which pitted the two codes against each other in a legal battle for authority in the matter.

The Monday before the game the NU Cup committee met and decided upon the punishment for Hull. The FA had an agreement with them to recognize each other's suspensions, but it was nevertheless considered only a theoretical possibility that such a draconian punishment would be inflicted on the Tigers, who were, after all, blameless in the affair, having a rental agreement of £100 per annum for three years for use of the Boulevard when not required by Hull's first team. Two days later on Wednesday 22nd the English Association officially informed the Tigers that the ground suspension was not binding on them, and City duly pushed ahead with preparations for their prestigious Friendly against the Cup holders. Late on the Friday afternoon, the NU held a meeting at Huddersfield and the Boulevard situation was discussed. The result of this was a telegram received at seven o'clock by a Mr A. Charlesworth (Hull's secretary) from Mr Platts in Huddersfield: 'My committee have decided that no match, Rugby or Association, can be played on the Hull club's ground tomorrow – Platts'. Whether this measure was designed to punish Hull or City or both is not clear. Perhaps the intention was purely to show the strength of the NU.

The effect of this late message was to create consternation in Hull. The Hull directors were convened to a meeting at the Liberal Club on George Street by their secretary Mr Charlesworth. The consensus of the meeting was sympathy for the Tigers' plight, but fear of the NU's reaction should the City match go ahead. A possible expulsion from the NU was one consequence. They reluctantly agreed to comply with the NU edict but made sure they placed the onus firmly on the NU for any consequences arising, and replied by telegram to that effect in the name of their President, Mr W.F.B. Eyre.

City's directors had learned of this news, and they were in turn summoned to a midnight meeting at the house of their Chairman Mr W.H. Gilyott at 207 Anlaby Road, where some strong opinions were expressed on the eleventh hour intervention of the NU. They decided that Hull FC as a limited company gave their tenants City a right to occupy the ground when not in use by the rugby club, and that they would proceed to play the game there the following day, despite putting Hull FC in a precarious position with their NU masters. Hull FC, in turn, informed City that they would forcibly prevent City from using it. Arrangements were made to have a large number of police officers in attendance outside the Boulevard to stop City playing their match there, indications being that a serious disturbance would ensue.

'Will your directors keep us off forcibly?' asked one of the City directors to Mr Charlesworth who was present at the midnight meeting.
'Yes, we shall have a posse of policemen' replied Charlesworth.
'And are you telling us this officially?' he was asked.
'Yes' came the answer, in a good-natured but resolute manner.
'It is a very awkward matter and we shall see it through', added Gilyott, equally aware of the need for diplomacy as well as decisiveness.

City wrote to Mr Wall, the secretary and barrister of the Football Association, and stated the facts as they saw them, effectively bringing about a confrontation between the FA and the NU. They received the following telegram by means of a response: 'Holborn, London, to Mr. Haller, secretary, Hull City A.F.C.. Suspension by Northern Union does not prevent your club playing your Association matches on the Boulevard on Saturday.' Wall had also had direct communication with Platt of the NU and his response to City was a considered one, formulated after due consideration of the pertinent facts. Saturday duly arrived and Mr J.H. Bielby, on behalf of City, attempted to assert formally his right of entrance at nine o'clock and was refused admission.

City acted with remarkable rapidity and energy. The citizens of Hull were greeted with a small army of sandwich-board-men with large notices giving the news that owing to the action of the Northern Union, City's game against Manchester City would now take place on the Anlaby Road cricket ground (the home of the Hull Town cricket team. City director Jack Bielby collected the goalposts from the Boulevard and helped carry them the short distance to the Circle.

Hull FC also organized numerous sandwich-board-men to walk the city's streets with the following bill: 'No football match will be played on the Boulevard today. By order of the Northern Union.' The battle lines had in effect been drawn, City versus Hull, football against rugby. Hull's president Mr W.F.B. Eyre was conciliatory and almost apologetic in his tone:

> "We have done everything possible, as far as we are concerned, to comply with the decision made by the Northern Union. As to the merits or demerits of this decision, I have nothing much to say. I do think, however, the sentence of the Northern Union is the most severe that has been passed since the formation of the union. It is drastic in the extreme, and, in my opinion, will be detrimental to the best interests of the Northern Union."

In a match reported as 'The Tigers' greatest game' some 8,000 spectators packed the Circle cricket ground on a bitterly cold March afternoon as

Hull's cricket and football teams, as depicted on Baines collectors cards of the period.

Paragon station witnessed a steady exodus of Hull fans journeying to Beverley to watch their side take on Swinton in what should have been a home game at the Boulevard.

The superior quality of the Anlaby Road playing surface was noted immediately and it was remarked that the legendary Steve Bloomer of Derby County and England fame, whose team had been defeated at the Boulevard and who had made disparaging comments about the state of the pitch, would have been favourably impressed. City had made tremendous efforts in putting the game on at very short notice. The Hull Daily Mail report of the 'Tigers' greatest game' was written by 'One of Athleo's staff' and remarked that:

> "Mr Haller, the City secretary, had a very busy time, but with the aid of the master of his art, Groundman Ford and his satellites, the crowd found splendid accommodation under the circumstances, and the game was started punctually to time, after a selection of music by the Newland Homes Band. Both teams were made comfortable, there was unlimited supply of hot water after the match and the Manchester officials were more than satisfied with the treatment their men received."

A keenly fought goal-less draw held the attention of the crowd until the final whistle despite the non-competitive nature of the match, and the 8,000 or so spectators did not include the usual proportion of Hull season pass-holders, who comprised part of normal home games at the Boulevard. Despite the bills round town advising 'no football on the Boulevard', City had obtained record receipts, impressed a large crowd against illustrious opponents and, more importantly, found an alternative to the increasingly uncomfortable tenancy at the Boulevard.

By the middle of the following month a public announcement was made detailing changes in the directorate: in short, various officials of the Hull Town Cricket Club had been invited onto the board. The rapidity and significance of these new appointments were an indication of where the club saw its future for the playing of home fixtures. Local MP Sir Seymour King was invited to become President of the Club (a symbolic figurehead role rather than an executive one), which it was hoped would raise the profile of the club in important circles nationally. Four Cricket Club officials now became directors:

Alwyn D. Smith – the new Chairman (replacing William Gilyott), the Hull Director of the Union of London and Smith's Banking Co., Whitefriargate, as well as a director of Hull Town Cricket Club. Smith had played football himself for the Old Etonians, the Casuals and for Trinity Hall College, Cambridge.

J. Bainton – the Chairman and President of the Hull Town Cricket Club, who was reputed to be 'a keen country sportsman'.

H. Ostler – the Hull representative on the Yorkshire County Cricket Club committee, as well as a Hull Town director and player, who had also played football.

Kenneth Wilson – director of Messrs Thomas Wilson, Sons, and Co Ltd and son of Mr Arthur Wilson. Reportedly 'a prominent figure with the Holderness Hounds, and if he has a hobby, it is that of watching a well-contested football match.' Wilson was a member of the famous Hull shipping family and his commercial activities included directorship of Ellerman's Wilson Line Ltd, and Wilson and North East Railway Shipping Co Ltd. He was also an underwriting member of Lloyds of London.

Commenting on these changes, the Hull Daily Mail's 'Athleo' portrayed an idealistic and selfless group dedicating themselves to the progress of Hull City as he wrote of the new additions:

> "All along it has been the spirit of the promoters of the code in Hull that they were bent on serving the game, and if they could be replaced by men who would be able to do more than themselves in office, or if they could be placed in other and more useful positions, then these changes were to be made. There has been an entire absence of selfishness and jealousy, and to these circumstances, and a splendid statesmanship and judgement, I attribute the onward march of the football club."

Certainly energy and ruthless ambition were evident in the constitution of this constantly changing directorate, as the club sought to increase its capital, its profile and influence, and its prestige, in order to assemble the most suitable group of directors possible for its attempt to gain admission to the Second Division.

As well as these boardroom changes, a document was being prepared for circulation to those league clubs with votes, in which the club sought to set out its credentials for election to the league. This was a handsome production with a white and gold cover, displaying the city arms in the centre, and contained, amongst other things, a coloured map showing the area of the clubs in the league, as well as an impressive array of statistics to support City's claims. Tracing the growth of the Association game in Hull, and City's prominence in that phenomenon, it gives details of the current playing arrangements and location of not only the Boulevard but also, tellingly, the Cricket Club ground. Directions from Paragon station ('not more than seven minutes') are given for these as well as details of the club's financial resources.

ANLABY-ROAD GROUND.

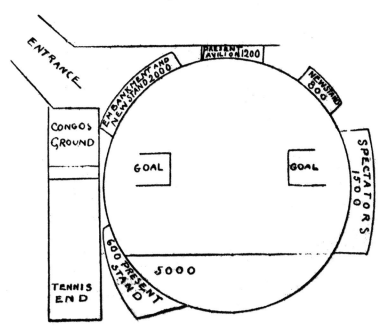

The proposed layout of the pitch and stands at the Circle, which was published with the following article: "The above rough plan gives an idea of the disposition of the playing piece of the Hull City A.F.C. next season. It shows how the cricket circle on the Anlaby-road will be arranged for the purposes of the game, and approximately there will be accommodation for 12,000 spectators to get a good view. The present pavilion will be the grandstand, and it will be numbered and reserved so that one will be able to go to a seat, as in a theatre. It should be noted that the county wicket will be in no way interfered with, for the spectators will stand at the other side of the dividing line. For season 1906/7 an up-to-date League ground will be laid out on the plot of ground adjoining the circle, and divided by a fence, and at present occupied by the N.E.R. cricket ground. Beside having the Congos ground for the reserve team, City will, according to the existing agreement, also have the use of the Boulevard."

'The Third Port' is presented as an accessible and well-connected city, served by the N.E.R, Midland, London and North Western, G.C.R, and Lancashire and Yorkshire railway companies. The coloured map showing all league clubs and their relation to Hull is given alongside details of excursion and pleasure party fares, and pains are taken to point out that 'natural resources and attractions of Hull' will draw visiting support, and by doing so lower the travel costs of the teams themselves. The document concludes by explaining that it is possible for Hull City to

"Little Willie" Foulkes; "Stop buzzing, Wilkie; back pedal."
"Wilkie": "Great Colossus! Have I struck the new Public Hall?"
Foulkes, the Sheffield United goal-keeper weighs 22 stones, 4½lbs.)

The famous Sheffield United goalkeeper William Foulkes was an attraction in the game against Sheffield United, his enormous size providing a comic contrast with the small Tigers' forwards.

take an average gate of £58 per match for friendly football with League clubs (including the 1,400 Hull FC season pass-holders with the right to 'free entry this season only') and so on that basis, a healthy financial success was foreseen. In the same week, it was announced that City would be playing next season at the Hull Cricket Ground, with the winter tenants – the Hull and East Riding Rugby Club – being paid off, as City, in effect, took over the third and final year of their rental agreement. City, as per the agreement, found a new home for Hull and East Riding at Dairycoates, which was deemed to be a better location in terms of catchment area and size of enclosure.

It was foreseen that City would actually play on a pitch laid out in front of the pavilion, like the rugby side before them. Care was taken to protect the wickets used for Yorkshire county cricket games in the centre of the circle by use of nets. Aside from other considerations about the venue, a real sense of satisfaction was apparent that the following season football would be played on a very level and well-kept pitch, in contrast to the Boulevard surface which had been seen unfavourably by some visiting clubs as uneven and not conducive to skilful football.

City also announced their intention to run a Reserve team (possibly to be called the 'Tiger Cubs', according to one director) in 1905/6 and that they would play either on the Boulevard, or if the NU forbade that, on a pitch just inside the Cricket Club's entrance gate used by the Congos team. In this way, football would be played in Hull every Saturday for the growing number of enthusiasts, and the idea of playing a game in East Hull 'for education's sake' was mooted. The Boulevard was also intended for training use during the week. The friction with the NU had intensified City's need to establish an independent base, and the well disguised animosity to the club served only to boost its growth and determination to prosper.

Back on the field, in their 41st game City then capped a momentous week by beating a full strength first division Sheffield United 3-1 at the Boulevard on the Saturday. Played in front of 10,000 fans, this was yet another record crowd, and a notable scalp. Reflecting on the inaugural season of friendly games, the Hull Daily Mail wrote in early May:

> "When one looks back over the season just closed it is remarkable to note how readily Hull spectators have come to appreciate skilful football such as that provided by the City team. Force and vigour have not been eliminated from the games we have seen, but what has been accomplished has been due more to adroitness than anything approaching the bull-rush or violence. What the sporting public are asking for is skilful football, in which one player does not calculate to cripple his opponent. The credit that comes from winning a game after such tactics is reduced to a minimum.
>
> The hustling, scientific and quick game is what our leading Association men have adopted, and the measure of a team's success has depended greatly on the combination the players could develop. Our own Hull City team have copied this well and the public apparently has appreciated they style of the football they have provided, for interest in the Association game in the city has never approached such a height as during the season upon which the curtain was rung down on Saturday. No club indeed, with the ambitions of City, could have desired to commence a career with more sincere or wide-spread wishes for future success amongst its followers that the 'Soccer' barque, with its enterprising crew, may be safely delivered into the desired port. It will be a trying time between now and May 29th, when the voting takes place." (sic)

WHO'S WHO in Advertising ?

MORISON'S ADVERTISING AGENCY, HULL.

Morison's Modern Methods Make Money.

Ernest Morison was one of the more influential early directors and one whose endeavours helped shape the club. His skills and commercial savoir faire helped to raise the Tigers' profile. He is also credited with having originated the black and amber stripes on the club's shirts.

Born in 1868 and privately educated, his occupation at the time of the founding of the club was 'advertising agent' and the agency in question was 'Morison's Advertising Agency' which he had founded in 1893.

Before this, with G.A. Shaw he had edited and published 'The Hull and East Riding Athlete' (headquarters at 50 Savile Street), starting in 1889, after having previously worked as a journalist for the Hull Daily News, penning articles under the pseudonym of 'Rambler'. 'The Athlete', as it came to be known locally,

combined local sporting stories and reports with advertisements, comprising 16 pages divided into 32 columns. Morison himself was a keen cyclist, holding the post of honorary secretary of the Hull Grosvenor Cycling Club in 1890, and as well as cycling 'The Athlete' featured rugby, field sports, hockey, swimming, cricket and many other Victorian competitive pastimes.

Articles appeared profiling well-known local sportsmen past and present (often illustrated by a portrait sketched from a photograph). Space was given to an 'Exchange and Mart' section in which readers could buy and sell sporting equipment, and a letters page printed correspondence from readers. Occasionally effusive sporting poetry was printed to add an

artistic flourish Football too featured occasionally in its pages but the lack of a thriving local league or 'class' team had restricted its coverage.

Morison's Advertising Agency was known locally and nationally in press and bill-posting circles. In addition to these activities, in 1893 Morison had also founded 'Amusements' – a publication devoted to entertainment information and a magazine which resembled a show-business version of 'The Athlete'.

City's directors, as well as providing funds, also represented a useful spread of trades and professions, which widened the influence and reach of the club. Local councillors, J Ps, freemasons, trawler owners, bankers and builders were just some of the roles and positions occupied by board members. As well as working in advertising, Morison appears to have been an enthusiastic and energetic participant in a wide range of commercial and social activities, enabling him to remain well-connected and influential well beyond the confines of Hull. His journalistic activities included frequent articles in the advertising press and he represented provincial advertising agents on the 'Advertisers' Advertising' committee. He was also Vice-President of the Yorkshire Association of Billposters. It was Morison who wrote the most authoritative version of the beginnings of the club – he was, after all, one of the founders.

His account is inevitably subjective, and he is somewhat vague about who belonged to each of the two factions involved in forming the club. (Were the two factions in agreement about everything? Was one faction over-represented in the running of the club?) Perhaps other founders, especially the younger or less affluent ones, may have had a different perspective on the origins. Unlike Morison, they did not have the opportunity or the means to recount their version of how the two groups became a single entity or how they viewed the evolution of the club. Nevertheless, Morison gives a typically energetic and upbeat version of the club's genesis and, in the absence of accounts from any other of the original 'promoters' or founders, it was one which was to become the definitive account:

> "The origin of Hull City; A romance of daring, pluck and luck.
>
> If ever there was a case where sheer, audacious, vaulting ambition did not o'erleap itself – as according to orthodox precedent it should have been – then most assuredly that example was the origin of the Hull City Football club. The reason for this remark will be readily understood when I say that it was only in July 1904, that some three highly enthusiastic but certainly indiscreet young men in the City of Hull divided to run a 'class' Association football team, for the benefit of all and sundry.

That there was no capital to back up their ambitious desires mattered not one jot! They entered into engagements with players, ground, and visiting clubs with a sublime indifference to all responsibility, and then, when the die was cast, and THEN only, decided to float a limited liability company! It was a bold stroke, but happily for all concerned, and the game especially, it is now a cry of 'All's well that ends well.'

Meanwhile, however, a remarkable state of affairs had arisen. Quite unknown to the original promoters of the City, but working quietly towards the same end, was another body of enthusiasts whose intentions were not quite so pretentious, inasmuch as they were to be satisfied with seeking admission to the Midland League. It may be imagined therefore that when the fact leaked out that a Board of Directors had already been formed to float a company and the articles of Association had almost been passed by the Football Association it gave one cause to pause, as it were.

However, as the intent was good, the would-be Midland Leaguers if I may so term them, readily agreed there should be no clashing of interests or display of diversity of opinion to upset the public mind, and so the new company came into being without opposition, as might have easily been unavoidably the case a few weeks later. The original directors were Messrs Marcus Andrews, J Barraclough, J H Bielby, J Emmerson, Ben Saunders Frost, W Gilyott (Chairman), W Hay, RH Hobbs, F A Levitt, G W Lilley (vice-chairman), E Morison, J Ramster, T W Shaw, A E Spring and PH Wrightson. Of these, I believe, I am quite correct in saying Messrs Emmerson, Hobbs and Wrightson never attended any meetings.

That there was no millionaire or other rich, sport-loving individual or coterie of individuals at the back of the scheme may be readily gathered from the fact that the capital was only fixed at £2 000 in 4,000 ten shilling shares. So matters progressed for a time, and whilst the public showed no overwhelming desire to take up shares in this, what has rightly been termed 'the stronghold of rugbyism' for almost half a century, there was sufficient money forthcoming to meet current liabilities, and great were the hopes that the 'gates' would do the rest.

When it is explained that fairly heavy guarantees had been given for friendly matches to such First Division clubs as Notts County, Everton, Middlesbrough, Derby County, and Preston North End, and Second Division clubs such as Leicester Fosse, Burton United, Bradford City, Burslem Port Vale, Grimsby Town, Glossop, Chesterfield, Doncaster Rovers, Gainsborough Trinity, and Barnsley, it may be imagined it required a fairly strong imagination and healthy optimistic temperament to face the situation composedly. However, as it happened, some very unusual conditions helped to contribute to success – success which was actually actively helped by the opposition code! It was this way.

One of the many agreements made was with the Hull Football Club (Northern version), to rent their fine ground on the Boulevard. They took the Boulevard for three years on reasonable terms for all occasions when the first fifteen should not be playing at home on League fixtures, or the ground be otherwise required for cup-tie or County matches. This cut two ways in the new club's favour. In the first place, it disposed of all initial difficulty in securing a well-accommodated ground, and secondly it brought directly before followers of the rival code the beauties of Soccer in such a manner which could not possibly have been done so rapidly otherwise, for every member of the Hull F.C. had free admission on their Rugby passes to all Association matches! Some hundreds of members were this initiated into the Association game without any proselytising effect whatever – and, needless to add, many who originally 'came to jeer, stopped to cheer.'

This is how it came about that, during its first two seasons, Hull City had two first-class grounds on which it could, and did, play as required – a rather unique position, I should imagine, for any Second Division club to occupy. But on the danger of such a situation I shall have a word or two to say later on. That the promoters knew how to get hold of the genuine Soccer footballer will be seen from the following selections with which the season opened: J Whitehouse (late Aston Villa and Grimsby Town), goal; T Jones (late Belfast Celtic and West Bromwich Albion), Andrew Raisbeck (brother to the Liverpool Raisbeck, late Queens Park Rangers and Liverpool), F. Wolfe (late Everton), F. Martin (late Millwall Athletic), G. Rushton (late Burslem Port Vale) George Spence (late Southampton), Peter Howe and Wilkinson (late Manchester United) and others.

There was an auspicious send-off by the then Mayor, Alderman Jarman, kicking off before some 4,000 people in the first Thursday evening match with Notts County, which ended in a draw 2-2. All in all, the success of the play was manifest by the following record for the season:- Played 45, won 26, lost 11, drawn 8, goals scored for 116, against 70. The original secretary was Mr Benjamin Crompton, but this gentleman's business not allowing him the requisite time for his duties, he resigned. It was at this period Mr J F Haller came upon the scene, but that he was not new to the game will be realised when I say he was really the pioneer of the opposition scheme referred to in the outset. At the same time a reconstruction of the board took place and Mr Alwyn D Smith, a keen supporter of the game and an old

Cambridge University player, who had been supporting Mr Haller in his efforts, was elected Chairman of Directors, vice Mr Wm Gilyott, a former strong Rugby supporter, who up to that time had safely steered the frail craft through its short but not wholly uninteresting career. In the meanwhile, with the City having 'caught on' much more strongly than was ever suspected would be the case by the Rugby landlords and other followers of the game, the Northern Union had the matter brought before them in decisive fashion – 'How far could Mr Rugby coquette with Miss Association without being irrevocably lost?'

The answer to this delicate problem was 'Henceforth, Mr Rugby must on no account philander with Miss Association', and so the Northern Union definitely decided there could be no such thing as half and half and that, under no circumstances, would they permit one of their clubs to benefit by any Association tenancy. Thus it is that Hull City was the means of settling one of the knottiest problems ever brought before Rugby legislators.

Before passing to the determination to enter the Second Division, I would just refer to the danger of dual grounds previously mentioned. Before taking the Boulevard, the original Hull City A.F.C. – from which the present club bought its name – had a ground at Dairycoates. Drawn at home against Stockton in the Cup-ties, City, debarred from playing on the Boulevard by reason of the Hull F.C. having a match, wished the game to be played at Dairycoates or the Hull Cricket club ground. But whilst Stockton was agreeable to the transfer, subject to the consent of the Football Association, the ruling books decided against the City, and declared the game must either be placed {sic} on their ground proper – the Boulevard – or at Stockton. Moral: Have one ground only.

With the new board also came the essential consideration of more capital and this was promptly raised to £8 000. The ground question was seriously tackled, and as promptly settled, to move to the Yorkshire county cricket enclosure on the Hull Cricket Club ground, for one season only, with a further ground newly laid out to be ready before the end of the season. No one can say after this Hull City has not had experience in tenancies.

This is, of course, as intended to be, only a skeleton outline of what happened when Hull City was brought into being. Of the thousand and one harassing and happy incidents that occurred during these momentous months, I am not now proposing to make mention nor do I refer to the career of the club since those dark days of 1904-5 when 'all seemed over' with a terrific adverse balance at the end of the first 'friendly' season of £1,857.

E.M."

The original directors were Messrs:

Marcus Andrews, certified teacher; 91 Blenheim Street
James Barraclough, shipowner; Holydyke, Barton on Humber
John Henry Bielby, builder; 479 Hessle Road
John Emmerson, assurance superintendent; 105 Albert Avenue
Benjamin Saunders Frost junior, fruiterer; 105 Charlotte Street
William Gilyott, wharfinger (chairman); 207 Anlaby Road
William Hay, advertising agent; 32 Chestnut Avenue
Richard Henry Hobbs, manager; 251 Boulevard
Frederick Arnold Levitt, furnisher and decorator; 17 Washington Street
George W. Lilley, J.P., surgeon (vice chairman); 22 Williamson Street
Ernest Morison, advertising agent; 106 Park Avenue
John Ramster, arts & sports club manager; 2 George Street
Thomas William Shaw, managing clerk; 83 Melrose Street
Alfred Edwin Spring, commercial traveller; 61 Blenheim Street
Percy H. Wrightson, coal exporter; 34 Beverley Road
Ben Crompton, honorary secretary; 11 Brook Street.

Scrutiny of the 16 men named as 'pioneers of Hull City F.C. Ltd' shows that no fewer than seven were active local players at the time of formation or shortly before; these being Messrs Andrews, Frost, Hay, Levitt, Shaw, Wrightson and Crompton. Of these only Marcus Andrews was deemed good enough to play for the new team, which must surely have been a source of disappointment for some of the others (Andrews had studied at Hull's YPI before going to college at St. John's in York, subsequently becoming Assistant Master at Northumberland Avenue school in Hull and then eventually Head at St Mark's in the Groves. He later became Head at Clifton Street school. His love of football remained together with a passion for yachting and yacht-modelling)

The first annual report of the club reported that the total net sum taken was £1,350 4s 8d and reflecting on this, commented that:

"Considering that all the matches were of the 'friendly type', and that the sporting proclivities of the present day spectator demands matches of a competitive nature, it is highly gratifying that such a total sum should have been reached. The team travelled 1,039 miles to fulfil fixtures, this accounting for £131 0s 4d (travelling) and £88 17s 5d (hotel) expenses. The loss on the first season's working account amounted to £1, 857 2s 8d, but the figure includes £852, a proportion of summer wages, transfer fees and bonus of the present team, thus reducing the said loss to £1,005 2s 8d. Of the amount £663 2s 11d was paid to visiting clubs as guarantees. This expenditure must be taken as for educational purposes."

With the season over and the AGM out of the way, there remained the most important event in the new club's short history – an appointment in London, to attempt election to the League by existing member clubs. Failure to be voted in would signal disaster for the new club, possible ruin for some directors and even extinction for the Tigers, so great was the gamble – and loss – after that first season.

The Tigers had missed the deadline for application to join the Second League in 1904 by a matter of weeks, and had set their sights on 1905's annual meeting of the Football League to be held in London on Monday May 29th. It is extremely doubtful that a new club founded only weeks previously with no ground to call their own, would have gained sufficient votes from league clubs to be admitted to the ranks of the second division. However, a season of friendlies had enabled City's directors to make the acquaintances of various well-connected officials, football 'worthies', sympathetic directors and secretaries of other clubs. Their support, lobbying, advice and connections would be of invaluable assistance to the Tigers in their bid for election to the league.

Buoyed up by the good wishes of this network of allies and contacts, the resolute City party steamed out of Paragon Station on the 11.43 train on Saturday morning no doubt also mindful of the consequences should their mission fail. The party consisted of 'the Chairman (Mr Alwyn D. Smith), the vice-chairman (Mr. W. Gilyott). Dr Lilley, Mr A E Spring (President of the East Yorkshire Football Association), Mr F G Stringer, members of the Board of Directors with Mr J F Haller, the secretary and Mr Langley, the team manager.' Mr Kenneth Wilson, another director of City, was also understood to be in the capital.

There was well-founded optimism on the train, as it was felt that the club had forged positive relationships with important legislators of the game who could be relied upon to back the club when the voting took place. If all the good wishes were translated into votes, City's election would receive an almost unanimous vote. The meeting was to take place at the Tavistock Hotel on Monday, leaving time for last minute canvassing by clubs seeking election or (re-election in the case of three clubs) on the day before the vote. Each member of the City party would have been given a list of 'allotted' clubs to court, followed by a comparing of notes at the end of Sunday, with all efforts then being concentrated on the 'doubtfuls'. It was reported that 'the City representatives are armed with handy-sized tickets, as a kind of business card, the contents recalling the old proverb that 'Brevity is the soul of wit'.

Grimsby's 'Mr Bellamy' worked on the Tigers' behalf as did several other people who threw their weight behind City's cause. As for the actual presentation of City's bid, it was to be left to secretary Jack Haller to expound on the reasons why the clubs should vote for City in his allotted three minute address to them. A key point of his pitch to the assembled throng would have been the fact that the club already had £2,000 towards the 1905/06 season, a squad of Second League calibre and 'a ground that can be transformed into one of the best in the Division'. It was thought that Leeds would be City's main rivals in the voting, ahead of the chasing pack.

The new clubs hoping for election were Hull City, Leeds City, Chelsea, Burslem Port Vale, Burton United, Doncaster Rovers, Stockport County and Clapton Orient.

When the time came for City to put their case, Jack Haller duly stepped forward to deliver his club's reasons to the meeting. There was a burst of applause as the City secretary spoke, and when he had finished several of the City party patted him on the back. A bell was rung at the start and finish of the three minute period but Haller made his points with several seconds to spare. It was thought to be one of the best speeches of the morning. But would it suffice? City had, it should be remembered, 25 promises of votes in writing.

The results, when announced shortly before midday, must have come as a bitter shock to the Hull party.

Leeds City 25; Burslem Port Vale 21; Chelsea 20

City came fourth with 18 votes and thus missed out. What happened to those seven promised votes?

It was revealed in the local press that both Chelsea and Clapton Orient had offered to pay visiting teams' hotel and other expenses when hosting clubs from the Midlands and the North. This appears to have worked for Chelsea but not for Clapton who only obtained one vote. City had made no financial sweeteners whatsoever.

The election bid was a failure but next on the meeting's agenda was a proposal (by Mr C E Sutcliffe of Burnley, seconded by Mr McKenna of Liverpool) to extend the Second League to include 20 clubs. Opinion among Football League clubs had previously been considerably divided as to the League extension, and it was decided that a 75% majority in favour was necessary to carry the proposition through. In the event a unanimous decision in favour was returned, and Mr J.J. Bentley, the president of the League, duly noted the verdict. By 12.30 City were back in with a good chance of election. Another poll took place of candidate clubs. The four extra clubs now admitted to the League were Burton United (36 votes), Hull City (36 votes), Clapton Orient (26 votes), and Stockport County (26 votes), with Doncaster Rovers thus falling out of the League. By 12.40 City had become a member of the Second League.

Clapton (attempting to match Chelsea's 'generosity' had even offered £15 to Midlands clubs and £20 to Northern ones towards travelling expenses for three seasons in a determined bid to 'influence' wavering voters, and it seems to have worked. City received 36 votes – unanimous backing – and had resolutely made no inducements. The view was expressed in some quarters that the second proposal to extend the League to 40 clubs was included specifically to take City in, their initial bid for admission having failed, to the surprise of many clubs.

Ernest Morison recounted City's admission to the League thus:

"Then came the all-exciting and anxious application for admission to the Second Division. Beaten on the post for first honours, things looked black indeed, but thanks to the enlargement of the Division by the admission of two extra clubs, City literally headed the list for second honours, and so was admitted. To those who have gone through this ordeal, it is quite unnecessary to say that City will make the most desperate efforts – should fate prove more unkind than at present – to avoid the necessity of ever again visiting the 'polling booth' under such circumstances."

It was a tired but jubilant party that arrived back in Hull at 10pm on the Tuesday evening, their objective achieved after tense and unexpected complications.

On Easter Monday 1904 City hosted Preston North End – giants of the Victorian age. Here the hungry Tiger helps himself to the Preston Lamb in another football cartoon.

1905 – 06

PLAY UP TIGERS

DAVY GORDON, Vice-Capt.

Read the "Hull Daily News,"
THE SPORTING PAPER.

The fixture list for the forthcoming season was compiled at Manchester on June 10th 1905 according to the Fletcher system. Clubs were permitted to modify the games in such a way as to reduce costs or increase crowds with the consent of their opponents. For City, Jack Haller attended, and was able to arrange a trip to Chelsea to follow a visit to Clapton Orient two days earlier. Similarly City's away game at Burslem Port Vale on Christmas Day was followed by a trip to Burton United on Boxing Day.

In recognition of his role in securing election to the league, Haller was presented with a large silver cigarette case and a silver matchbox by the City directors. Both gifts bore the secretary's monogram and the day in question (May 25th 1905). The cigarette case was inscribed with the words 'Presented to Mr J F Haller by the Directors of the Hull City A.F.C. Co., Ltd.' Haller's unceasing and relentless endeavour in lobbying and canvassing members, involving countless hours and miles, was recognised by both Alwyn Smith and William Gilyott. By common consent, the work and sheer determination of the secretary was an important factor in the club's election to the league.

At a shareholders' meeting at the Grosvenor Hotel, Carr Lane, on July 20th, the main resolution carried was that the share capital of the club be increased to £8,000 so as to build up the club's strength and share the load among more investors. The prices of season passes for the first league season were set at 6s, 8s 6d and 12s 6d – aimed at enticing members of the wider sporting community. Ladies and boys would be admitted at half price. As a sign of the club's vision and ambition, it was revealed that the club hoped to have 'accommodation on the ground for thirty to fifty thousand spectators. A large amount would also be spent on the stands.' No timetable or further detail was given, but such plans would surely have aroused great interest and curiosity in a city in which the existing largest stadium would have been tiny in comparison.

With the approach of their inaugural league season, City strengthened their squad as they contemplated the rigours ahead and assembled for pre-season training. It was reported in the local press that:

> "By arrangement with the Hull Cricket Club the team are to train on the cricket ground, and naturally they are delighted with the prospect, for the accommodation and the surroundings are ideal. Probably some of the training would have been done on the Boulevard, but seemingly, suitable days could not be arranged."

There was perhaps the faintest suggestion of the Tigers being denied access to the Boulevard in the wording, and the enforced training at the Circle would have accentuated any rift between Hull FC and their Association tenants. The same article waxed lyrical about City's defence:

> "To return to the team again – the defence can be described as equal to the best in the Second League. In the middle division we have the pick of six half-backs including Gordon, of Leith Athletic, and in the front rank, in one of our captures' we have Wilson of the Heart of Midlothian, who went through the South African War with the Black Watch Regiment. I might add that City's first trial match will probably be at the Newland Orphanage in aid of that Institution, on August 19th; the other will be on August 26th on the cricket ground after the An Eleven match. It will however be necessary to be there before six o'clock, as the English Association allow no charge to be made, and the gates' will be closed after that hour. Those, however who pay their threepence to see the cricket match will be able to remain for the football."

Modest enough preparations and opposition, and to twenty-first century eyes, a surprising piece of legislation that forbade football clubs to charge for admission to pre-season warm up games.

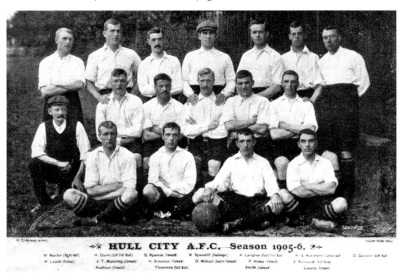

HULL CITY A.F.C. Season 1905-6.

City line up in their training shirts in a pre-season photograph taken by Robert T. Watson in a field between the Circle and West Park.
Back Row (left to right): Billy Martin, Harry Davis, George Spence, Martin Spendiff (goalkeeper), Ambrose Langley (player-manager), Billy Robinson, Davy Gordon. Middle row: Bill Leach (trainer), John Manning, Harry Simmon, Davy Wilson, Peter Howe, Andy Raisbeck. Front row: George Rushton, Billy Thornton, Jacky Smith, Patrick Lavery.

Reflecting on a year's work by the directors and the careful progress made, a local journalist observed that: "... no parent ever watched his child grow from babyhood to man's estate with more anxiety. It would hardly be possible for any board of directors to hold more meetings than that of City; every little detail is carefully attended to at these, and the time that has been devoted all round must be very considerable." With the second and final practice game against a Reserve XI over, one supporter (signing himself 'Felix Tigris') felt compelled to write to the Hull Daily Mail to name the players he believed would best represent the club – as well as detailing their perceived failings:

"With your kind permission I should like to express an opinion as to the exhibition of the latest rivals in the field of sport, viz., our 'City' club. Having seen the two practice matches, and also a good number of last season's as a supporter, I would suggest to the directors the advisability of selecting the following to meet Barnsley next Saturday:- Spendiff in goal.(Up to the present we have not seen anything like the best of this player). Full backs, Davies (who plays with judgement, and who's (sic) only fault lies in the direction of speed, for if he is beaten by an attacking forward, he is slow in recovering. Mr. Langley is considerably faster than his partner, and with his experience of class football, as a power of strength to the team.

As to the halves, here is where the strength is concentrated, and in Martin, Robinson, and Gordon we have three reliable players. The forwards are somewhat of a mixture, and Rushton will have to play up if he means to keep his place, and remember that his position is within an inch or two of the touch line: Spence I would put in inside-right, and is certainly slow but sure. Our new centre Wilson, shows considerable control of the ball, yet strikes me as being a trifle selfish, and does not shoot at goal. No doubt this will be remedied in the serious games to come.

Howe, inside left, appears to dally with the ball at his feet, yet when he shoots he puts his weight behind. Raisbeck, after his play this evening, shows promise of retaining his new position as outside left, and it is to be hoped that both wings will improve in the centring game. One of the gratifying features is the form shown by the reserves: Smith calls for special mention, as also our locals Cook and Frost. I would conclude in congratulating the directors on the improvement of the ground, and sincerely wish them and the players a most successful season."

City made their League debut on Saturday 2nd September against Barnsley on the Anlaby Road cricket ground, almost a year to the day after their inaugural game against Notts County at the Boulevard. Some had predicted that the club would fold by Christmas, certainly in the New Year, but the game – and the club – had taken root in the city (no doubt to the disappointment of some). The arrival of yet another Yorkshire team in the Football League was further demonstration of the round ball game's rapidly growing popularity east of the Pennines, and the determination of the Association game's administrators to invade

The Newington Hotel, Anlaby Road in 1905. Popularly known as Parker's after its landlord Ernest Parker, the long-established pub was now ideally situated to cater for thirsty City followers.

areas previously thought to be rugby strongholds. City's team, like those of Chelsea, Leeds City and Clapton Orient consisted of a few well-known players and a group of unknown ones. Their prowess would soon be revealed. The opening game would be followed not just by those paying their 'tanner' at the Circle on Anlaby Road, but by others much further afield. The Newland Orphanage band once again entertained the gathering crowd from 2.30 onwards on a warm late summer afternoon. As the buzz of the expectant crowd mingled with the music, City's players prepared in the Circle cricket pavilion which served as their dressing room. In a city once described as a 'hotbed of rugbyism', the numbers of the paying public for this first game would be closely scrutinised.

The Newland Orphanage Band.

The pitch, with its short grass and smooth flat surface would prove to be a very fast one for the teams. Just as well that trainer Bill Leach, who had been at the Barnsley club for two seasons, had the players in the peak of condition. The superior fitness of the home side was evident in the afternoon's proceedings.

Surveying the scene some twenty minutes before kick-off on an afternoon 'far too hot for football', a reporter described the pitch as being 'like a billiard table and the markings are as clear as on a tennis court'. The ground was filling up nicely with some 4,000 people estimated to be present. News of Barnsley's late arrival did little to spoil the occasion. Chairman Alwyn Smith used the slight delay to make a visit to the home dressing room and addressed the players, telling them that 'Soccer is the game' and to play it for all they are worth, no doubt mindful of the importance of a successful start to league football in Hull in a city with two rugby teams. The players were told that if they won it would go well in the city, and they were encouraged by his remarks and applauded them. A pleasing unity between players and officials appeared to exist.

Davy Gordon depicted on a Baines card and wrongly described as G. Browell.

HULL CITY
v.
BARNSLEY
ON THE
ANLABY-ROAD CRICKET GROUND.
KICK OFF **3.30** P.M.

THE FIRST SECOND DIVISION LEAGUE PLAYED IN HULL.

ADMISSION 6d.   STANDS EXTRA.
PASSES MAY BE OBTAINED ON THE GROUND.

After a 15 minute delay, the game finally started as fullback and captain Ambrose Langley led his team down the pavilion steps and onto the pitch in front of 8,000 spectators to a 'hearty reception' – Barnsley having 'incurred a fine equal to the time elapsed'. The game started with City having won the toss and Barnsley kicking off to what was quaintly described as 'the bowling green end'. The Tigers soon gained possession and began to press the Barnsley goal. First George 'Geordie' Spence ran at the visitors' defence and shot hard against Hay the Barnsley defender and into touch. A minute later the City attacker received a fine pass from the left wing and placed his shot firmly into the net to 'loud cheering' – goalkeeper Thorpe just getting a touch. After just two minutes City's whirlwind start has been too much for Barnsley, the impetus and desire transmitting itself from the directors and home fans to the players themselves, who attacked relentlessly.

Barnsley then shook the home side by pulling level after ten minutes when Beech gave Tigers' goalkeeper Martin Spendiff no chance. City regained the lead before the interval through Davy Gordon, a Scottish discovery of Messrs Stringer and Langley, who was proving himself to be an energetic half-back with unselfish passing skills and an eye for goal.

HULL CITY v BARNSLEY.
COME ON, MR MAN, AND BE CHAWED!

A hesitant Barnsley miner approaches the Hull City Tiger.

In the second half City increased their lead after 55 minutes through another newcomer – David 'Soldier' Wilson, who converted from an awkward angle after some neat passing with George Rushton. City's stout defence resisted the sporadic Barnsley attacks and ten minutes from time, Davy Gordon scored his second goal. The Tigers showed no signs of letting up, and Barnsley would have been relieved to hear the final whistle to spare them further embarrassment. A resounding success from all aspects, and the occasion must have given immense satisfaction to all involved with the club. Players, officials and well-wishers must all have found their expectations exceeded by some measure.

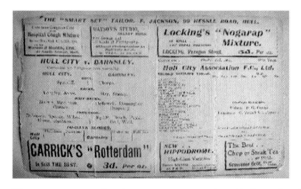

With the arrival of League football in Hull, the club started to issue match programmes through Ernest Morison's advertising agency.

The programme for the opening match with Barnsley (shown above) was a simple affair. Apart from the team line ups, the results from the previous season of Friendly games were given as well as the list of fixtures for the current one. The surrounding space was given over to advertisers – among them the official club photographer Robert Watson, City director John Locking's tobacconist shop and the Grosvenor Hotel grill. All were closely associated with the early years of the Tigers. The club's ground is given as 'Cricket Ground, Anlaby Road and Boulevard, Anlaby Road' in recognition of the fact that they were still paying Hull FC a rent for the use of the Boulevard.

City's win was described outside Hull in glowing terms, as periodicals further afield digested the opening day's results which saw the Tigers as the only newcomer of the four to gain a victory. The Athletic News commented 'Hull City have made a very auspicious commencement, and every real enthusiast will wish them continued success.' The positive start was greeted in West Yorkshire thus: 'By the decisive manner in which they disposed of their visitors, the men of the Third Port have already shown that they are worthy of a very wholesome respect.' (Yorkshire Post). The Leeds Mercury said: 'Their victory over such an experienced side as Barnsley stamps them as an eleven capable of creating for themselves a prominent position amongst their rival competitors ... provided they can maintain their form, the crowds are likely to grow in numbers every week.' Over in Bradford the view of the Observer was that: 'They are trying hard, are these Hull Soccer people to make a name for the City club, and if

capable and smart management counts for anything, the Association game in the East Riding is in for a flourishing time.' Down in South Yorkshire, where football had deeper roots, the Sheffield Telegraph wrote: 'Hull City could not have wished for a better send-off, than they received in their initial venture. A large gate, perfect weather, and withal, a first-rate victory – a truly happy augury for the future.'

The following Saturday the Tigers travelled to their first away game against fellow newcomers Clapton Orient. The trip down to London was the furthest yet for the club whose previous games had encompassed only friendlies in the North and Midlands. A game on the Monday had been arranged against Chelsea (another newcomer) to defray travelling expenses, and the 'mini tour' attracted the interest of the curious, or wealthier, fan.

"For the benefit of the party (which is growing to fair proportions) going up to London on Saturday morning, it may be as well to outline the programme. The train leaves Paragon Station at 6.30 and will arrive in London about 11.30 a.m. From there the gathering will go the Charterhouse Hotel, Charterhouse-square, Oldersgate (sic) where luncheon has been arranged for 12.30. After a rest the team will set out for the Clapton ground in time for the kick off at four o'clock. As the party will return by 6.30 there will be ample time to visit an evening entertainment.

On Sunday there is to be a trip by steamer to Hampton Court, leaving London Bridge at 9.45, with luncheon at the celebrated Mitre Hotel. The evening will be spent quietly at headquarters.

On the Monday as much of London as possible will be seen before the game at Chelsea, which commences at five o'clock. The return to Hull will be from Marylebone Station at 10pm on Monday, and this city should be reached at 3.30. Messrs Dean and Dawson, of King Edward-street are arranging the tour, and will be able to answer all questions concerning it. It might be added that the fare is only 12s 6d and the Charterhouse Hotel account will be about 17s 6d inclusive. This is a chance for a pleasant three days' jaunt to London."

The Clapton game was another triumph – having won the first home game, the Tigers then secured their first away victory.

"At the first time of asking Hull City captured two League points away from home. The news was received with great rejoicing in Hull.

The feelings of the little party that drove through London after the stiff mill in the depressing district of Homerton – which is in the district of the Hackney marshes – are not easy to describe! Points obtained away from home are a wonderful tonic.

In fact every club wants a little luck to get them. Obtaining them as we are, right at the beginning of the season, too, is quite an excuse for almost delirious delight at the result, for points are always terribly harder to secure towards the end of the season, when the clubs are anxiously seeking them, and every match is as strenuous as a Cup-tie, than at the beginning. Certainly we have 'surprised the natives', whose expressions in the unadulterated dialect of the Cockney I should like to be able to produce. But then, as a Scotch member of our team would say, 'We went down to town to do a wee bit of damage.' That the Tigers – and I was glad to hear some of our sportsmen cheering them on by that name – did so magnificently after the fatiguing journey and the brake rides both from Marylebone to the Charterhouse Hotel, and thence to the Homerton ground, is remarkable. At Paragon we had a surprisingly good send off, despite the early hour of starting, and although Mr. Haller, the secretary, could not accompany us, he was there to see everything was in order. In Messrs Barraclough and Locking, two of the directors, we had efficient conductors, and the men (all as fit as fiddles) were having breakfast before the train had started. There was perhaps some risk in taking such a journey on the day of the match, but fortunately the G.C.R. realised its responsibility, and ran us through very expeditiously on their picturesque route, with hardly a stop.

There were aboard the crowded train, too, some who might have been suspected of Rugby tendencies, possibly 'converts' who, as they were going down to London, evidently intended seeing the matches. Amongst the party was Mr Smith, the new President of the East Riding Football Association, Mr Morison, another director, and an ex-director in Mr Smurthwaite, who saw that there was a liberal supply of City buttons. Of course the colours were largely worn, and when a placard had been affixed in the saloon window to show who we were, I imagine everything was complete to make an impression on this, our first away league engagement.

At Doncaster we certainly did, but fortunately there was not time to stop to explain why the Rovers had been ousted to make room for the new arrivals, including Hull City! Arriving in London to find it raining hard, there was another cramping journey across the city to headquarters, which we find very comfortable, with a square of grass and trees in front, which is by no means suggestive of the crowded heart of London. There was plenty of time after dinner to get down to the ground, which meant another four miles drive for the team, who were still reported fit, although there was little time for rubbing down. The rain was still coming down in torrents, and one would not have been surprised to hear that the ground was under water. It was not so sodden as might have been expected, although it was too heavy for the liking of the Hull men. I was also much astonished to find that there

was absolutely no stand for the spectators, and the accommodation was not at all suitable for a Second League team. Talking to the Orient chairman however, before the game, he told me that from the present state of upheaval the ground is to be converted into one suitable for the First League, with plenty of stand accommodation.

The 'O's', as they call them, were fully expected to win, but their rushing tactics, without combination, were not effective, and though they are a heavy lot, they are suggestive of size without symmetry. Not that City could be expected to combine on soaked turf, and in a storm that wetted them through in the first few minutes.
But considering that they were not too fresh, they did not give the Orientals any rest. In fact they kept with them in the good old way, like old League hands. There were no liberties on either side, and each team in turn made the other fight hard. There were no pretty movements to speak of on either side – just that exciting strenuous effort to get through goal somehow or other. It is a long time before those of us who witnessed the last two or three minutes will forget the experience, and how City kept their opponents off the mark, with Spence helping the half backs. It seemed an interminable time, but the defence proved sound and Spendiff emerged from the fray one of the heroes of the game. The only goals of the game resulted from one of the brightest bits of passing of the afternoon, for the trickiness of the Tigers enabled them to get down to within ten yards of the goal, where Howe, seeing his opportunity, shot into the net. An easy goal it looked certainly, but it was one of those where the slippery ball hangs on the ground all the way and goes through at an awkward, oblique angle. There was quite an aggressive shout of 'Tigers !' at this in which several Hymers lads distinguished themselves, and I heard one Clapton enthusiast make use of an expression he had not learned from the Psalmist. On this occasion City had not got their cornetist, and probably discretion was the better part of valour, for I have never forgotten the angry demand to 'put it i' the bag!' when we defeated Leeds City last season."

The Chelsea game on the Monday provided the first sobering defeat – a heavy 5-1 scoreline at Stamford Bridge in front of a modest 6,000 attendance, the game kicking off at the relatively late time of 5pm to enable more spectators to attend.

This London trip was the most ambitious yet for City followers and was an indicator of the interest in travelling to watch the team, using England's extensive railway network. The involvement of agents to book saloons, the advertisement of rail travel for important games and first-hand accounts by journalists, all helped to make away match travel an important part of supporting Hull City in the club's early years.

FOOTBALL PICTURE POSTCARDS.

"Sports Express" Series of Cartoons Published To-day.

The Pictorial Postcard craze has extended to footballers, and the "Sports Express" has supplied local followers of both games with the very article they desired.

The first two of what will be known as the "Sports Express" series, shown below, were issued this morning, and there was at once a keen demand.

Everyone was delighted and asked for more.

HULL CITY'S LONDON TOUR.

Clapton were attacked first, and brought down with a long shot, though the day was more suitable for fishing than shooting. At Chelsea, where they met the Pensioners, their reception was decidedly rough; for as the story tells of the veteran fighting his battles o'er again, "Shouldering his crutch, he showed us how the battles were fought and won."

A LITTLE ADVICE.

OWD THIRD PORTER: "I'm watching the fortunes of all of ye, sonny, an' I don't like that stain on your brother Rover's record. You're paying a visit to Leeds; remember, you're to wipe out that stain with blood."

Our artist has some more attractive ideas for the future, and you should look out and send them to your friends.

Booksellers, Stationers, Newsagents, &c., desiring a supply are requested to apply at the head office.

To capitalise on this wave of enthusiasm for league football, Hull's weekly sporting paper The Sports Express ran an advertising feature on Saturday 23rd September which read:

> "The Pictorial Postcard craze has now extended to footballers, and the 'Sports Express' has supplied local followers of both games with the very article they desired. The first two of what will be known as the 'Sports Express' series, shown below, were issued this morning, and there was at once a keen demand. Everyone was delighted and asked for more. Our artist has some more attractive ideas for the future, and you should look out and send them to your friends. Booksellers, Stationers, Newsagents, &c., desiring a supply are requested to apply at the head office."

As shown left, one card depicted a Hull City footballer in two scenes from the 'London Tour'. The first one has the player beaming proudly, having just shot down Clapton, whilst the second shows the same player coming off second best to a bearded and battling Chelsea pensioner. The second card alludes to Hull Kingston Rovers' recent defeat at Leeds, and depicts an 'Owd Third Porter' encouraging the Hull City tiger to avenge this loss and the city's sporting honour, on his forthcoming visit to play Leeds City. Alas, these two cards appear to be the only ones issued in the series and no further cards are advertised.

A topical profile of club secretary Jack Haller written by 'Athleo', appeared in the weekly Hull Times on September 9th:

"A STRENUOUS SECRETARY
MR HALLER AND THE RISE OF CITY

Now that the Hull City club is fairly and firmly set upon its feet I think that a few words about its secretary (Mr J. F. Haller) will not be out of place. Of course it will be more of a personal impression, for he who accepted the onerous commission on September 8th, 1904, when interrogated about himself smiles in his good tempered way, and talks about anyone but himself.

Yet although one who has personally canvassed nearly every club in the First and Second League, and has become acquainted with many of our leading Association football legislators, the Tigers' secretary practically ignores his share. At the League meeting, too, he had the distinction of being chosen by the Board as the spokesman when the City application was put forward. On that memorable occasion, in fact, he could hardly be persuaded to go to bed, fearful that he might be missing someone with a vote who required canvassing.

Determination is, in fact, one of the traits of Mr Haller. A whole-hearted optimist in matters concerning 'City' he is to the fingertips, and when the local Associationists were passing through some of the

Club Secretary Jack Haller

early trials those concerned used to say sight of his cheerful face took a load of care off their minds. But the crisis now is past, and there is every prospect that the game will go on and flourish like a great green bay tree. Mr Haller is quite a young man – but 31 – and for the past 13 years has been actively associated with the dribbling code.

He undoubtedly had the game at heart from the first, and when the present vice-chairman (Mr Gilyott) and Dr. Lilley waited upon him last September and asked him if he would accept the secretaryship of the new club, in place of Mr Crompton, who was resigning, he promised to consider it. And because Mr Haller – though at the time he was thinking of retiring from football affairs – desired above most things to see a 'class' Association club in the city, he accepted the position. Endowed with that quality of taking infinite pains, he has been working hard at it ever since. But it's the continuous sticking at it that tells. Some of us may perhaps require reminding that the Tigers' secretary was also associated with a Hull Association Club, which (excepting the present City organisation) may claim to have been the finest combination in the city. I refer to the team which arose out of the amalgamation of the original Albany and Kingston Rovers in 1895, the arrangement being that Association should be run on those days when Rovers were playing away.

That club entered for the English Amateur Cup, the East Riding Cup, and the Scarborough Hospital Cup. In the first-mentioned competition, though, they were beaten by Grimsby All Saints, a club which in those days almost equalled the League team, although the final was reached in the other two cups. But the Albany-cum-Rovers club, in which were the clever brothers Robson, Waterstone (late professional for Grimsby Town), and Wallace (of Kirkcudbright), had a short life of but a few months. It was three years previous to that, at the age of 18, that Mr Haller started on the path of Association football and largely through the instrumentality of Mr Will Robson (then captain of Albany, who, with Kingston Amateurs and St Paul's led Association in the city), Mr Haller was appointed treasurer

of Albany the first year he was connected with the club, carried through the amalgamation with the Rovers, and also terminated the arrangement.

The Tigers' secretary has served on the Council of the Hull and District Football Association, which was dissolved in favour of the East Riding Football Association for a number of years, and also on the latter body. On the resignation of Mr C.E. Hampton, the hon. secretary, he took over the secretarial work till the close of the season, and was subsequently appointed vice-president. That position he held until appointed secretary of the Hull City A.F.C. Company, Ltd. Mr Haller, it should be added, was one of the original members of the committee of the 'Hull Times' Charity Cup Competition, the first final being between the Hull Town Club (of which he was then hon. secretary) and Grimsby All Saints. The following season (1898-9) he was appointed hon. secretary of the Competition. He succeeded in turning an adverse balance sheet into a credit one, and that after certain donations had been given to charities. For three years Mr Haller was secretary, and was then appointed vice-president.

As secretary of Hull City, the work could not be in better hands, but Mr Haller says that the success of City has been largely attributable to the energy and forethought of the directors, with Mr Alwyn Smith as chairman."

Their inaugural season had seen the Tigers eliminated at the first qualifying stage of the FA cup in somewhat unsatisfactory circumstances as Hull FC's match calendar took precedence over their own. City conceded ground advantage to Stockton. A draw meant that the replay was also to be played at Stockton. A defeat meant that any chance of the Tigers advancing and generating revenue from ties against illustrious opponents was extinguished. For a club seeking to publicise itself and its attempts to be elected to the football league, this summary exit was a depressing setback. Their status as a new second division club meant that City were not considered among the 32 automatic entrants for the first round proper of the FA cup, so the Tigers had to progress through the four qualifying rounds starting in early October at the Circle against Grimethorpe United when they cantered to a 8-1 victory.

The next round saw an away game against Denaby United, on the same day that Manchester United were to be the visitors to the Boulevard in the league. Unable or unwilling to re-schedule the games (playing Manchester United in mid-week would have meant a much smaller attendance), City were faced with a fixture clash and opted to field their strongest team for the second division match and sent their reserves – popularly known then as the Cubs – to face the hitherto-unbeaten amateurs of Denaby, hoping they would be able to see off the non-leaguers' challenge. Despite the big game at the Boulevard, it was reported that the reserve side were followed by supporters on the 11.43 Hull to Doncaster train using 'a special saloon provided through Messrs Dean and Dawson's agent, Mr Butterworth.'

At the Boulevard, the absence of any rugby matches in the city saw the attendance soar to 12,000 (the largest home crowd of the whole season) as the Tigers lost to the eventual runners-up Manchester United by the only goal of the game. The rougher playing surface of the Boulevard would certainly have levelled the technical skills of the two sides, and Hull FC's home would be more accustomed to hosting larger crowds than the makeshift football enclosure that the Circle had become. The hard-fought game was a good advertisement for football and the Tigers, as the home side tore into the Manchester team. 'Even followers of the Rugby code became vastly excited, and cheered the Hull men to the echo. The roar that burst from the throng at times was deafening', reported the Hull Daily Mail in its coverage of the game, noting that 'Hull City seem to have attracted a new class of follower – some of whom have not attended football matches before – as a glance at the stand at the cricket ground will show'. City laid siege to the Manchester goal but the visitors held firm with their goal advantage to leave the Boulevard with the win. Many spectators at the Boulevard would have found their minds wandering to events at Denaby and the progress of the second string in the more glamorous FA cup. They need not have worried, as the Tiger Cubs disposed of Denaby with two unanswered goals.

It was not uncommon for local sports journalists to display their poetic prowess in print when a significant event was felt worthy of celebratory verse, and the victory at Denaby by a young City team was deemed a fitting subject for such an honour. To this end, the following lines attributed to 'Zealander', about events at the Boulevard and Denaby, were printed the following Monday in the Hull Daily Mail:

TIGER "AT HOME" AGAIN.
City returned to their birthplace, the Boulevard, this afternoon.

"WELL-PLAYED, TIGER CUBS

BOULEVARD, 4.35
'What of the Cubs?' The whisper dies
O'er the massed expectant throng
'No score at half!' But hope soon dies
For 'The Colliers going strong!'
A loud and deep roar of might and main
Speeds from Hull to Denaby,
That Airlie Song with chaste refrain
'What a r- - - - n re - - - ee!'

Cruel fate and wall-eyed luck had told
Their tale of honours dashed
Against the Tiger, striving bold,
Grim, desperate, unabashed.
'Good lads! Well fought!' the people roared
Tawny Tigers left the field.
'We'll bear in mind the goal you scored,
Though ne'er a point it yields!'

DENABY, 4.35
'Now, lads, for glory and for fame,
And for revenge as well!'
Thus Captain Davis, as the game
Wore to its final spell.
''Twill be a great and splendid thing
For us to snatch the match!'

'You're right!' his players' voices ring,
'We're game from boot to thatch.'

Two goals to nil the Cubs have won!
On that weird and tilted ground;
Shattered is Denaby's record run,
With groans the pits resound,
Oh, Glorious Cubs! We sent thee forth
With best wishes but faint hopes,
But now thy grit and sterling worth
Have cheered our football mopes.

HULL, Always.
A toast, my friends. Now fill your glass,
And raise it to the sky!
'Tis not the team of name or 'class'
I give you to drain dry,
But the gallant whelps of prize-bred sire,
GENTLEMEN — 'THE TIGER CUBS!'
Their name shall live and fame inspire
As long as clubs are clubs."

A home tie, this time with the full first team, awaited in the third qualifying round. But the Tigers could only manage a disappointing draw with Leeds City, and were forced to replay the tie at Elland Road on the last Wednesday of November. Supported by followers who had travelled on the N.E.R. or Hull & Barnsley rail excursions, the Tigers took the field, watched not only by the directors but also by the reserve side, conquerors of Denaby, whose transport and admission to the game had been generously paid for by the same directors. Against a team who had already beaten them easily 3-1 earlier in the season, City prevailed in the second half on the rough and sticky pitch, and beat their hosts 2-1 to the delight of all visitors from the Third Port, bedecked in amber and black neckties, ribbons and buttons – 'the Hull big excursions delighted beyond bounds'. Davy Gordon opened the scoring after the interval before John Manning ran with the ball from well within his own half on the soft turf ('a lightning bull-dog run') and passed it to 'Stanley' Smith to convert a simple goal. Despite a late goal from Leeds, the Tigers prevailed. 'Athleo' in the Hull Daily Mail was so enthused that he declared the day 'would live and linger in undying memory as long as Hull is a city, which is as long as Hull City will be a club.' In concluding his ecstatic report of the game he wrote:

'Tigers, you rose to a great occasion. You wrung admiration and the acknowledgement of superiority from your keenest, most critical foes. Above all, you justified in the West Riding the claim which the years have reduced to such a meagre shade that Hull can play football.'

The Hull Daily Mail reported the enthusiastic scenes at Paragon station at 10.15 that night as the train carrying the players arrived home to be met by approximately 4,000 happy supporters. In scenes more redolent of a cup final victory, the train's arrival was met with 'a prolonged roar of applause' by the enthusiastic waiting crowd:

"At 10.25 it drew up at the platform, and the passengers on detraining immediately found themselves in the midst of a surging crowd. "Three cheers for the Tigers!" was called on all hands and then followed a shout that made the rafters ring. The players were lost at first in the great throng of cheering supporters, but one by one were recognised and warmly shaken by the hands. Manning vainly endeavoured to lose himself in the pack, but he was eventually 'spotted' and carried out shoulder high into the street. 'Stanley' Smith also had to undergo the same ordeal. As for the rest of the players admiring groups followed them all the way up Paragon-street."

No such scenes followed the victory in the fourth qualifying round against Oldham on the Circle on 9th December, which allowed the Tigers to take their place in the first round proper – a sporting milestone for the city as well as the football club. A tie at the Circle against Reading in early January awaited and the chance of a record crowd. Hull Central MP Sir Seymour King and his wife Lady King were present at the game, indicating the importance of the game at a civic level. Mention was also made in the local press of the difficulties of access to the Circle for the

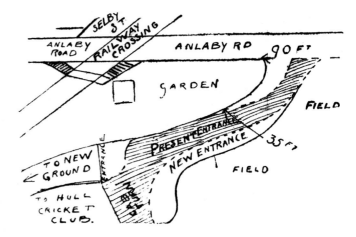

The Entrance to Hull City's New Ground at Anlaby-road.
The shaded portion shows the present entrance, and the wider lines indicate the new boundaries of the entrance.

An artist's impression of the entrance to the 'Cosy Corner' that was the Anlaby Road ground.

large crowds who were starting to attend games and the solutions that had been provided, specifically:

'... the tortuous passage has been considerably widened, so that it now has a trumpet-shaped entrance 90ft. from Anlaby-road, with nowhere a less width than 35ft. It was fortunate that the weather was fine, for, as it was, the present arrangements were taxed to accommodate everyone, and there is no doubt that hundreds stopped away because they imagined they might not be able to see the game.'

Some 10,000 people (the highest recorded for a football game at that venue) crammed into the cricket ground to see City go out to a single goal 'from a free kick at the bowling-green end', this despite their landlords playing a rugby game at the Boulevard some five minutes away. Not the outcome that the directors and players had hoped for, but

still significant progress and cause for satisfaction. The enthusiasm of the large crowd 'which could be heard a mile away', the receipts of £263 15s and the increased profile of the club locally, all signified meaningful progress for a new club striving to make an impression in its first year in the league, and faced with an established alternative sport competing for the public's affections and funds. The attendances, the heightened press attention, the fervour of the fans all confirmed what was already known in other towns and cities in the land – that the English Cup was the most glamorous and exciting football competition in the world. The league was important but didn't possess the charisma and allure of the cup, which had been competed for since 1872, some 16 years before the founding of the Football League. The romance and prestige of the cup, and the perceived unpredictable nature of the games it produced, had, as elsewhere, captured the affections of the Hull sporting public.

The club had arranged to play three away games in four days over the Christmas period. Lincoln away on December 23rd was followed by Burslem Port Vale on Christmas Day and Burton United on Boxing Day. City set off by ferry from the Pier at 9.15, accompanied by a following of supporters who had taken advantage of a cheap organised trip.

The game had seen mention for the first time of the son of the Vicar of Ferriby, the Corinthians' outside-left, E.G.D. Wright. It had been revealed in the local press that he 'might have participated in the tour' but was unable to. He had however undertaken to 'assist the City at Hull against Clapton Orient on January 6th'. Wright had turned out occasionally for Portsmouth in the Southern League and was now offering his services to City when asked.

THE SATURDAY SIXPENCE.
FOR WHO GOT THE SIXPENCE, PLEASE REFER TO OUR ESTIMATES OF THE RESPECTIVE ATTENDANCES AT THE BOULEVARD AND ANLABY-ROAD.

The continuing battle for the public's affection – and money – between City and Hull FC.

THE REV. W. H. WRIGHT, M.A., New Vicar of North Ferriby.

Mr E. G. D. WRIGHT

The vicar of North Ferriby, the Reverend Wright and his son.

Chelsea were the penultimate visitors to the Cricket Circle on February 10th, and William 'Fatty' Foulke as usual figured in the match-related cartoons.

"Little Willie" Foulkes: I'm certain I saw a forward with the ball just now.

"Denaby" Smith: If you can't get past, go underneath.

THE NEXT BIG EVENT.

THERE WAS A YOUNG LADY OF NIGER WHO WENT FOR A RIDE ON A TIGER

THEY FINISHED THE RIDE

WITH THE LADY INSIDE AND THE SMILE ON THE FACE OF THE TIGER

CHELSEA'S HEAVY-WEIGHT: So that's supposed to be a funny picture about our next week's match, eh? But don't you forget, I'm going to be in that affair.

City easily beat Lincoln 4-1 in front of a paltry 1,500 spectators, their fleet forwards bewildering the home side's defenders. Victory at Burslem Port Vale 3-1 and at Burton by 3-0 underlined the impressive form and fitness of the City players as well as their determination and resilience away from the Third Port.

Back at home early in the New Year, the Tigers continued in their rich vein of form against Clapton and then Burnley, both of whom conceded three goals as they slumped to defeat. A goal-less draw with Leeds in front of 10,000 at Anlaby Road was followed by another high-scoring home win – 4-3 against Chelsea on February 10th. A glance down the fixture list of 19 opponents revealed plenty of opportunities for trips to towns in Lincolnshire (Grimsby, Lincoln and Gainsborough), Yorkshire (Leeds, Bradford and Barnsley) and Lancashire (Blackpool, Manchester and Burnley), as well as trips to Stockport, Chesterfield, Burton and Glossop.

The away fixture at Gainsborough Town on the 17th February 1906 was one such trip. A vivid and detail-filled account of the departure on the day of the game provides an insight into the workings of a football club in the early twentieth century, completely reliant on public transport and travelling alongside their supporters. The Hull Daily Mail opened its match report as follows:

"When Hull City departed for Gainsborough this morning at 12.25 they received a splendid send-off from a number of supporters who had assembled at the Corporation Pier. 'Now, Tigers! Play up City' were the departing greetings as the packet left the Pier, and some of the company on the steamer fluttered back a reply with their handkerchiefs, not in the Morse code. Someone spied Browell and Gordon, like two mariners at the helm in the stern, and a special injunction was given them. The Chairman (Mr Alwyn D. Smith) and Mr. A.E. Spring were amongst those who saw the team off, but a large number of supporters went on with them to Gainsbrough. Amongst them were many of the directors, including the new one from Holderness-road (Mr G.J. Kennington), Mr Barraclough (the Lincolnshire director), Mr J. Haller (the secretary), and Mr. Langley, with others who were interested in the early promotion of the club. As enthusiastic for the welfare of the Tigers as ever was ex-Director Smurthwaite, who, with Mrs. Smurthwaite, accompanied the party, who constituted one of the largest to go away with them."

(N.B. George Kennington, of 350 Holderness Road, was a builder, and was the only City director with connections east of the river).

The unexpected 3-1 defeat no doubt made the return journey a bitter one, and it signalled a change of fortunes for the team who then went on to lose the next three games, thus wasting the promising platform for a promotion push that their previous results had provided. The home defeat the following week against Bristol City on the Circle cricket ground was to be their last at that venue. A 5-0 defeat at Manchester United was to follow seven days later.

IN DISGRACE.

This cartoon appeared after a hefty 5-0 defeat at Manchester United on March 3rd.

City's agreement with Hull Cricket Club to use the Circle had expired, forcing the Tigers to return to the Boulevard for one last time against Glossop on March 10th. This also ended in a home 2-1 defeat for the Tigers, and with any hopes of promotion disappearing, attention was now shifting to developments on the north side of Anlaby Road. Hull Daily Mail's 'Athleo' provides a progress report on City's new stadium taking shape next to the Circle:

"Considerable progress has been made with this new ground of late, and on the opening day, it is stated, it will be ready for the reception of a crowd of 20,000, if that number turned up. One does not say that there will be ample stand accommodation by that date, but the stand (186 feet long) erected by City adjoining the Pavilion on the Cricket Ground is now being dismantled, and will be bolted together on the new ground by the date mentioned. It is also proposed to cover in the east side of the ground next to the allotments, and it may be that in time a stand may be erected on the North side.

There was a kind of net work of pipes beneath the surface of the ground, which had been levelled, so that a perfect system of draining has been ensured, whereby the water that falls on to ground will be carried away to gullies at the sides. The playing area is what may be termed the average size-in fact larger than many League grounds – and the novel expedient has been adopted of raising it. In other words, the bottom of the terracing, which has been carried all round the ground, is sunk quite eighteen inches below the pitch, so that whilst spectators can stand all around the enclosure rails, they will not interfere with the sight of the occupants of the first row or two of the terracing.

The main entrance, as has been indicated, will be down the present aisle and along the side of the advertisement hoarding, instead of through the Cricket Club gates. About 130 feet wide at the entrance to the ground proper there will be room for a dozen turnstiles, although only half-a-dozen will be requisitioned at first. It has been argued that this passage, though wide, is long and roundabout, but the writer is assured by those accustomed to deal with crowds that the new City ground will all the better for this, for the supporters will be able to leave quicker without crush, and the traffic of a main street will not be interfered with. There will be an entrance to the ground for members, who will enter through the present gates of the Cricket Club."

Other reports indicated that J.H. Carr and Sons, of Alexandra Road were the contractors for the stand; Messrs J. Taylor and Sons, of Caroline Street, the contractors for the new entrance, and the contractors for the fencing and playing area were Messrs. Barker and Sons, of Smeaton Street. The whole of the woodwork was treated with Messrs Major's green 'Solignum' anti-weathering agent.

The opening game a few days later was played against a backdrop of wintry showers, as the ceremonials associated with the ground opening took centre stage. The occasion was described in the local press, providing a detailed account of the day's events:

"OPENED IN A BLIZZARD

The Hull City ground at the opening received a baptism of rain, sleet, snow – call it what one likes.

Nothing daunted there was though a large gathering of ladies, officials, visitors and home directors A number of enthusiasts were only waiting to have the distinction of being among the first to pay for admission. The first portion of the ceremony was a happy little speech by Mr Gilyott the vice-chairman of the club, who presented to the chairman, Mr Alwyn D. Smith, a golden key. This bore the inscription on one side:-

'Hull City A.F.C. pass key, March 24th, 1906,' and on the other 'Presented to Mr. Alwyn D. Smith, chairman of the directors.' Mr Gilyott referred to the pleasant duty he had to perform in handing over the key. They would agree with him that Hull City, like the weather, has had its ups and downs, but he was sure they would have good sport. They had had bad times in the past but with the united efforts of the worthy chairman, the enthusiasm of the Board, a generous public and an equally generous Press, the time had arrived when they had got out of their troubles. In the past they had great difficulty in arranging for their English cup-tie with Stockton, notwithstanding that they had the use of three grounds. On the day their match was to have been played, the engagement could not be fulfilled in Hull. But that had been all done away with (applause), Mr Gilyott referred to the indebtedness to the ground committee, Messrs Bielby, Locking and Glossop, especially Mr Glossop, the chairman of the committee and the clerk of works (applause).

He was sure when they saw the ground they would agree that it was in a most forward condition, and what it would be next season one could scarcely grasp. Their chairman, they would agree with him, was full of enthusiasm for Association football, and he had a most enthusiastic board. It was fortunate that Mr Smith took the reins when he did (applause). Mr Alwyn Smith was then handed the key, with wishes for prosperity of the club. With this he opened the main gates which are painted in yellow and black stripes, paid his sixpence and was the first to enter the ground, remarking before doing so, 'I am exceedingly obliged to the board for the splendid gift of the key.' He thought they would want to see the ground, and so he would not detain them with a speech.

Everyone else then paid for admission with various coins, and next made a thorough inspection of the ground, the weather now clearing.

At the luncheon the Chairman referred to the exceptional work done by Mr Bielby, and said that he had the greatest pleasure in informing him that there was a writing table waiting for him. This bore the inscription:- 'Presented to Mr J.H. Bielby on the occasion of the new Hull City Football Association ground as a slight recognition of his valuable service, 24th March, 1906.' He asked him to accept with the best wishes of the club, and hoped he would make a heap of money at it. Mr Bielby replied, and remarked that his ambition had been realised in the establishment of class Association football in Hull. He hoped the Corporation would be as progressive as Hull City. They intended to make the ground one of the best in Yorkshire and there was to be erected on the north side a boardroom, and a billiard room for the players. The Sheriff also spoke and at the close, at the request of the Chairman the toast 'Success to Hull City' was drunk. A telegram of congratulation was received from Leeds City by the Chairman."

Finally the Tigers had their home, a purpose-built one, which would serve them well as they attempted to gain promotion to the first league. The sense of optimism imparted by this development would help the club to become established second league campaigners, usually nearer the top than the bottom of the division.

The new ground would eventually have four sides; a covered main stand with seated accommodation above a lower paddock for standing spectators, an open end nearest the main entrance and Anlaby Road, a low side terrace, covered for approximately half its length and a covered north terrace (sometimes referred to as the 'railway end' on account of the carriage shed directly behind it and the N.E.R line to Scarborough.

The Spion Kop, as the open end was also sometimes referred to, was the most basic of the standing areas, the largest and the cheapest. As well as being nearest to the entrance turnstiles, it would probably have been home also to the earthier and more vociferous elements of City's support. Scant protection from the elements would have been available for the Spion Koppers, as they looked across to the left and saw the wealthier patrons of the Best Stand snug in their newly erected wooden structure. Entry to the Spion Kop was through an opening in the terrace which led from the turnstiles.

The roof of north and east stands would, with time, become adorned with advertising for local shops and businesses (butchers, the local brewery, the local paper etc.) as the club's commercial director Ernest Morison sought to increase revenue. Pitch level advertising boards for, amongst others, Fry's chocolate and 'Amusements' magazine would be mounted on the wooden picket fencing. This use of stand and pitch-side space for advertising was commonplace in football grounds of the era. Morison himself recalled the opening a few years later and his own small piece of history, writing of it:

HULL CITY'S NEW GROUND.

An artist's impression of how the new ground would look, which appeared in the press.
A rudimentary truncated main stand, and a pitch enclosed by white picket fencing,
were recognisable features of the Anlaby Road ground.

"The new ground was duly opened on March 24, 1906 on the visit of Blackpool, and the first admission money taken – a new sixpence, which I had the pleasure of paying, still hangs on the walls of the Directors' room on the ground."

Following the inaugural game at the new ground and the associated opening ceremony, further details were made public in local papers. The poor condition of the pitch after its first game – played in snow, sleet and rain – meant that consideration was given to playing some games back at the Boulevard if need be, now that the two clubs were not condemned to be playing at home on the same day. Talk from director Jack Bielby of a barn roof erected over practically two thirds of the ground, making it one of the best in Yorkshire, was reported.

As well as this improvement to the spartan facilities, ambitious developments to the main stand had been conceived:

"The proposal to build a sort of club for the players, with a billiard room, naturally will be a welcome innovation, but I am afraid the players will have to wait some time for that. As far as one could judge, the sight from every part of the ground is excellent, though probably iron supports in front of the grand stand might have been better. But these could not be obtained in time, and so wood had to be used. There is one point however – the stand is a remarkably stable structure, for to the uninitiated there seems to be a forest of timber and steel beams sufficient to erect another. The directors have a board-room beneath, which they have furnished. Mr Haller and team manager Langley have an office fully equipped, the referee and linesmen are accommodated in another room, whilst there are a couple or rooms where the visitors and the home team can retire at half time. Under present arrangements, the men dress and have their baths in the pavilion, and the crossing of the cricket circle to get on to the playing area reminded our Blackpool visitors of junior football days."

But by next season or so, we are to have our own ground, the possibilities of which we can hardly grasp yet, according to Mr Gilyott, the vice chairman, who – he will excuse me for calling him so – is the orator of the club. The Sheriff (Mr E. Gosschalk) was especially impressed with the progress made, and it was a memorable day for him, as representing the occasion on which he saw his first match. He was, too, impressed with the enthusiasm of the City directors, one of whom is, however, retiring on account of pressure of business; and a word of praise has to be said about the N.E.R. on this occasion, although the fencing that has been erected on two sides of the ground does not appear to be high enough to prevent athletic youngsters scaling it."

The new ground was the latest in a long line of firsts for Tigers followers that season, as a succession of new opponents and grounds awaited them.

Support at away games had been steady in the 'Friendly' season as the games had been played almost exclusively at grounds in the north, but the first season in the league had provided the opportunity for City followers to visit venues much further afield. To cater for this demand, and to muster support, trips by train were publicised extensively in the local press. In the case of games at Grimsby, Gainsborough and Lincoln, the Humber ferry was used to access the railway network south of the Humber, at New Holland.

Hull at the time was served by two main railway stations and two railway companies. These were Cannon Street – the departure point for trains of the Hull and Barnsley company – and Paragon which was a terminus for the North Eastern Railway. Thus fans, as well as having access to a ferry, had an enviable choice of railway companies and routes for their excursions following the Tigers.

In a letter entitled 'Hull City Club – Some Criticisms', and published in the Hull Daily Mail of October 23rd, Mr. Sydney T. Smurthwaite sought to give his side of the recent developments among the directorate and the shareholders. Apart from detailing the minutiae of company protocol which he felt had not been observed, Smurthwaite gave some insight into the rapid succession of intrigues and alliances which characterised the directorate of the club at that time:

"... I content myself by pointing out for the delectation of the directors, the following lines:- Matters appertaining to, and the way the resignations as Directors of the Board of Messrs Crompton, Levitt, Andrews, Hay, Shaw, another, and another were obtained. Also the disqualification of two directors at least under Rule 21, Paragraph 3 or 4."

Smurthwaite then goes on to accuse the club of sharp practice by wilfully misleading the public before the Chelsea game in which the visitors' star goalkeeper had been expected to play, thus boosting the attendance and swelling the club coffers:

"Also I complain that, though the Chelsea directors and team, minus Foulkes, arrived on Friday night, yet Foulkes was advertised by sandwich boards on Saturday morning to play."

He then returns to his main argument – the running of the club by the directors, and concludes with some damning accusations:

MR SIDNEY T. SMURTHWAITE,
New Candidate Botanic Ward.

Fancy goods dealer, councillor and prominent City supporter Sidney Smurthwaite – more often identified as Cyd.

"I desire to point out that this letter is not penned with animus or in pique at my non-success in the voting, as I proceed to prove by stating that a non-retiring director of Hull City so recently as the afternoon of the meeting, without any hint from me, offered to vacate the seat on the Board if I would be nominated for the same. This I refused with thanks. I only allowed my name to come forward at the last moment as a protest against the policy adopted by the Board throughout this meeting, and noticed with amusement how anxious certain parties were that the late arrival, Director Locking, should be allowed to vote. I noticed with regret the chairman made no mention of the original promoters. By promoters I mean the gentlemen who first had the requisite pluck to start the Hull City Association Club. Surely they were entitled to a vote of thanks and musical honours, as accorded to others.

I add a word of thanks to Mr Hay, who refused to go to the vote in order to give a chance for a rebuff to the packing of the Board, which I offered to do either for him or Mr Levitt. I am fully aware that to be a director of Hull City, with its cliques and its you-pat-my-back-and-I'll-pat-yours system is far from being a bed of roses for a free lance. In conclusion praise can only be sarcastic if given to someone as regards the well-cooked dish served up to the shareholders."

SPENDIFF.
Hull City's fine Goalkeeper.
(From photograph by H. Harrison, New Cleethorpes.)

Martin Spendiff, the new goal-keeper, who soon established himself as a firm favourite with supporters.

MARTIN SPENDIFF.

The apparent ousting of some of the original enthusiasts associated with the formation and founding of the club in favour of other directors' allies was a sure but depressing indicator of the growing size and status of the club. Money, fame and prestige were starting to accumulate around the directorate of the club, as its evolution continued apace. Inevitably, it seemed, there would be casualties.

The second game played at the new ground was against West Brom' on April 7th 1906. The satisfying 4-0 win was also the occasion when Edward Gordon Dundas Wright played his first game in Hull City's colours. This fact alone was thought to have been responsible for increasing the gate from 5,000 against Blackpool a fortnight earlier to 9,000.

Playing on the left wing and forming an effective pairing with Davy Gordon, the Cambridge Blue made an immediate impact with his precise passing and the ease with which he beat his opponents. To cap his impressive start and to the delight of the crowd, Wright scored with a curling shot direct from a corner past the West Brom' goalkeeper Springer. As well as being notable for Wright's debut, the antics of Martin Spendiff in goal for City and his psychological games with opponents were reported in the press. As the Tigers conceded an early penalty, the goalkeeper started to do 'that jig of his which set the crowd laughing and cheering' as West Brom's Pheasant prepared to take the kick. The ball then went wide of the goal, and the Tigers went on to gain the ascendancy.

Wright had played for England less than a month earlier on March 9th against Wales and it was hoped that he would be able to appear more regularly for City, his other engagements permitting – and there were plenty of those other engagements, either College-related or playing for the famous amateur team Corinthians, composed mainly of players from solid middle class and public school backgrounds. Wright's Corinthian team mates had a purist vision of football that frowned upon cheating and held the values of playing in the correct spirit over winning. These values were increasingly marginalised as the sport became more competitive, and amateur 'gentlemen' became something of a rarity.

Professional 'players' were the norm and were referred to by their everyday names, unlike the 'gentlemen' who were known by their initials followed by their surname. This distinction was to be seen in programmes, newspapers and cigarette cards. Wright was, more often than not, referred to as 'E.G.D. Wright' rather than 'Gordon Wright'. This unusual arrangement (Wright was an amateur in a team of professionals, and reckoned to be the outstanding player associated with City at this time) was compounded by the fact that Wright's father was the Vicar of Ferriby. It was reported that Wright was 'assisting Hull City through the instrumentality of Mr. Alwyn D Smith, the chairman and he signed a City form some time ago'. This would seem to confirm that he was affiliated with City as a club even if he had not yet played for them at the time of his appearance against Wales in March.

If the nickname of 'The Tigers' had gained immediate and enthusiastic acceptance, a name for the new enclosure was not so easily decided upon. 'The Cosy Corner' was rumoured to be favoured by some of the senior directors, owing to the ground's sheltered and compact location. This somewhat fanciful title did not appear to win widespread approval and was quietly forgotten.

On the evening of Saturday 28th April, after the final game of the season (won 2-1) at home against Lincoln City, the club held a farewell dinner at the Imperial Hotel, to which players, management and directors were invited. The directors present were Messrs Kennington, Locking, J. Spring, Morison, Bielby, Stringer and Barraclough. The secretary J Haller was also there with manager Ambrose Langley. The newly elected director Mr Kennington chaired the proceedings and 'bid farewell to the men, wished them a pleasant time during the close season, and hoped they would come back to play for City next season as fit as they were going away'. He touched upon the very creditable position the team had won in the first season of Second League football, and remarked that there was no reason, with the same spirit displayed, why they should not finish even better next.

"The health of the men was proposed by Mr. Locking, who referred to the performance of the Cubs in winning the 'Hull Times' Cup, which occupied the place of honour in front of the chairman. With a smile he remarked that the winning of the 'Times' Cup might be the preliminary to lifting the English Cup sometime in the future. He and his fellow directors had been struck with the general behaviour of the men both on and off the field, and declared that the reason Hull City had done so well was because they had been a team of tigers in the very best sense.

The lid of the cup was removed, and the trophy having been filled with champagne, was passed around and 'Success to Hull City was drunk' – 'Andy' Raisbeck, the City half, and brother of the International, proposed a vote of thanks to Mr Smith, the chairman, and the directors, and that genial back (Davies) seconded. Neither said much, but it was evident their remarks were earnest. The vote was carried with musical honours, Browell leading the singing with even greater ability than he shows in his rendering of 'I wouldn't leave my little wooden hut for you' after City have captured both points away from home. Messrs Bielby and Morison were associated in the vote of thanks to the Chairman, and the company separated early with many expressions of goodwill."

Pondering City's first season in the league and the progress made, one local journalist summed up the state of affairs thus:

"Hardly has any club commenced a career with more sincere wishes for future success, both locally and amongst some of the leading clubs in the country. The interest in the game was never greater or keener in these parts. It, of course, remains to be seen whether the increase of spectators in Hull will command a First Division club in the not too distant future. Amongst those who ought to know opinions differ on the point, but it may be that City will gain promotion without the many winters of toil such as fell to the lot of Woolwich Arsenal for instance"

City's finish of fifth in their inaugural season was bettered only by Chelsea of the new clubs, but the gap between the Tigers and second-placed Manchester United was a massive one of some 18 points. Promotion had never been a serious possibility despite some good results and sequences of victories. Improvements and reinforcements were necessary before a concerted assault on the Second Division table could be contemplated. The fixtures for the 1906/7 season were published within a month of the end of the season, putting the onus on the two rugby clubs to arrange their fixtures around those of the football club. Hull had approached Rovers a year earlier with the idea of putting up direct competition to the City games for all home fixtures. This policy was tried and the respective balance sheets of the rugby clubs at the end of the year showed which sport was the winner. The Hull Daily News commented that '... we are informed unofficially that the Hull F.C. intend next season studiously avoiding clashing when Hull City are at home. The onus of competing with Hull City, therefore, looks like being left entirely to the Rovers.'

The City Board of Directors.
Back row (left to right): F.G. Stringer, A. Bulay Glossop, A. Langley (manager), G.J. Kennington.
Middle row: J.F. Haller (secretary), E. Morison, J. Spring, A.E. Spring, J. Barraclough, J.W. Locking
Front row: J.M. Bielby, W. Gilyott (vice-chairman), A.D. Smith (chairman), Dr. G.W. Lilley, E.K. Wilson.

Shortly after, a rumour in and around Hull that Hull and Rovers were to merge was picked up on by the press. In an article entitled 'Will Hull and Kingston Rovers merge?' on 16th May, the possible sources and motives were explored, City being identified as the party with most to gain from such a merger. City were also identified as the wealthiest of the three clubs as evidenced by attendances and recently published balance sheets. There was allegedly a prevailing belief among those running the club that for City really to prosper, one of the rugby clubs would have to close its doors. Such boldness or mischief making in the Press would surely not go down very well at the Boulevard or Craven Street, and would probably galvanise the rugby clubs into a stubborn defence of their sport and interests.

City were now in the final year of their three-year rental agreement at the Boulevard and intended their reserve side to play there in the Midland League when Hull were not using it. This meant that Hull's A team would have to play at Dairycoates – hardly a satisfactory state of affairs for the rugby club. The positive appraisal of the season continued at the shareholders' AGM held at the Grosvenor Hotel in early July. Chairman Alwyn Smith drew the attention of the directors to 'the way in which the men had played'. He went on to say 'They had been most energetic and enthusiastic, and the shareholders ought to be gratified at having such a hard-working set.' He also outlined ground improvements: they proposed before the next season to cover in the north and east side to accommodate 6,000 people, so that with the present grandstand they would be able to shelter 7,500 in wet weather.

A modest but wholly satisfactory profit on the year of £76 19s 9d was announced, and optimism for the coming season abounded.

One of the most consistent performers that season (and the previous one) had been Andy Raisbeck. He had amassed an impressive amount of appearances in these two seasons, often on the left wing – the position also favoured by Gordon Wright. Perhaps Wright's arrival influenced Raisbeck's decision to leave the Tigers the following season.

Andrew Brown Raisbeck was a pioneer. Not only had he represented City in their first ever game against Notts County at the Boulevard, but he also took the field for them in their first-ever league game in 1905, playing in every match that season. He left City early in the 1906/7 season. His pioneering instincts again became evident when left the Tigers, and Britain, to take up a mining post in Canada – or at least that was the plan. As tenth child of a Scottish family, all of whose male members toiled down the mines, it was no great surprise when Andy joined his brothers down the pit aged 13. However, notable football talent was a family characteristic, and Andy's older brother Alex built an illustrious career playing for Liverpool and Scotland.

During his time in Hull, Raisbeck went to Mansfield at 245 Anlaby Road for this portrait of himself wearing a white City shirt. The photographer's premises were on the south side of the road, approximately between Coltman Street and Bean Street – within easy walking distance of the Boulevard or City's enclosure at Anlaby Road.

Another brother William also played professionally, and another – Luke – had qualified as a mine manager and moved to Southern Alberta in Canada to take up a vacancy. At Luke's urging, brothers Andy and William decided to join him working out there. It was this job offer that signalled the end of Andy's career in black and amber and appeared to offer him a more prosperous long-term future than the modest salary of a footballer.

By the time Luke arrived in Alberta, the managerial job opportunity had disappeared and the brothers had then to make other plans.

These naturally enough included mining, but would not have promised the rosy and relatively secure future they had perhaps envisaged for themselves.

With the outbreak of the First World War, Andy, by now a father of two young children, joined up and enlisted in the Canadian Army – the 28th Battalion (North West Rifles) – in early 1915. His wife and children returned from Canada to Hornsea for the duration of the war.

A crowded Spion Kop photographed by W.H. Duncan, with the usual rich variety of characters and faces.

1906 – 07

"What a marvellous change has come over the football public of Hull! A couple of seasons ago Association football was only visited as a novelty, and when a serious effort was made to introduce class Association football into the City, but few were confident of the ultimate success of the effort. Now, however, the game has come to stay, and thanks to the grand show given by the Tigers last season, it has gained a hold upon the public of Hull which it is impossible to shake off. The progress of the City club has been not only rapid, but sound."

Match report, Hull City v Clapton Orient
Hull Daily Mail 8th September 1906.

The Tigers played their first home game against Clapton Orient, with all the usual early season bustle and optimism apparent. Cyd Smurthwaite's lorry full of boxes of his novelties could be seen near the ground, ready to sell to supporters arriving for the match. As the crowds rolled up, secretary Jack Haller was busy selling passes for the best stand, as the strains of 'My Molly, oh' filled the air. The playing surface, as was to be expected, looked immaculate and the ground itself had various minor innovations such as a dedicated telephone box in black and amber colours for use by the local newspapers. City's two nil victory in front of 5,000 fans would have been an encouraging home start to the Tigers' second full league season ...

The season team group pictured in front on the Best Stand at Anlaby Road was taken by R.T. Watson, the Anlaby Road photographer, who had many years experience of capturing sporting activity. Robert Watson's picture of a Hull City team in front of the Best Stand was reproduced and printed as a supplement to the Sunday Chronicle, a weekend paper with a strong sports bias, published in Manchester.

In the photograph energetic secretary Jack Haller takes his place among the players, manager and trainer. The seated players take their positions on individual wooden chairs, with a rug placed on the grass, lending a genteel Edwardian feel to this team group picture – possibly the earliest taken inside the new ground. Frank Pearson, the forward signed from Chelsea, is seated second from the left on the front row.

In his thanks at the beginning of his 1892 book, 'Football: The Rugby Union Game,' the Reverend Frank Marshall states: 'Especially would I acknowledge my indebtedness to Mr. R. T. Watson, Anlaby Road, Hull, who generously placed at my disposal the whole of his stock of photographs of football teams.' Given that the work was the earliest published complete history of the oval-ball game, such a reference to a local photographer gives an indication of the quantity and quality of the sports-related photographs taken by Robert Thomas ('Bob') Watson in the latter years of the nineteenth century, and of the importance his work must have had within rugby circles. He attended the international game between England and Scotland at Leeds on 4th March 1893 and photographed the teams together, pre-match. His energetic and resourceful approach to his craft was exemplified by an advertisement regularly placed in local sports periodical 'The Athlete' throughout 1890, which read:

"WATSON'S ART STUDIO, ANLABY RD, HULL

FIRST CLASS WORK DONE AT MODERATE CHARGES

FOOTBALL GROUPS A SPECIALITY

THIS SEASON'S WORK: YORKSHIRE, LANCASHIRE, DURHAM, NORTHUMBERLAND, SURREY, CHESHIRE, MIDDLESEX, SOMERSET — ALL ON SALE."

In March the same year, he is mentioned in the same publication thus:

"Mr Watson of Hull journeyed specifically to London to photograph the England and Ireland rugby international fifteens at Blackheath. I should imagine that Mr. Watson has travelled more miles in search of fizogs to photograph than any man in England."

Supplement to the "SUNDAY CHRONICLE."

HULL CITY F.C.

Mr. A. Langley (Manager), G. Browell, M. Spendiff, H. Davis, J. E. Smith, Mr. J. F. Haller (Sec.), W. Leach (Trainer).
J. T. Manning, F. Pearson, E. G. D. Wright (Captain), D. Gordon, W. S. Robinson.
G. T. Hedley, A. Raisbeck.

Engraved, Printed, and Published by E. Hulton & Co., Ltd., Manchester.]   [Photo by R. T. Watson, Hull.

Clearly distance was not an obstacle in the pursuit of an important team photograph.

Watson was born in 1854 in Porter Street – some 11 years before the formation of Hull FC, and 50 years before the formation of the Tigers. The town of Hull, surrounded by green fields, into which Bob Watson was born would have been markedly different from the important city and third shipping port of the country that it had become by the time he started taking photographs of early Tigers team groups in the first decade of the twentieth century. He would have witnessed at close hand not only the birth and development of the Airlie Birds and the Tigers, but also the steady growth in popularity of photography and its central role in the rise of the postcard as a cheap and fast means of communication.

Watson occupied a shop at 70 Anlaby Road, which was close to the building used by emigrants as they awaited their train to Liverpool (and ship to America). He practised his profession for some 63 years before his son took over the business in the early 1930s. As well as studio portraits, he photographed events such as the mammoth Trades and Friendly Society processions, with their lavish banners and decorative regalia, which wound its way from the city centre to the Botanic Gardens running track (now part of Hymers College).

If photography was his profession, music was his hobby as his founder member status in 1884 of the Hull Musical Union testifies and indeed he became their conductor shortly before the First World War.

Pictured left to right are Chas. Saner, Jack Townend, Dick Thornton, J. G. Saner, and Bob Watson as part of a five-man cycling team on the Gladiator Quintet Cycle. They were unsuccessfully attempting to beat champion track cyclist Dick Norton (also pictured) in 1898.

His musical activity started at the tender age of eight in 1862, in the Holy Trinity choir, then in 1864 he joined the St. James choir. In 1873 as a member of the Moore and Burgess Minstrels, he blacked his face every night and became a singing 'negro'. A chorister, singer and musician, he was also a member of the Holy Trinity congregation, as well as occupying the role of choirmaster at St Barnabas Church on Hessle Road and later, in 1885, at St John's, Newington.

As if this professional and artistic activity was not enough, he had taken up track-cycling at 40 years of age with the St. Andrews cycling club and quickly came to prominence, becoming established as the best in Yorkshire in terms of number of prizes won. During one season alone, he won prizes to the total value of more than £3,000 – a considerable sum of money to win in the late Victorian era, especially for a 'mere hobby'. Riding his Nelson cycle, he competed in events as diverse as 100 mile races as well as one mile time trials, entering road races as well as track races. Such was his success that he had to rent a house in which to store his trophies. It was said of him that he had more marble clocks than most jewellery stores and the combined weight was such that the shelves in the house had to be specially strengthened to bear them. He accumulated a large number of gold medals and when a national appeal was made for old gold, he sold some for a value of over a hundred pounds. Such was his fame that he was asked to ride competitively in America and Europe.

A parade passes Watson's Anlaby Road studio c.1914

Bob Watson officiating at a
Boulevard sports event.

'I preferred to stay and keep on winning in England' he said. Nevertheless, his keenness to compete in cycling events and to photograph rugby teams led to a nickname of 'The Wandering Jew'.

His energy and enthusiasm continued to take him into unusual situations, one of which was the task of photographing prisoners on remand at the Hedon Road prison. This meant wheeling a pram from his studio on Anlaby Road at 4.30 in the morning to the jail. He was also staying up late into the night working on his photography, which led to fatigue and illness. 'I sat up till four or five in the morning working, not wanting any sleep' he once remarked.

It was reported that even after his 80th birthday, he would continue his daily sprint around the Boulevard stadium followed by a cold shower, and had contemplated a book of reminiscences on his eventful life.

Perhaps his extremely lucrative cycling activities curtailed his photographing of sports teams and events, as no doubt the two would sometimes clash on Saturdays. His Anlaby Road studio continued with its photographic work and he found time in his fifties to take pictures of early City teams. Watson also advertised his services in the very first Hull City programme on the 2nd September 1905 for the game against Barnsley as the club's 'Official Photographer', and advised potential customers to 'See Windows for Specimens' of his work.

For whatever reasons, the role of official photographer would soon pass to photographer William Harper Duncan on the other side of Anlaby Road, a short walk away at number 15.

Absent from the win against Clapton Orient was the captain and winger Gordon Wright. He had played only one game in City's colours in March earlier in the year – and scored on his debut at Anlaby Road. The public were aware of his particular circumstances – an amateur who often travelled abroad with the famous amateur club the Corinthians; an educated middle-class son of a vicar with a Cambridge University degree who was only intermittently available to play. They also knew that he was a potential match-winner, a player of national profile and a figurehead. Wright had plenty of options, sporting or other, open to him and so his intentions and priorities were not those of the average footballer.

He returned by boat from America at Liverpool in late September after more duties abroad with the Corinthians, to be met by a welcoming

City directorate, anxious to see the winger add his considerable abilities to their cause, as the Tigers made an excellent unbeaten start to the campaign. They need not have feared, as Wright declared in early October that he would play in almost all the home matches and in as many away games as he possibly could. By now permanently resident in North Ferriby, his teaching duties at Hymers College on Saturday mornings (for him) took priority, so the club had to be grateful that he had agreed to play for them in the afternoon. In early October he spoke with 'Athleo' of the Hull Daily Mail about his involvement with the Tigers:

"You can depend upon my turning out as often as I possibly can."

"Then you like playing with City?"

"Yes, they are very good fellows, and they play very hard."

"And what is your opinion of the team?"

"Well, I haven't seen much of them except in the Stockport and Chesterfield matches, but in my opinion, they ought to do well."

Wright revealed that he would be available to play until Christmas, after which he would then be away for ten days. In February his commitments to the Corinthians meant he would play some games for the amateur side. If there were doubts about his popularity with his professional team mates at Anlaby Road, they had not been evident when he had scored his debut goal against West Brom'. After the goal, every member of the team ran up to shake his hand and the crowd 'raised a cheer that might have been heard in the city.' Wright was described in the article as 'of a quiet type, has very little to say on the field or off, and carries such an impassive face through the ups and downs of an exciting match, that one could never guess his feelings.'

Hull's football fervour continued to grow in measurable terms – attendance records were broken and receipts continued to increase. This consistent expansion of profile carried with it levels of increased expectation, as the aspirations of the local footballing fraternity soared. To satisfy the public's demand, local newspapers often featured articles on interesting or influential sporting personalities, which sometimes included directors and administrators.

One City director so profiled was Alfred Spring, who as the piece revealed, had solid local football credentials. Described as being of a 'genial disposition', Spring had played the game in the Hull area in the late 19th century before becoming involved as an administrator first at local level and then at national level. His time as a senior part of the City directorate would last several years.

Mr A. E. SPRING.

"MR ALFRED E SPRING – sketch of a popular Hull Association official.

Mr A. E. Spring, who has been elected to the charmed circle of the English Football Association, is one who has done much to foster the Association game in the East Riding, and the honour which he has received is a fitting reward for a long and active service in connection with the winter pastime. He has been connected in an official capacity with the managing body in Hull since its establishment, and he has held alternately the position of committeeman, vice-chairman, chairman, president, and secretary under the Hull and District Association, afterwards styled the E.R.Y.F.A., and he is, as everyone knows, a hard-working director of Hull City F.C.

At the end of last season, he relinquished the secretaryship of the East Riding F.A., and for his services was unanimously elected a life member of that association. When East Yorkshire recently obtained direct representation, the Council fittingly nominated Mr. Spring to represent them on that body. It was comparatively late in life when Alfred began to evince any liking for football. His first experience was that of a spectator at a rugby match when 19 years of age.

The following season he journeyed across the Humber with the Hull Town Association second team to play Barrow, and although his knowledge of 'Soccer' was absolutely nil, he took up the duties of referee. He candidly admits he blew his whistle when the Hull captain held up his hand; needless to say there was trouble, and Alfred was threatened with a ducking in an adjacent brick-pond before the game was over.

The following year (1889-1890), Mr Spring joined the second string of Hull and played at full-back. The season 1890-1 saw the formation of the old St. Paul's Club, whose first ground, by the way, was on the Hull bank, twenty minutes' walk from the tram terminus at Newland. A.E.S. was now playing forward on the left-wing. Fixtures were bad to arrange owing to the small number of clubs Kingston Amateurs, Grammar School, Hull Town, and St Paul's, practically composing the whole of the clubs in Hull. Season 1891-2 saw the first attempt at a league, the clubs included being those named above, with the additions of East Hull and H.M.S. Guardship teams. St Paul's finished second. The ensuing season saw the subject of our sketch accept the office of secretary of St.Paul's Club, which position he held until the club's demise nine years later. During this period his club had a successful career, and won the Senior League twice, receiving neither cup nor medals for their achievement.

In 1893 A.E.S assisted his team to win the first cup (given by Sir H.S. King) which was ever offered for competition in Hull. After innumerable objections and re-plays, St Paul's met Hull Goughs in the final tie, which was played on Beecroft's Farm [an old farm directly opposite the West Park on Anlaby Road] before a couple of thousand spectators. The result was a goal to nil, and although Mr Spring did not score the winning goal he had a big hand in it.

While never a brilliant player, Mr Spring was always a welcome and useful partner, and during St Paul's last season he held the goal average. We believe he holds the record (locally) for the number of goals scored by one player in a single match, namely, nine, against a team called 'The Critics.'

It is as an organiser that Mr Spring, perhaps, is seen to the best advantage, and his name for many years has been a household one amongst the followers of Association football in Hull. He has seen the number of clubs in Hull increase from a matter of half-a-dozen to over a hundred at the present time. We sincerely hope that Mr Spring will have the same success on the English Football Council as he has had in local football."

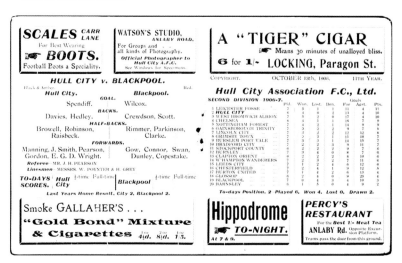

The unbeaten start to the season continued well unto the autumn. On October 8th, Blackpool were the visitors at Anlaby Road. Another goal from Frank Pearson helped the Tigers to a 3-0 victory as the bandwagon rolled on. Messrs Wilson's Prize Brass Band enlivened the pre-game atmosphere with their programme of music, which consisted of:

"1 March 'Anon'; 2 Selection (prize winner) 'Carmelite'; 3 Intermezzo 'Hypatia.'"

The crowd was further entertained at half time by the march 'BB and CF' – the 'British Band and Contest Field March' written by James Ord Hume. As if this wasn't enough, Hull Fair week was in progress at nearby Walton Street, although it was reported that the players had resisted its 'temptations and distractions' to concentrate on their promotion push.

Local newspapers, as well as reporting the Tigers' activities in word and depicting them in cartoons, would use City's increasing popularity to exploit a commercial opportunity if available. In October 1906 the Hull Daily Mail offered 'picture postcards' of 'coloured character cartoons' (drawn by R.W. Lawson, one of their cartoonists), at the price of 4 for 3d or 1d each. Initially four cards were produced; 1) Gordon Wright, 2) Martin Spendiff, 3) Frank Pearson, and 4) Harry Taylor (then a rugby player, and later a trainer of City).

The cards, three of which are shown below, came with 'verses': typically a popular music-hall song modified to extol the virtues of the player in question. Keen students of music-hall song will recognise the verse on the Frank Pearson card as a variation on Ernest Shand's 'Oh! Isn't it singular!'

The Mail used a network of newsagents, hawkers and mobile boy-vendors to sell the cards, and subsequently asked purchasers to write limericks on the reverse and send them back in to the paper in a competition with ten shillings at the prize money. On October 27th, the paper reported that 'the number of Football cards sent in has been extraordinary' and that the ten shillings that week was to be divided jointly between John Witty of 20 Burleigh Street and a Mr Hutton of 221 Walton Street, respectively the senders of the following:

"The game fore and aft, he's been taught,
So with Spendiff in goal City ought,
This season to pass
From II to I Class,
for he's proving himself a Dreadnought"

Bravo Captain Gordon Wright,
To see you playing is a sight,
When you're running down the wing, oh dear!
You make the opposition look so very queer.
We doff our hats and raise the cheer,
"Hurrah for Captain Gordon Wright."

Wot cher, Martin, I've parted wi' a bob!
Wot cher, Martin, to see you on the job!
You're a clever box o' tricks,
You're a Tiger 'tween the sticks,
One what holds the double six.
Bravo, Martin!

"OH, ISN'T IT SINGULAR!"
There came a new forward from Chelsea to Hull,
Oh, isn't it singular;
To Glossop we took him, of confidence full,
Oh, isn't it singular.
Oh, isn't it singular, awfully, very peculiar;
He scored three out of four,
He'd played football before;
Oh, isn't it singular!

Coloured Character Cartoons
(with verses)
Of Famous Players.

No. 1. GORDON WRIGHT.   No. 3. FRANK PEARSON.
No. 2. MARTIN SPENDIFF.   No. 4. HARRY TAYLOR.
Others to Follow.

4 for 3d.   1d Each.

From All Newsagents and Boys.   Now on,

Special Terms to Wholesalers.

Agents, Boys, and Hawkers should Apply at once to
PUBLISHER, "Mail" Office.

and ...

"There's a Tigerish howl of delight
For opponents a funeral rite,
As he slips round the backs
And for goal he makes tracks
I'm right when I write he's all Wright."

Other contributions included:

"Here's health and success Gordon Wright,
Your men lead the list with delight
Fight your way to the goal
Find the net with the ball
Then the First League will soon be in sight."

... by Albert Wilson of 5 Ann's Place, Raywell Street, and ...

"There is a fine forward called Pearson,
With City this is his first season,
He is tricky and cute,
He can dribble and shoot
In the net with a very swift fierce 'un."

... by E.A. Foster of 21 Grove Street.

To continue the success of the cards the paper next changed the competition to a 'Picture puzzle competition of local players' names', in which readers wrote in their answers on the cards in response to published cartoon depictions of local sportsmen's surnames.

All three City players were prominent at the time, Pearson scored a hat trick in his debut at Glossop on October 6th 1906, Spendiff being the established goalkeeper from City's start in Division Two and Wright was arguably the club's most famous player, having played for his country on several occasions. Writing of Pearson on the Monday after his explosive debut in black and amber, a local journalist wrote:

"Solid and squarely built, he is one of the steady and resolute type of centres, with plenty of confidence, but none of that flashiness of the dapper type of forward, who reminds one of a cat treading on a glass roof. An ideal centre forward must be possessed of a sound constitution, a sturdy physique, and a calculating brain, and City's new man appears to possess all three qualifications. He does not seem to mind helping a hard wrought centre-half, although a centre forward who has to out-sprint the backs has plenty to do without going back and wearing himself out in helping the defence. Pearson's idea seems to be to be well up the field, just sufficiently inside the backs to keep onside. He likes, he told me, to have the ball passed to him slightly ahead, and then he endeavours to slip between the backs, out-sprint them if possible, and shoot. He is also partial to a ball, that comes breast high, and, as those who saw the match last Saturday realise, has a knack of shooting on the run so that the goal has little chance of steadying himself."

Pearson's promising start in black and amber and his high profile transfer was insufficient to create a place as a notable player in the club's early history, for despite his eventful debut, he managed only 12 further appearances and three more goals. Despite a massive transfer fee of over £800 paid to Chelsea on the basis of his impressive scoring exploits the previous season, he failed to live up to expectations. He disappeared quietly from first team reckoning, the reasons for which culminated in a suspension sine die later that season. The experience of this costly gamble was a harsh lesson for the club. With an International winger and expensive goal-scorer in the middle, City were seemingly set fair for a serious promotion challenge as they topped the table, but four straight defeats revealed hitherto hidden weaknesses and their campaign faltered in the late autumn. On 1st December the Tigers made the short trip by boat and railway to Cleethorpes to take on Grimsby Town.
Along with the Leeds City matches, games against Grimsby Town had started to be relished by local fans and press as local derbies.

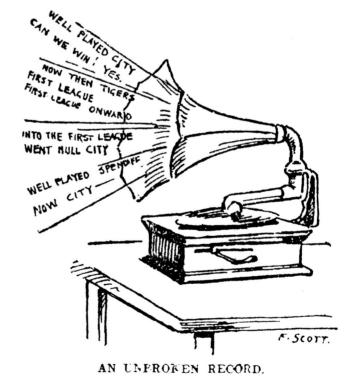

AN UNBROKEN RECORD.

City's invincibility in cartoon form

Proximity and traditional rivalry ensured the games were keenly fought in front of partisan crowds. City had not yet beaten Grimsby so the win there was particularly relished. An account of the day's proceedings on the following Monday graphically reported the joy of the travelling supporters, prefaced with tongue-in-cheek, quasi-biblical prose:

"How doth the Mariner sit solitary that was full of egotism! How are they become as a potsherd, that were great among the Soccers and princes aforetime among the First Division! Among all their supporters there were none to comfort. They have gone down into captivity and are held by the yoke, fourth from the bottom of the table. All their strength is departed. Their forwards are like harts that find no pasture, they search in vain for the goal net.

If Association football had been the national pastime in the days of Jeremiah, the great prophet must have been impelled to bewail the result of the great encounter which seven thousand people witnessed at Blundell Park. The Tigers' was a great triumph, and it was the more acceptable because they had never beaten the Mariners before. It was a Gala day for Hull supporters who, to the number of 2,000 went to Grimsby. The second trip was run in duplicate and New Holland Pier was suggestive of a Bank Holiday. Nearly five thousand of the crowd left the ground absolutely despondent. The remaining number were intoxicated with the exuberance of delight, and after carrying Spendiff off the field shoulder high, came down Cleethorpes-road making the air ring with their songs of gladness. Hull City's visit was a holocaust for Grimsby."

SPENDIFF ("LET 'EM ALL COME.").

Goals by Pearson, Manning and Robinson helped City to a 3-1 win, but ex-Grimsby goalkeeper Martin Spendiff was regarded as the match-winner with his two penalty saves.

The visit of promotion-chasing Chelsea on Christmas Day for an 11.30 kick-off drew 16,000 to the Anlaby Road ground, beating the 12,000 Manchester United had drawn to the Boulevard the previous season as Hull's

A GOOD MEAL.

THE CITY TIGER: Um! a bit fishy perhaps, but not quite so tough as I expected.

Games against Grimsby were to provide a rich source of inspiration for cartoonists over the years. This one was published after the 1-0 win on December 1st.

highest football attendance (providing record receipts of some £380). Elected into the Second League with the Tigers some 18 months earlier and possessing a huge stadium with accompanying financial backing, the visitors would have been a crowd-pulling opponent.

The attendance was some 6,000 more than the previous best at Anlaby Road. Gordon Wright played in spite of some concerns that as the son of a local clergyman, family religious convictions would prevent him doing so. The players accompanied by directors Spring, Glossop and Bielby, as well as Mr and Mrs Cyd Smurthwaite, had attended the service at St Augustine's Church in Queen's Road, and a seasonal atmosphere prevailed as the selections of Wilson's Prize Band encouraged the vocal participation of spectators in the grandstand and enclosure. Before the game:

"From all quarters of Hull spectators arrived. Tram loads arrived from the Newington end, and it was quite a sight to see the crowds arriving by East Hull and Beverley-road and Spring-bank cars at the

City-square terminus, and sprinting across to catch the Anlaby-rd cars for the new ground. A band helped to interest the vast crowd, which but for energetic stamping might have been frozen in the biting cold, and on the best stand the noise was like the intermittent rattle of a Gatling gun. There was not long to wait for punctually to time the City captain led the team on to a ground as hard as cement, which the sun feebly smiled at."

On a frozen pitch and with a gale-force northerly wind blowing the ball repeatedly into touch, the game was a dismal spectacle. City's careless passing also contributed to the seemingly incessant throw-ins. Although some Chelsea players had brought boots with rubber soles with them from their Hornsea hotel, they opted to play with normal studs and in jerseys – 'that would have been an advertisement to Reckitts Blue.' City won the toss and chose to attack the Anlaby Road end, believing the wind favoured this option. Having failed to capitalise on this advantage by the interval, City knew they would have to withstand Chelsea's exploitation of the conditions.

There was an air of inevitability about Chelsea's winning goal from Windridge. Wright was virtually a spectator in the second half as City struggled to construct any meaningful attacks in the strong wind and left their most creative attacker starved of possession, as Spendiff and the backs continued to slice the ball towards the opposite wing. An idea of the strength of the north wind can be gained from the goal kick count in the two halves: in the first, with City attacking the Anlaby Road end, Chelsea had 16 goal kicks and City had eight. In the second half, Chelsea had one and City had 19. Wright's Christmas Day commitment to the team was not rewarded by the result for which he had hoped.

The Tigers, by virtue of their status and league-placing at the end of the 1905/6 season, avoided having to compete in the qualifying rounds of the FA cup, and found themselves drawn to play Tottenham Hotspur early in January. Tottenham, although not a League side had won the cup in 1901 as a Southern League side, and were regarded as tough opponents to be approached with trepidation. Having suffered a 2-1 defeat at Clapton Orient the previous Saturday, the Tigers, accompanied by manager Ambrose Langley and director Cyd Smurthwaite, spent the night in the capital before making their way from London Bridge to Worthing, their training base for the Spurs game.

Before departing from London, the group found time to visit the Drury Lane pantomime where the artiste Miss Queenie Leighton honoured them by gaily waving the 'Amber and Black' colours (supplied to her by Smurthwaite) in front of a packed house before returning to the Charterhouse Hotel.

Gordon Wright's old club had allowed City to make use of their ground for training, which together with the breezy beach, would ensure the players were rested and in the best condition for their biggest game of the season against the Southern League club that had won the competition in 1901. Tottenham, in the meantime, had gone to Leigh-on-Sea to finalise their preparations.

The large number of fans from Hull expected to make the trip meant that special arrangements had to be made to ensure the railway companies could cope with the extra passengers, and three services out of Paragon station were advertised accordingly- the 11.25 pm Friday night train, and the 6.25 am and 9.45 am on the day of the game. In addition, Thomas Cook also operated a train out of the Cannon Street station of the Hull and Barnsley Railway Company leaving at 11 pm. Secretary Jack Haller had a supply of reserved seat tickets for those wishing to watch the game in style.

Frank Pearson's knee problems kept him out of the game at White Hart Lane where the home side were strong favourites to progress, having won the tournament in 1902 as a Southern League side. In his absence, Jacky Smith, George Rushton and Stanley Smith finished tamely and their lack of conviction contrasted with the more forceful efforts of Tottenham's Walton, Woodward and Hewitt. Despite this, a draw was adjudged to be just about a fair result – City having more chances, the Londoners having the better ones. Tottenham's science and invention dismayed their supporters, but the direct bustling style of the Tigers seemed to enthuse them more. Gordon Wright's Corinthian background was evident in his playing style and his application of their straight-ahead theory, but there was more to City's game than kick-and-rush haphazard play. They worked very hard to nullify Tottenham's attack and restricted them to a minimum of clear-cut opportunities, which made their own tame finishing all the more frustrating.

City's half-back line of Browell, Robinson and Gordon was rated as one of the best in the Second League that season and their display on the day was faultless, with Davy Gordon's tireless industry and relentless probing outstanding. Bill Leach's efforts and the Worthing sojourn appeared to have made the difference as City appeared more energetic and sprightly than their metropolitan counterparts. The general impression was that Tottenham, who had won all of their previous home games that season, had underestimated their young opponents, or as one local paper put it:

"But we saw the Tiger at his best. His fur bristled, and his tail was always out at an angle of 45."

For the replay, City based themselves at Hornsea to prepare, and Tottenham went to Withernsea, interrupting their stay to visit the Turkish baths in Hull's George Street.

To Tott'nham, to Tott'nham, to play a Cup-tie,
Home again, home again, to have one more try.

FAIRLY UP A TREE!
SHOOT STRAIGHT, MR TIGER!

TIGERS AT HORNSEA.
Spendiff: "Can you see anything!"
Captain Wright: "Yes; I can see the Wreck of the Hotsupurus."
Martin: "Marvellous!"

The highlights of the season were the three FA cup ties played against Southern League Tottenham Hotspur. The games captured the imagination of fan and cartoonist alike.

Mr A. Stapleton, described as 'Hull's blind musician', wrote the following lines which were to be sung to the tune of 'My Irish Molly':

"City, dear, just come and hear
I'll sing a little song;
You pleased us in the first round,
And now we shan't be long.
Yes, every night I go to sleep
I see the English cup
And dream of Crystal Palace, boys-
I wish the Tigers luck,

Chorus:- Tigers, the famous Tigers!
Hull City is the team;
They've got the strength and science-
Password - defiance.
They are the cream;
Spendiff, the fine goalkeeper,
Gordon Wright, of course is full
Of the game and football fame:
The 'Spurs of Tottenham cannot tame
The Tigers we've in Hull."

Many drawings depicting tigers and cockerels in a variety of situations appeared in the press. The cockerel was eventually to triumph but the tiger, too, played his part – and was well paid for it.

For the Thursday afternoon 2.30 pm replay, the gates opened at 1.15 and to watch the game spectators had the following options:

"... prices of admission, 6d ; to east side, 3d extra; to north side 1d extra; to west side enclosure, 6d extra; to grandstand, admission by ticket only, price 2s, which includes the enclosure. It has been decided to issue 1,000 tickets for this stand, which accommodates 1,300, so every purchaser should be sure of a seat."

These tickets could be bought from two of the directors; Jack Haller in his office at 26, Scale Lane or from John Locking in his tobacconist's shop in Paragon Street. The competition rules stipulated that no half-price admission was allowed, which would have disappointed many younger or female spectators. Pre-match music was once again to be provided by the prize-winning Wilson's Band. A local newspaper report described the scene:

"The very atmosphere breathes of the match and everyone talks of it. Everyone was bent upon seeing it. From all over the city, from all over Yorkshire, and many parts of the South came football enthusiasts, who were intent on seeing the Tigers and the Hotspurs try conclusions for the second time. All along the Anlaby Road remarkable scenes were witnessed. Cars were at a premium, and many pitched and hasty battles were fought for possession in the square. Tram after tram was crowded with human freights. From one end of the road to the other extended a great procession of people. They entirely flooded the entrance to the ground. Money takers had not known what it really was to be busy till then. Coins after coins rolled in through the wicket gate, and the great wonder of it all was where did the multitude come from. Surely the Thursday half-holidayite could not muster in such illimitable numbers. Employers could early find an answer.

Many applications had they received from their employees for a few hours off, and it was rumoured that several offices were closed, so few hands were left. Thus it was when 2.30 arrived there was not a vacant corner in the ground, and an air of expectancy was apparent all over the enclosure, and there were impatient cries for the teams to make their appearances."

On a dank and misty Thursday afternoon, Rushton kicked off for City from the Anlaby Road end in front of an expectant capacity home crowd which included representatives of Blackburn Rovers, the team drawn to play the winners of the tie in the next round. The pitch was on the heavy side and slippery, and there followed a game similar to the first one at Tottenham, with ineffectual shooting by both sides. As they realised the unsuitability of the pitch for their quick-passing game, Tottenham started to play the long passing tactics adopted by the Tigers in London and employed again at Anlaby Road. This was due to the unyielding nature of the City half-backs as much as the pitch.

As the players visibly tired on the heavy pitch, and the chances of a victory diminished, the teams agreed to an extra 30 minutes of play to settle the tie. As the gloom intensified, the referee, Mr Hines of Nottingham, decided to abandon the game after only ten minutes as poor visibility meant that play had become impossible. It was reported that – 'a weird effect was produced by the spectators striking matches to light their pipes, the lights looking like will o' the wisps.' The murky mid-January light had curtailed the game by half past four.

The London team, as in the first game, had played with intricate footwork and what was referred to at the time as 'combination' (meaning cohesive teamwork and mutual understanding) that had been cancelled out by the Tigers' wholehearted endeavour and bustle, but there was a widespread perception that City would struggle to win with their lack of goal-scoring talent, which meant that a single goal from Tottenham might suffice. After this abandoned replay, a weary City went down to an abysmal 4-2 defeat at home to a modest Gainsborough Trinity side. Despite seeming to be far superior to the Lincolnshire team in the opening exchanges, the Tigers contrived to waste chance after chance and give away goals, due to slipshod defending. The buoyant early season promise seemed to

be evaporating and fans jeered openly at George Rushton, guilty in their eyes of missing several chances.

Despite the supportive and positive tone of the local newspapers, who continued to reflect a largely uncritical view of the club, sections of the support, usually portrayed as equally enthusiastic, showed signs of impatience and disenchantment. Directors as well as players came under critical scrutiny by frustrated fans, who expressed a more direct appraisal of the situation than the journalistic diplomacy evident in match reporting of the Tigers' games. One fan wrote in a local paper after the Gainsborough game:

"What a match! What a display after Thursday! There are people who will probably say I am too hard on the players but are there any who can deny that one particular forward should himself have scored three easy goals in the first half alone! Let City drop that man at once.

I think the public ought to be enlightened through the Press as to why some good class men cannot be got into the forward line? Every match shows plainly for itself where the weakness lies. Teams that are aspiring for First League honours have met City here, and have been practically penned up around their own goal for half the game. The half-backs are responsible for this, and are a good set of workers, but the forwards cannot put on the finishing touch.

I myself, as a younger man, played soccer, so of course know the game. In fact I am heart and soul in it, and it grieves me to see such displays as are given sometimes on the Anlaby-road, especially when everybody can plainly see (including the directors, unless they are blind) that Soccer is a coming game. Give the public a good game, and they will roll up in their thousands. If funds are low then wait a bit, but there should be got at once, at least one good back, one half-back, and three forwards, and to get good men they would cost at least £1,000. The directors should spend that amount if they can, with a view to a good game, good gate, and good dividends in the future.

When the first team has been put in good working order, then attention should be paid to the reserves. A clean sweep wants making of about half. Replace them with good ones who can step into the first team any time in case of an injury. To-day a man may be injured and there is not another to take his place unless it be one who is practically useless.

Honour and great thanks are due to Mr. E.G.D. Wright for the way in which he sticks to the team, but he cannot really do his duty in such company. His partner of to-day cannot either receive or give a good pass.

Further comment is unnecessary, and in conclusion I think City directors have, in obtaining men, been penny wise and pound foolish. What on earth is the use of having 30 men on their books and playing gates of 2,000 – that is what it will come to – when, with 30 good men they would get honour and never play to less than 10,000. I enclose my card, I am, Sir, etc — SOCCER"

For the second replay, the Tottenham directors induced City to play at White Hart Lane on the following Monday (the third game in five days) for a consideration of £150 in addition to a half share of the gate receipts. City players also reportedly preferred Tottenham to a new unfamiliar neutral ground.

The Tigers' weary limbs were rejuvenated at the electric baths on Anlaby Road owned by a Mr Blackburn, and the party of players and directors left Paragon Station at 4.30 on the Sunday afternoon for their familiar London quarters – the Charterhouse Hotel. City were followed by supporters on the excursions run from Paragon at 6.25 and from Cannon Street an hour later.

In the poorest of the three games, weak and ineffective finishing was again evident, City missing three glorious chances in as many minutes – Jacky Smith (twice) and John Manning were the culprits. George Rushton had been dropped following his poor display against Gainsborough, but no improvement in attacking incisiveness was evident.

A goal on the half-hour from Herbert Chapman of Tottenham, who had freshened up their team with new and younger players, put the home side ahead. Rather than demoralising the visitors, this provoked a spirited response from the Tigers who set about Tottenham with renewed vigour. But the greater speed and skill of the Spurs players, allied to their greater strength in depth, meant that City were unable seriously to threaten Reilly in the Londoners' goal. The Tottenham supporters gave the departing City team and directors a rousing cheer, as the visitors drove away from White Hart Lane, under mounted police escort and with many more officers on foot, to catch the 5.45 train from Kings Cross.
It was reported that funeral cards of Hull City decorated with a mourning coach and verse: 'Por ole Hull City ...,' were finally able to be sold outside the ground, having been on sale before the first tie as well as outside the Anlaby Road ground for the replay. It added that the Tottenham street hawkers showed no bias and offered favours mingling 'the orange and black with the blue and white'.

For these three cup ties City received £475 for their first match at Tottenham, £249 for the second match at Hull, and £500 for the third match at Tottenham, making a total of £1,224. This would have cushioned the disappointment of the early exit, as well as easing some of the financial burden on the club in the wake of the expenditure incurred in establishing the Anlaby Road ground.

SHOWN THE DOOR.

CITY TIGER: This not a very dignified position; but it has its compensations.

Detailed criticism of the club in the local press was starting to become a regular occurrence, as supporters started to compare City with other clubs and evaluate the success of the club's decisions in that light. Some fans were disgruntled specifically about boardroom affairs and disliked the idea of rugby men being allowed to join the board, given the obstacles placed in front of City by the Northern Union. Such views found their voice in a letter published in a local paper in the spring of 1907:

"HULL CITY FOOTBALL CLUB DIRECTORATE
Hull Daily News 8th April 1907
Sir,
I see by the 'Sports Express' of Saturday last that there is a likelihood of another ex-Rugby Director seeking a place on the Hull City board. Now I don't know who the gentleman is, but if he is rash enough to seek re-election, I do hope the shareholders will refrain from supporting him. No matter how estimable a man he may be in other respects we don't want the Hull City board crowded with disappointed officials from other clubs- especially rugby clubs. The Hull F.C. had their opportunity when the Association game was first played at the Boulevard but they would not risk anything and some of those Rugby people who sat on the fence want to jump over to the Anlaby-road side now that the Association garden is in order. Let us vote some practical men on the Hull City board, and not men

who want to run away from rugby. If they cannot run their own club successfully we don't want any more of them fingering in our pie. I am glad to see that some of the original directors of the City are coming forward again, and I hope the shareholders will support these instead of voting for 'turncoats'.

The men who first set the Association game on a substantial footing in Hull in the face of so many difficulties are the men who deserve to get back in office. Their choice of players was a credit to them. I wish we had a forward line like the men we had the first season, I hope the directors will get more players of experience, and not wait till they are all booked by other clubs. We want some live players and live officials next season.
Yours truly, VIGILANT"

City wound up their season with a visit to Leeds City's Elland Road ground on April 27th. It was a chance once again for many Tigers fans to visit what had been a happy hunting ground for them in previous meetings. The colourful exodus is detailed in a match report by the Hull Daily Mail's 'Athleo' two days later:

"Whenever the Tigers journey to the West Riding, they are always accompanied by a big following, but on Saturday the number of trippers who travelled to Leeds in order to bid farewell to their favourites beat previous records. This fixture is being looked on as a 'local Derby' more than ever and I shall be surprised if the dates on future occasions are left until the 'fag end of the season.' There was no necessity for the flag edge retailer to greet us with his familiar cry 'Tiger colours, 1d each,' as nearly every one of the faithful trippers possessed a button, neck-tie, or muffler of black and amber.

The excursionists wending their way along Boar-lane and Briggate shortly after two o'clock (thanks to the railway companies, whose trains only occupied about an hour and a half on the journey) caused many of the natives to wonder who these invaders were, and what their business.

A party of 25 were mistaken for Congregational Sunday-school trippers, and I really began to realise how easy it is for people to make ridiculous mistakes at such times. All roads led to Elland-road: the Leeds Corporation tramway officials, who cater so admirably for the public, found they were unable to cope with the demand for seats, and a number of City officials, officials of other concerns and 'yer 'umble,' marched like the dismissed Woolwich workmen to the scene of the action."

City quickly raced into a two-goal lead to the delight of their travelling followers...

"The Hull crowd applauded as only Hull crowds can; the strains of 'Hello, hello, hello' were heard on all sides, and for several minutes the Tigers enthusiasts would not be silenced with their 'One, two, three. Well played, Stanley Smith'."

Leeds fought back to parity but an entertaining draw was a satisfactory finale to the season. The Tigers' final league position of ninth was a disappointment after the previous season's fifth placing. Inconsistency, a vulnerability at Anlaby Road and a continued goal-scoring weakness were the hallmarks of a modest campaign. The Tottenham cup-ties, as well as providing an enthralling spectacle in front or large crowds, enabled the club to make a very healthy profit of £635 on the year.

Having started in promotion-winning form, City suffered their first defeat as late as mid-October at the hands of Bradford City. The quality of the opposition up till then had not been the highest the division had to offer and other defeats quickly followed. Dreams of promotion evaporated as seven defeats by the turn of the year signalled that the Tigers were not among the strongest group at the top. The trio of cup games against Spurs in January temporarily revived a flagging campaign, even if defeat was the outcome.

HULL CITY'S FIRST DEFEAT.

KATISHA (Bradford) sings:
" Yes, I like to see a tiger
From the Congo, or the Niger,
Especially when a-lashing of his tail."
—The Mikado.

Gilbert and Sullivan's The Mikado provides the inspiration for this cartoon on City's first defeat at Bradford

A new ground attendance-record was set as 21, 975 fans crammed into the Anlaby Road ground for the replayed first round tie, which took place on a Thursday afternoon, but after that City won only once up to Easter Saturday. To put that attendance in-perspective, some 60,000 spectators attended City's game at promotion-aspirants Chelsea on Good Friday. The Tigers rarely played in front of five-figure crowds, and then only when the opponents were near the top of the table or local. Hence the match with Grimsby and the Chelsea game on Christmas Day duly attracted five-figure attendances at Anlaby Road. A late run of victories hauled them back up the table and a spirited display at Leeds on the last day ensured that City finished one point above the West Yorkshire club.

As the club endeavoured to build its support in the face of weekly competition from older established oval ball attractions, the novelty was wearing off, and floating fans started to show they could be discerning in selecting which Tigers games to attend. The home gates however never sank below 5,000 even though at many of the clubs they visited attendances failed to reach this level.

The signing of the ex-Chelsea centre forward, Frank Pearson, had been a significant investment for the club and his hat-trick at Glossop augured well, but his appearances became sporadic. Matters deteriorated to the point that the club had no other option but to suspend him sine die and the local press, perhaps mindful of the importance of their relationship with City, declined to go into 'undesirable details', as they coyly described the cause of this suspension. Instead John Smith, commonly referred to as 'Jackie', emerged the main goalscorer with 19 goals in 38 games. City experimented with various players in the centre forward role. As well as Pearson, George Rushton and 'Stanley' Smith also wore the number nine shirt.

The Pearson affair and the Tottenham games seemed to take the wind out of the Tigers' sails, perhaps the large amount of gate receipts from the cup-ties offset the loss made on the Pearson signing, and helped pay the increased wage bill that City were now facing. As well as increased wages, the expenses associated with a growing club started to appear on the balance sheet. The cost of running a Reserve team competing in the Midland League (2,202 miles travelled) and a third team (220 miles travelled), as well as the first team (3,946 miles travelled), added up to a total of £448 18s in travelling and hotel expenses. This figure also included some 4,520 miles travelled by the club officials on business, which all worked out at about a halfpenny a mile.

But at least the £100 per annum rent payable to Hull FC was no longer being paid, and no doubt that money could be utilised for strengthening a team that had fallen from 5th to 9th. At the shareholders' AGM in June, Chairman Alwyn Smith was of the opinion that the overall quality of play in the division had improved markedly in one year, though they were extremely happy with the players they had, and 9th place in that context was more than acceptable.

As regards new players, Smith related that people in the past had advised 'Get stars'. He continued that he did not like stars – 'there were three kinds of stars – planets, comets and fixed stars.' At which his colleague William Gilyott interjected, to general laughter – 'and shooting stars.' 'Solid, good, hard-working, sound' players were to be preferred – players such as new signing Tommy Nevins from Washington Athletic. The value of City's players, according to Smith, stood in their books at £265 – that was 20 players, working out at about £13 each.

The priority, as indeed was the case a year earlier, was now the signing of a class centre forward (of the type Pearson had briefly promised to be) and a reserve back. With these positions strengthened, and the promoted duo of Notts Forest and Chelsea no longer an obstacle after their elevation to the First Division, the way seemed to be clear for a determined promotion campaign.

1907 – 08

William Harper Duncan, also known erroneously as William Arthur Duncan or William Hooper Duncan, and more familiarly as Billy Duncan, would have been 30 years old and married with two small children when Hull City was formed in 1904. By 1907 he had established a photographic business at 15 Anlaby Road, on the south side of the road opposite the entrance to the College of Art. He was to trade from this location until the early 1930s when he transferred his business to 102 Hessle Road.

Much of Duncan's life around the first quarter of the twentieth century was spent in a succession of houses in the streets south of Anlaby Road. He is known to have lived successively at Ruskin Street (1900), Bacheler Street (1907), Cholmley Street (1911), Arlington Street (1919) and his longer term residence at 148 Boulevard from around 1920 onwards. This last address was significantly grander than his previous ones and overlooked the ornate fountain placed at the Boulevard's intersection with Cholmley Street and Gordon Street.

Most of these addresses are a short walk from each other and less than five minutes' walk from both the Boulevard home of Hull FC and the Anlaby Road ground of the Tigers. In an era when most of the players also lived near their place of work, not only would Duncan be steeped in the day-to-day happenings at both clubs, but he would be handily placed with his camera to record crowds and events at their respective stadia. The noise generated by a goal scored for City at Anlaby Road or a try scored for Hull would certainly have been audible in the Duncan household.

The photographic recording of goings-on at City and Hull was only a part of Duncan's business. Apart from his bread-and-butter studio portraits, he was also a conventional commercial photographer who was able to record a wide variety of activities, parades and public events, perhaps reasoning that the more people featured in the picture, the greater the number of potential customers for prints of that photo. Hull Fair crowds, visiting London Policemen engaged in policing the Hull Docks strike, company or works dances, soldiers training locally for the Western Front, school and amateur sports teams – any group represented a photo opportunity. For this reason, the courteous and kindly Billy Duncan would have been a familiar face to thousands of Hull people, and his photographs would have had their place on their walls, mantelpieces and sideboards, as well as in countless family albums. He also had an association with the Hull Territorial army and its annual training camps, becoming more familiar to the men than some of their sergeant-majors, as his permanent presence lasted longer than many of their corps commanders.

As the advent of the reproduction of photographs in local newspapers coincided with his increasing activity with the Tigers and the Airlie Birds, Duncan's work started to appear regularly in the sports pages of the local press. Even fringe or reserve players would appear in the midweek editions when news was thin on the ground, usually pictured posing at Duncan's Anlaby Road studio. The local papers had not yet employed their own sports photographer(s) and would not do so for several years, enabling Duncan almost single-handedly to provide a visual chronicle of the players of Hull City, Hull FC and Hull Kingston Rovers for approximately a quarter of a century. These photos, as well as being sold to the newspapers, were sold in his shop to fans of the three clubs, and it is these early examples of supporters' memorabilia which provide his lasting legacy. Sold as postcards, but almost never sent as such, they were kept by enthusiasts of the clubs or even by the players themselves and their families.

Crowd scenes would also be kept as mementos of big games and cup-ties in family albums, as well as providing good business for Duncan since dozens of spectators would be featured in any single crowd scene, and a walk around the perimeter of the pitch at any of Hull's three clubs for a big game would provide several of these populous groups. Around 1930 however, with the so-called Golden Age of postcards long since over, his photographic output of the city's professional sports clubs gradually dwindled.

City's relegation to the third tier of English football meant declining crowds and interest. Local newspaper mergers and acquisitions meant that the Hull Daily Mail emerged as the sole potential publisher of Duncan's work – and the volume of photographs they

although he did remarry in 1940. William Duncan died on October 25th 1944 at his home, by then at 2055 Hessle High Road – a long way from the densely populated streets linking the Boulevard and Anlaby Road grounds in which he had lived and where he had captured the leisure hours and sporting enthusiasms of his fellow residents.

Despite his death, the business was carried on in his name from 102 Hessle Road for some ten years after the end of the war. This address was later also registered as a draper's, trading simultaneously from the same premises (which suggests Duncan's studio was on the first floor) before finally ceasing all activity.

Billy Duncan opted not for the customary team group in two or three seated or standing rows, but instead issued these two artistic postcards comprising the first team players with trainer Leach, and the second team with their trainer Massie. Sharing the same format, these elegant cards required that the players and trainers be photographed individually in Duncan's studio, and then mounted in a composite image including the head and shoulders of each as shown above. The names of the individuals were written in slightly-dated (for the time) mock-mediaeval style script beneath their pictures, rendering their names slightly difficult to read. The name of the issuer was printed in the bottom right corner, so small as to be barely visible to the naked eye. Duncan's studio compositions also demonstrated eye-catching compositional flair. Additionally, Duncan would also have been able to use the individual player portraits for sale in their own right to the public or press, not just as mere component images for his team card.

printed was such that they would have been able to employ their own photographer(s). The established cinema newsreel coverage of sports events meant that the public had access to ever more sophisticated national footage, and were therefore less obliged to focus on purely local sports events.

In 1930, William Duncan would have been 54 years old and in all probability less inclined to venture out photographing sports teams and crowds as he had done so energetically 10 or 20 years previously. Fewer postcards from this era remain. Very few, if any, postcards of players photographed in his studio at 102 Hessle Road exist. Team groups taken at Anlaby Road, The Boulevard and Craven Park testify to his continued activity in this period. The death of his wife Louisa in 1939 and the advent of the Second World War provided a sad end to this period of decline,

the FA cup was also on view – a draw in itself, given the trophy's near legendary status – and where after the first innings, City players and their Sheffield counterparts would race against each other in a series of sprint competitions. Should this glimpse of the precious cup not suffice, a further opportunity to see it displayed in a prominent position at the Hippodrome theatre in Porter Street presented itself, as the management had invited both teams to the second-house performance.

The Tigers had a modified strip for the 1907/8 season, and it was reported that:

'the display of the new jerseys of the Hull City team in the windows of Messrs Ward and Abercrombie, Silver Street, are an indication of the approach of the new football season. This firm has supplied the jerseys during the past two years,

Duncan was to take many more studio portraits of City players, but from 1909 onwards took the annual pre-season team group picture and issued cards showing the team group in classic standard two or three row shots. Although Bob Watson had taken the original photograph, it was another local photographer – Charles Pinchbeck of West Park Studios in nearby Walton Street – who actually issued the coloured postcard shown above. For Charles Pinchbeck, this foray into football postcards appears to be an isolated one, and the fact that the photo is not attributed to Bob Watson anywhere on the card may well indicate that the photograph has been used without permission. The tinting or colouring of the card to create, in effect a new image, would tend to confirm this. Watson's photo appears (correctly attributed) as part of the local press coverage of the City versus Arsenal FA cup replay taking place in Hull in January 1908 that day.

Pictured are: (standing) Ambrose Langley (manager), 'Tot' Hedley, George Browell, Martin Spendiff, Davy Gordon, Billy Robinson, Bill Leach (trainer); (sitting) 'Stanley' Smith, 'Jacky' Smith, Gordon Wright, Joe Shaw, Arthur Temple; (seated on the ground) Frank Martin and 'Jack' McQuillan.

City's pre-season preparations included a cricket match and day of sporting events against Ambrose Langley's old club, the current English Cup-holders, Sheffield Wednesday, on Saturday the 15th August at the Circle. For sixpence, spectators could gain admission to the ground where

TIGERS' HULL FAIR DRESS.
"THE TIGERS WILL WEAR JERSEYS INSTEAD OF SHIRTS, AS JERSEYS MAKE THEM LOOK BIGGER."—Vide "Daily Mail."

and this year they obtained the order after facing keen competition, including that of well-known London houses. The jerseys are knitted, and the whole outfit looks exceptionally neat and well made.'

Essentially the strip dispensed with the collared shirts of the previous year in favour of a round-neck design with drawstring. This change prompted local cartoonist R.W. Lawson to depict a humorous exchange between a new jersey-wearing player and a team mate sporting the previous season's shirt style. Lawson drew City cartoons in the Hull Daily Mail in the years before the First World War. A commercial traveller by trade, Lawson lived in Raglan Street in the city and his cartoons illustrated light-hearted moments from games, as well as skilfully-drawn likenesses from photographic portraits.

As the first game approached, attention turned as usual to the prospects for the forthcoming season and what improvements (if any) had been made to last season's squad. Secretary Jack Haller was characteristically guarded about what lay ahead for the club on the 22nd August in an interview with a local paper:

> "We are looking forward to the coming season with a quiet confidence he stated, before going on to expand on the nature of the directors' labours during the summer months. Six new players had been procured to reinforce the weakest positions in the team. Attention was paid not only to securing men whose playing abilities improve the team, but also to ensuring that the players were of the right character to keep 'the morale of the team at a high standard'. This was considered to be a very important point and the present players were determined to assist the directors in this respect. In their turn, the directors were quite satisfied that they had secured good men, who were described as being 'not internationals, but young, promising players, who are anxious to do their best for the club."

Regarding the progress made since the founding in 1904, it was felt that this had been remarkably rapid. The successful first season in the league was achieved by playing in a style referred to as 'bustling' football. The following season (1906/07) saw an attempt to play in a more sophisticated style, with a consequent lower league position. The club had no generous financier behind it in its early efforts to build up a team, and the management were to be congratulated upon building up a team which ranked among the elite of the Second Division at a very low cost. The six new players were the defenders Nevins and Stephenson, and the forwards Shaw, Temple, Hunter and Hanns – all recruited from the North East. Missing at the start of the new season were Davis, Brooks, Romig, Dixon, West, Ahlberg, Dagnall, Rushton (joined Swindon), Raisbeck (emigrated to Canada), Pearson (joined Luton), Thornton, Howe and E.G.D. Wright.

Action from the first home game against Barnsley on September 7th. Match scenes of this type were a novelty for the local newspapers and this game is one of the very earliest to be featured. This picture shows a midfield battle, with the Best Stand as backdrop.

The Paralysing of Barnsley, on Saturday Last, By the Tigers.
(AN IMPRESSION BY ERNEST NOBLE.)

Ernest Noble drew this unusual cartoon, after City's victory over Barnsley.

The vexed question of who would score the goals that had been missing in the previous season was addressed in the article thus:

> Although the officials are on the look-out for another good forward, they have not been able to procure one. There are dozens who would like to come to Hull, but it is of no use bringing men who are no better than those they have, and any further importation must be of First League strength, with plenty of experience and of good morale. The directors are determined at all costs to raise the tone of Association football, and in this they desire hearty support. Perhaps the most prominent feature of this season's opening is the confidence of the players in the management, and the members of the board, and the managers of the team feel they have the hearty support of the men. This is as it should be, and I am hoping to see the same conditions throughout the season."

The new players would strengthen the squad and it was envisaged that the second team (or Midland League team as they were known) would contain the majority of the new players.

> 'Last season the back division of this team was very weak and on many occasions let the team down rather heavily. The introduction of Nevins (who is 21 years of age, and sturdy built, in fact a mass of muscle) and Stephenson (who is only 17 years of age) will remedy this defect. In fact, the Midland League team promises to be a remarkably warm lot."

The City Juniors, managed by director Jack Bielby, trained on the Dairycoates ground and it was reported that they were 'remarkably keen even to the extent of stopping their 'cigs' between Thursday and Saturday nights. They take their training seriously and if the other Hull clubs did the same there would be no necessity for City to go out of Hull for players.' This pointed remark confirmed the previous details about the non-local origins of the new recruits.

City started the season with a 1-0 defeat at Clapton Orient on September 2nd, however they followed that up with five successive wins in which Jacky Smith netted five times. A sobering 3-0 reverse at Oldham finished the run of positive results, before Clapton were thrashed 5-0 at Anlaby Road with no less than four coming from Jacky Smith. The following week saw two more from City's free-scoring forward but could not prevent Leeds from winning by 3-2. City shipped five goals at Glossop on November 9th to lose 5-1, the consolation goal coming, inevitably, from Smith.

The attack-minded Tigers were also prone to conceding goals in quantities that damaged their league placing. In the month of December, City played six times, winning three and losing three. In the process they scored 11 and conceded 12. It was a microcosm of their form – unpredictable, rich in goals at both ends, entertaining but ultimately frustrating. Throughout the inconsistency, Jacky Smith produced a steady supply of goals – some 18 in the first 22 games, and the goals continued to mount up against the Tigers, hampering any attempt at a concerted attack on the upper reaches of the Second Division. City rounded off their year with a 4-1 defeat at Derby (scorer Jacky Smith) and started 1908 with another heavy defeat against Barnsley at Oakwell (4-2, with Frank Martin and the consistent Jacky Smith on the mark for the Tigers). City's porous defence was fast becoming their Achilles heel.

The previous season's FA cup draw had seen City paired with Tottenham Hotspur, and in early January they travelled to the capital once more, this time to play Woolwich Arsenal at their Plumstead ground. There was no doubting that the tie away to First Division opposition was one that would have been attractive for City fans – combining as it did, a trip to the metropolis, new opponents and a chance of the cup glory

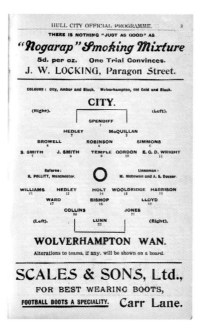

This postcard of an Anlaby Road crowd shows an advertisement for Ernest Morison's 'Amusements' magazine, with St Matthew's church in the misty background.

that was already an established feature of that competition's appeal. Despite fine but freezing January weather, enthusiasts were not deterred and to accommodate this, a number of rail excursions were organised, leaving late on Friday night from Cannon Street station (used by the Hull & Barnsley Railway) or Paragon Station (the North Eastern Railway's terminus). Both railway companies arranged departures for fans leaving late that evening, and the N.E.R also had a train leaving Paragon at 6.25 am on the day of the game. It was reported this was because supporters had 'expressed their intention of availing themselves of them in large numbers'.

Certain patterns associated with City's cup games were starting to become established. The team had gone to the seaside (Worthing) to prepare for the game. Gordon Wright's connections with the football club there from his early playing days were no doubt a factor in this choice. This ozone-rich environment away from the distractions offered by well-meaning fans was to become a standard preparation for all cup games, be they home or away. The supporters, on the other hand, succumbed to the special allure of the FA Cup, which pre-dated the establishment of the Football League by some 16 years, and was thus firmly embedded in

national consciousness as the more glamorous and exciting competition. This meant that cup games tended to attract far bigger crowds than league games, with all the accompanying publicity and excitement.

Fans responded to the competition's charisma, and City's were no exception. For those who didn't travel to Plumstead, the game was reported in detail in the local press. The next best thing was attending the Reserves game at Anlaby Road against Leicester Fosse. The following excerpt from a contemporary press-cutting illustrates the wit and lively humour of City fans present on that cold January afternoon, and able to follow events in the capital thanks to the ingenious use of telegrams and megaphones, and the good-humoured resourcefulness of City directors Messrs Locking and Spring, with events unfolding as follows:

"2.50 — Hull City attacked at the outset. Stanley Smith narrowly missing at goal. Much applause by the crowd, and some mirth, at the shouting through the megaphone.
2.54 — Woolwich attacking strongly. Forced two corners. There was silence at this and someone else shouted, 'Get another trumpet, please.' Director Locking bowed his acknowledgements.

3.10 — Woolwich pressing, Spendiff playing splendidly. 'Well played, Spendiff!' rejoined the boys on the popular side.

3.15 — 'Secretary' Locking is getting famous. Director Spring has offered him a trawler captaincy.

3.20 — Half-time: Nil-nil. Tigers making a solid defence. Can't break it. The crowd, 'Is that a bit of your own?' Arsenal struck the crossbar, after Spendiff had saved. More applause.

3.30 — Director James Spring relieves the man with the megaphone, but finds it too cold, and goes for a cup of tea. Director Locking once again. No score; both teams attacking in turn. 'Hooray, hooray' and 'Hullo, hullo.' What excitement !

3.40 — 'Well played, Roughley,' shouts the megaphone man in absence of news. Indignant sport: That is not a telegram.

3.55 — City pressing: no score. Cry of 'Keep on pressing.' Megaphone again: 'The second half did not commence till half-past three.'

4.0 — City are reproducing their Tottenham form. Still no score. Great applause, and 'Give us a limerick.'

4.3 — 'Woolwich peppering City goal. Spendiff playing splendidly – no score.'

4.7 — A man in the crowd 'Hull City,1; Woolwich nil.' Cries of 'Rats' and 'Book your seats for Thursday.' The Reserves match being over, the crowd have swarmed round the stand.

4.10 — 'City have the best of play; attacking briskly. No score yet.' 'What ho,' and choruses.

4.12 — Only a few minutes to go.

4.13 — 'Woolwich force two corners.' What excitement! A Voice: 'Liar.'

4.14 — 'It's the truth. City having the best of it, no score.' Chorus, 'Chase me round the building.'

4.15 — 'We want them here.' Chorus 'You want the money.'
All together:
'I'll tell Jacky on the telephone;
I'll tell Jacky to score another goal;
I feel so shy when Jack is nigh;
So I'll tell Jacky to score another goal.' *

4.17 — Now's your time to book your seats for Thursday. Final: 'No score.'

Three cheers for City and much excitement."

(*Harry Castling's popular Music Hall song of 1907 – 'I'll tell Tilly on the Telephone', being adapted to include a reference to City's Jacky Smith by the club's fans).

THE RETREAT OF THE GUNNER.

THE CITY TIGER: My word if you are not off!   And he was off: Hull City, 4 goals; Woolwich Arsenal, 1 goal.
(With apologies to Otto Monstad, Limited.)

City had held their First Division opponents away from home, and having journeyed to Woolwich to see City hold the Gunners to a goal-less draw, delighted travelling fans would have returned to Hull late on a freezing Saturday, savouring the replay to be played the following Thursday.

City visited Withernsea the day before the game for some sprinting practice, as temperatures started to rise, leaving the Anlaby Road pitch soft. This must have suited the Tigers who quickly raced into a three-goal lead within the half hour, and won by four goals to one in front of 16,000 spectators (the largest gate of the season). To celebrate this feat of giant-killing, the City players were invited to the Empire theatre on the evening after the game by the lessee of the theatre, a Mr Slingsby, who was a keen sportsman and fan.

January 18, 1908.   THE PENNY ILLUSTRATED PAPER.

UPS AND DOWNS FOR T' COOP.

The Mascot of the Hull City team on the ground.   Ashcroft and Temple do a little wrestling.   Kyle heading the ball in front of the Hull goal.
ENGLISH CUP: WOOLWICH ARSENAL AND HULL CITY DRAW.

The performing artistes that evening made reference to the victory, in their attire during sketches (City and Arsenal shirts) and one – Cliff Dixo – wore a City badge. It was reported that 'portraits of the team were displayed on the screen, and as each succeeded the other, there was considerable cheering. They were capital likenesses.' Yet more verse was penned in local newspapers, this extract summing up the euphoric mood as a visit to Aston Villa beckoned:

> "...And when the strife was ended,
> And the Gunners were undone,
> All England praised the Tigers,
> For the victory they had won.
> Quoth the Captain of the Gunners
> 'They've o'er us fairly run.'
> Here's to ye Martin Spendiff!
> Here's to ye, Gordon Wright!
> And Shaw and 'Jack' and Stanley,
> All heroes of the fight.
> Hurrah for 'Geordie' Browell,
> Robinson, Hedley and 'Mac,'
> Good luck t'ye, Temple and Martin
> And may ye ne'er look back!
> A stiff task yet awaits you,
> At Joey Chamberlain's town;
> But the men who spiked the Gunners,
> Need not fear the Villans frown.
> And remember Withernsea's ozone,
> It has helped you to renown."

Villa were one of the founding clubs of the Football League with an already illustrious history. The opportunity to see the match (in what was then the world's most prestigious competition), at their hugely impressive stadium would have been the type of game that City fans had longed to attend. The club's directors must have had exactly this type of fixture in mind when they were striving to set up a professional league club in Hull – a huge crowd, the focus of national attention and the chance to measure up against the best. As for the Arsenal game, supporters journeyed by various special trains to Birmingham to be part of a 35,000 crowd (an estimated 1,500 from Hull), this time with a disappointing if not unexpected outcome. Lavish coverage in the local media furnishes a wealth of detail about the day. One journalist en route to Birmingham reflects on the mood in the city during the week and contemplates events unfolding around him:

"The success of the (shall I say unexpected success?) of the Tigers in the first round of the great National Cup has taken Hull by storm and all classes have to-day a bad attack of football frenzy ... the team had

a fine send off yesterday noon, and the cheers of the workmen at Sculcoates and Springhead must have given them great encouragement ... There was a big crowd at Cannon Street this morning and the colours of the Tigers were freely worn. The following is a list of saloons and engaged carriages, each representing a party:- Messrs Locking, Tholander, J. Smith, W. Wulff, Looath, W. Johnson, Bottings, Maggs (2), Johnson, Westmorland, Taylor, Priestman, and Glossop. And what a lot of Rugby supporters were there! Is this a sign of the times? Mr Syd Smurthwaite had with him his famous mascot cat, which, by-the-bye, has never seen the Tigers lose. It has been to Leeds, London and other places, and the Tigers have always come out on top or drawing. Surely the Tigers will not break the run of success this afternoon? Only one train left Cannon Street this morning but it was an extraordinarily long one, and we had two engines to take us there. The Tigers had a 'splendid following' and 'they did not half make themselves heard when the teams entered the ground.' 'Three cheers for Gordon Wright!' yelled a Hull enthusiast, and it was heartily given."

Clerk: "Return to Birmingham, Sir?"
The Tiger: "Confound you, Sir! No! I'm going right through."

The Tiger goes to Birmingham – a whimsical way to capture the excitement of a tie against one of the best Edwardian teams, Aston Villa.

Another local paper also supplies vivid descriptions of the fans' experiences, starting with the writer's own account of the journey to Birmingham on the same 8.37 Special train from Cannon Street, which also included City captain Gordon Wright as a passenger. The train was almost an hour late into Birmingham, and the journey was a very spartan one in the 'ice-cold' carriages. The train was met at the station platform by 'many old Hullites' waiting for friends arriving on the Special. The scenes outside and inside Villa Park are described in depth:

"The Brummagen gutter merchants were driving a prosperous trade, and are smart and up-to-date business men. They pushed their wares upon you with a stubborn persistency which was most successful, and among their varied wares were the colours of either teams with a cup attached, and they guaranteed that a purchase would ensure your favourites winning the cup. The funeral cards of either team (pay your penny and you get your choice) and the official teams (which were official only in name, and gave Gordon as playing) were also specialities. There was a big rush for the cars, and it was strange experience for the Hull people to have to stand in a queue down Slaney-lane and wait their turn, although the arrangements were really excellent. When I was watching this scene, the Tigers in a four-in-hand, went by, the guard loudly blowing a long horn.

Loud were the cheers which greeted the Tigers, and they responded with one equally as hearty, to be replied to with that pathetic ballad 'I'll tell Jacky on the telephone.'

Villa Park proved an eye-opener to the Hull visitors, who looked around the vast amphitheatre in amazement, but it does not take the average football-spectator long to get accustomed to his surroundings, and they were not long in making their presence heard. They had found great difficulty in finding their way into the ground, especially the ticket-holders, and many were the enquiries as to which was entrance B, D, G, etc. But the arrangement of the ground is excellent, and before long everyone was comfortably settled.

'1, 2,3 , good old Haller!' '1, 2, 3 for Mr Smith!' In fact it was '1, 2, 3' for everyone connected with the City club who made an appearance on the track which surrounds the playing area. Several telegrams were handed in to the team- one from the Cubs to Mr. Gordon Wright being especially welcome, whilst the ones to Jacky Smith and Browell determined these quiet youths to deserve the honour thrust upon them. The appearance of the Tigers from the dressing rooms was the signal for loud and hearty cheers, not only from the party from Hull, but also the home supporters, who appreciated the Tigers' victory over Woolwich."

In bright sunlight and with a brisk wind, Villa treated their visitors as a threat, they knew that City had led the Second Division table for a long time earlier in the season. Their programme notes described the Tigers as 'one of the most consistent sides in the country' and added 'it reads like a fairy tale when we consider what Hull City have accomplished to learn that they have only been in existence a little over three years.' Villa's intricate passing game made little impression on City's goal in the first half, and Villa adopted a far more robust approach in the second half as the game degenerated into a bad-tempered affair and a 3-0 defeat for the Tigers. After the game in the dressing room, George Browell attempted to raise spirits. It was reported by a local journalist that:

"... his warbling fell upon unsympathetic ears, and ended in a dismal failure. But the Tigers were by no means done with and strongly resented the advice of the driver not to play the horn upon the return journey. They returned with flying colours. In the New Street station at night, I found that the Tigers' supporters were not down-hearted. In fact, they said so on more than one occasion. They were a lively and noisy crowd, bubbling over with harmless gaiety, and as each player came down the staircase leading to the platform they cheered again and again. Trainer Leach was the recipient of a special ovation, which he gratefully acknowledged by raising his hat and giving a most elaborate bow. What would have happened had the Tigers won, I know not, but Birmingham would not have been big enough to hold them. There was another cheer given when the players entered their saloon. Then following the long and cold journey home, which was reached in the wee small hours of the morning, and further cheers for the team in Cannon Street station. Defeated but not disgraced, the players will go again to Withernsea for another week's special training."

Such detailed anecdotes of the travelling supporters' exploits would have no doubt whetted the appetites of readers for travelling by train to major games. As well as providing an insight into some of the earliest big games played by the club, as viewed through the eyes of travelling spectators, the rich detail offered in these newspaper reports give informative first-hand accounts of early twentieth century football spectating.

The advertisements placed in the local press by Paragon Street tobacconist J.W. Locking reflected his passion for the club as many of his tobacco products carried names referring to his favourite local sporting team. His city centre retail business was yet another field of activity in the range of businesses represented on the City board. He soon expanded into confectionery and his business continued to grow; he would later become involved in the wholesaling as well as retailing of tobacco. Aside from his commercial interests, he was to play a prominent role in civic life and was to become a Sheriff of Hull, a Freemason of the Wilberforce Lodge, and a vice-chairman of the Hull Motor Club.

SMOKE TALKS.
No. 15.
THE CRITICS.

When we introduced the Tiger Cigar, we wondered how it would be received by the critics. The critics are the very particular people, you know. We were a bit anxious about the critics.

But, strange to say, the critics are most enthusiastic about Tigers. They say the Tiger Cigar exactly meets their idea of what a cigar ought to be. So there must be something in what we say.

Try a few.

Tiger No. 1, 4 for 1/-   21/- per 100.
Tiger No. 2, 5 for 1/-   18/- per 100.
Tiger No. 3, 6 for 1/-   15/6 per 100.
Tiger No 4, 7 for 1-   13/6 per 100.

Tiger Whiffs (Little Tigers). 7 for 6d.

___

J. W. LOCKING,
Paragon St., Hull.

City director John Locking advertised his own tobacco products in the local press, as well as the club programme.

Locking was also involved in local politics as a member for the Paragon Ward, and his zest and keenness for the minutiae of procedure and management brought his talents to the attentions of a wider audience. Because of his involvement in municipal affairs, local bodies sought his recognised skills and expertise on their committees. These attributes were also used to improve the lives of the elderly, whom he entertained in the grounds of his large Cottingham home, or disadvantaged children, for whom he organised trips to the countryside.

The Tigers returned to the business of the league, scoring freely, conceding many and rarely drawing. After 25 games and the Villa defeat, they had lost nine times and only drawn twice. Too many losses to threaten the pace-setters but a respectable record, and one which guaranteed entertainment for the crowds. A further four defeats and two draws in the remaining 13 games ensured that City didn't trouble the teams at the top of the table, but maintained a respectable placing, eventually finishing in eighth place. Only once in these 13 games, did the Tigers manage to keep the opposition out. Little Jacky Smith scored no less than 32 goals in the season, the type of deadly expertise which characterises top of the table teams, but the consistently inconsistent team and its vulnerable defence ensured his efforts remained unrewarded.

Having secured 8th place in the table, the team rested for a few days before embarking for the first time on an end-of-season trip to the continent. The first week of May saw the Tigers play two games in Belgium and one in Holland. This trip to the Low Countries or to Scandinavia became an end-of-season tradition for the Tigers, who enjoyed an annual jaunt to play friendly games against opponents eager to measure themselves against players from the acknowledged motherland of football.

The tours also provided a chance for City's players to visit other countries, not a readily available opportunity in the early twentieth century for people without funds or benevolent employers. This annual tour-cum-holiday must have been popular with the players as it soon became an established finale to the season for them, and their exploits between games made lively reading for supporters back home.

As well as match reports detailing the peculiarities in style of their continental opposition and the quirky local refereeing standards, accounts were also published of the sightseeing activities, the lively nights out and good-hearted camaraderie of the squad and the directors who accompanied them. Insights into their musical abilities and their performing talents are also given, providing a vivid picture of proceedings. The Tigers left Hull on Saturday 2nd May and the Hull Daily news reported on the arrival the next morning in Belgium:

"We sighted Zeebrugge Lighthouse at 9.14 a.m., and landed at 9.37, being 2 hrs and 37 minutes late, which was caused by a very heavy fog and we stopped three times during the night. We left by express train for Bruges at 10.15, and arrived at the station at 10.39. Just a few words about the voyage. The send-off from Hull from our friends, wives, and sweethearts gave the boys heart for any kind of passage. Stanley Smith thought he was going to be ill about 4 o'clock this morning, but it all turned out to be nothing. Trainer Leach, who as mentioned in these columns before, has had some experience of the sea, made certain of shipwreck, as he wore a lifebuoy nearly all night. McQuillan, Martin, Cook, and Stephenson, thinking of his welfare, and that he might be floating on thin air, put him in a bunk and sat on him.

McQuillan thought he (McQuillan) was on watch as he got up at 1 a.m. and went on deck, but returned two hours later, having 'watched' long enough. Manager Langley came on deck this morning looking in the pink of condition.

We had coffee and rolls at 6.30. as we were late, and our breakfast was waiting at Bruges. At 8.15 the captain sounded, and found he only had 10 fathoms, to which he remarked – well, think of what the London bus driver calls the taxi-cab, and you will about hit it. Roughley, good-natured. as usual, tried to soothe him by saying he would order some more fathoms. The Tigers are certain they heard boys selling Sports Expresses' off Yarmouth.

Leaving the boat there were some good-byes to get through, as some of the Tigers made friends -of course purely platonic. The Customs didn't bother us with our baggage very much, as they saw the Tigers' skins – I mean jerseys – in the bags, and that was quite sufficient."

The group arrived in Bruges, beat the local side 3-0 and proceeded on the Sunday evening to enjoy themselves at a local fair, amusing the locals 'helped by a barrel organ and two Italian singers by giving a concert-no charge.' The following day saw more sightseeing by the Tigers, as they witnessed Bruges' 'Procession of the Holy Blood' and the crowds who thronged the streets.

Some of the Tigers this morning went along the 'Walk of Love' to see the Lovers' Well, where the local maidens are supposed to follow their sweethearts through the water, and if they drink together they will love each other for ever. Well, it might be a nice game in the summer on a very hot day, but it would be disagreeable in the winter. One of the party who shall be nameless, remarked that 'there were no gas lamps.' Talking of the weather, it was glorious yesterday, and quiet hot. To-day it is quite cloudy, but very stuffy. Roughley has been made head cashier, as he is quite a good hand with Belgian money, and always ready to help and see that we get the right change, but then goalkeepers always are quick you see.

Manager Langley is doing very well with the language, and is getting along splendidly; but then I think his nice kind ways get him through. 'Geordie' Browell soon made himself understood. He asked for pickled onions and got them, and I helped him to eat them. Then he wanted a wash, he called it 'Washee, washee.' The waiter was ready to oblige him, and I think Geordie's size got him through. All the Tigers are wishing that their captain E.G.D. Wright, was with them. What a time they would have given him. There is no mistaking his popularity with the players. Some of them coming across wished they had E.G.D.W's sleeping capacity, as they said he could have slept on the deck and then not be disturbed."

The Tigers then played for the second day running on the same pitch, this time against a team referred to as 'Belgium' but containing several of the players from the Bruges team the day before. Despite possessing a fair pitch, the ground had only one covered area for 100 people under a small pavilion and the dressing rooms were in a cafe ('equivalent to our public-house') opposite the ground. The Tigers won this game 3-2.
The group from Hull left Bruges for Brussels that evening, and enjoyed a great send-off from the committee of the Bruges Football Club as they did so.

"The Tigers' glee party sang 'Auld Lang Syne' and 'God Save the King' outside the hotel. In the station they sang a hymn that was sung in the procession in the morning, so that the crowd would know the tune. Then they gave them 'Zuyder Zee,' which told very well: and to finish up with, they sang a real English comic song, with chorus, entitled 'We all came into the world with nothing.'"

A morning exploring Brussels with the 'Man from Cook's' before continuing on to The Hague, for the final match against the local club, which they duly won 3-0. Three victories in four days, hectic sightseeing and travelling schedules, many friends made and good fun had. It was to prove a great reward for months of effort by the players and the fact that the club was to repeat it at the end of every season demonstrated recognition of this by the directors, some of whom always accompanied the group.

The commercial exploitation of the growing public hunger for football was in its infancy and existed in relatively rudimentary forms. The concepts of 'disposable income' and 'marketing' held little or no relevance to the men running the game or the clubs of which they took charge. Aside from paying their admission fee at the turnstile, any fans with either the money or the inclination to show their support for their favourite team had limited opportunities to do so.

Some national postcard producers however spotted this underdeveloped commercial opportunity and produced comic cards with a common scene but with a variety of teams to appeal to the maximum number of potential purchasers. One such card was the one issued by Scarborough publisher E.T.W. Dennis, forming part of the 'Dainty Series' and bearing the slogan 'I fear no foe'.

It showed a small ragged boy in front of a makeshift goal, with the slogan 'Play up Hull City' written at the base, by the famous postcard illustrator Jack Broadrick. The card would probably have been produced in several variations, detailing many of the League clubs of the day.

"TOMMY" NEVINS

'Ma Foi!' it is surprising, isn't it? As a full-back in purely a 'football' sense Nevins has many superiors, but in the art of stopping a misguided forward who lingers occasionally to juggle with the ball for the edification of the 'gallery,' then the ubiquitous 'Smiler' needs no coaching from any 'armchair critic' bursting with technical knowledge, or anyone else, for that matter.

Hull City's full back is a man with his heart in the right place, who 'fears no foe in shining armour' – or football clothes – and whose loyalty to his team is not exceeded by that of any player wearing a black and amber jersey.

In a Cup-tie, or any match of that description, the muscular Nevins is a man to have on your side, and in the past, when 'Tommy' has been an absentee, opposing teams have been known in an 'absence makes the heart grow fonder' spirit, to breathe a sigh of relief.
You see, the burly Nevins is rather robust, and is apt to take risks which cause ordinary men to feel a tremor.

What's that? You don't know him? Then come with me to Anlaby-road. It is near the hour of kick off, and the crowds are streaming through the turnstiles in their thousands. We take up position on the top of Spion Kop, and gaze down upon the level stretch of green turf far below.

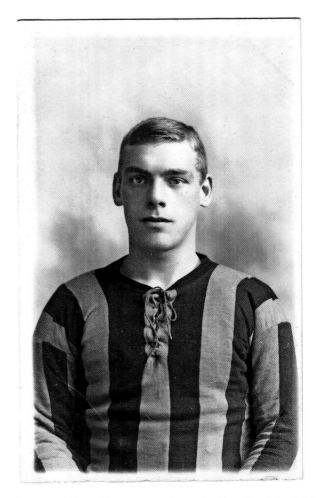

"SMILER" NEVINS
FRIENDS OF "SMILER" NEVINS SAY HE WOULD CHARGE A BULL IF
NECESSARY. THE BULL MIGHT GET "KINKED."

Here they come! From that gate yonder at the far side of the field the players trot forth eleven sturdy men and true. They spread out in the shape of a fan and make tracks for a vacant goal. See that last one, that rather short, bow-legged figure, with broad shoulders and stout, muscular legs? Watch him!

The ball is kicked off and play has begun. The game waxes faster and more furious, and amid a roar from the crowd the visiting forwards come tearing down the field, full pelt for goal. The inside left gets possession, and is about to shoot when – thud! A clearance follows the shoulder charge, and a mud-bespattered forward picks himself up ruefully, and wonders vaguely what struck him-an earthquake or an express train.

And that sturdy stiff-built figure of a man who walks back with a rolling gait towards his goal, a good-humoured smile on his rugged face – that's Nevins!

The Annual General Meeting at the Grosvenor Hotel on June 11th was a cheerful event, as Alwyn Smith presented the balance sheet and stated that they (the directors) might congratulate themselves on the workings of the past year. He also noted that since City's inception, each season had been an improvement on the last and that the quality of the team's play was greatly improved. He believed that this had helped to contribute to the increased gates, which on League attendances alone, were up some £400 on the previous year. He recounted that money had been spent on improving the ground once more, namely the enlarging of the embankment at the Spion Kop end, which was then able to accommodate more people. Stands were now being erected at the back. As well as this, the east side of the ground was being enlarged to take 1,000 more fans for those that preferred to stand there instead of on the Kop. Proposals were made to increase accommodation in the Best Stand by lengthening it at the end so that it would meet with the stand to the north. This would cost £400. Tributes were paid to director Jack Bielby for his work on the east side – given free of charge. The club had finally wiped out what was termed 'formation expenses' and the item would no longer appear on the balance sheet – a minor milestone in itself.

Turning to the players themselves, Smith lavished praise on them, citing their 'earnestness and enthusiasm'. He further added that they were 'the best and most whole-hearted set of boys he had ever seen in his life. They had the city at heart and always played with the object of winning', which drew cheers from the assembly. Gordon Wright offered his services for the whole of the following season.

Director William Gilyott followed Smith and declared (again to cheers), in recommending the adoption of the report and balance sheet, that the First Division might not be today or tomorrow but it was looming in the near future ... and the sooner they put their house in order the more prepared they would be.

Jack Bielby spoke to laud the contribution of Gordon Wright saying that he was one who instilled good clean play into the men, and was himself one of the best and cleanest footballers on the field.

Wright himself was present, as he had been at the previous year's AGM, and responded saying he had enjoyed heartily his two seasons with the club – it was a privilege to play for them. Applause greeted his statement.

STANLEY SMITH.

The flowers that bloom in the Spring, tra-la,
    Have nothing to do with my case.
It's of "Stanley" Smith that I sing, tra-la,
A forward that blooms on the wing, tra-la,
    Who can beat all the rest in a race.
And that's what I mean when I say or I sing,
Here's luck to young Stanley who plays on the
  wing,
    Tra-la, tra-la, lah-lah-ah.

THE DAILY GRAPHIC FOOTBALL ALBUM, 1908-1909.

E. G. D. Wright (Captain), J. McQuillan, E. Roughley, D. Gordon.
Mr. A. Langley (Manager), F. Martin, J. Morrison, G. Browell, G. Lindley, W. S. Robinson, A. Browell, T. Tildsley.
J. Taylor, Joe Smith, John Smith, J. Shaw, A. Temple, E. Neve, A. Pace, W. Leach (Trainer).
E. Gordon, A. E. Gilberthorpe, T. Nevins, W. Stephenson, J. E. Hall.

HULL CITY. Photographed by Watson, Hull.

In the Second Division of the League last season Hull City secured eighth place. Results of matches—21 won, 4 drawn, 13 lost. Goals scored—For 73, against 62. Colours—Amber and black, black knickerbockers.

"I like young players because they are much easier to manage. They are not nearly so troublesome as the older ones, and you are able to train them into the way they should go. Past experience proves to me that if a club can wait for the men 'coming on' they reap a big benefit and find they are far more successful than continually changing. Remember, every star has been developed by some club, and we are developing our own. I understand the Hull public are clamouring for new players, but where are we to get them from, and do we require many? We are told we require more inside forwards – so does every club in the kingdom. They cannot be found, although by chance if there happens to be one in the market, no price appears too big to ask. A class centre will fetch £1,200 to £1,500 and there are plenty of clubs willing to pay this ridiculous price. We have not been asleep during this close season, and are not the only club who have been disappointed. We have some fine, promising lads, but the public have not the patience to wait for them to develop.

We have young Gordon, who is only 17 years of age, but the public will expect him to play as well as a fully-developed player. It is most ridiculous to expect these youngsters to shine against the more robust and experienced players they have to meet. Look at the success which has attended our efforts in procuring young players and developing them. When Jacky Smith first came to Hull, it was said he was too small and light to play football. He then weighed 9st 5lb but now he weighs 11st 6lb and, far from being too small and light to play football, he last season proved the top goal-scorer in either League, and was chosen to assist the English against the Scottish League. Another player who, at first, failed to satisfy the Hull public was Joe Smith. He was not said to be too small, but was described as being unable to play centre or outside. In fact, he was no player. But we now find that Joe Smith has proved himself a most capable player. These lads, when we get them down, are not class players; they have had no experience of class football. But you never know what they can do until they are tried. Arthur Temple is another example of how the public are not the best judges of a youngster's abilities. Temple was too slow and clumsy, according to the critics, but let me assure you that Temple will make a fine player. Nevins is another youngster who has not received sufficient encouragement from the public. This lad only wants the chance to gain confidence, and he will prove his value. I wish that the public would remember these players are young, and do not worry them, but rather encourage them. I cannot see why the public are shouting out for new men. What is the matter with the old ones?

I have seen football for 17 years all over the country, and if our team were to be sold today we should have three-parts of the First League clubs all over us, and Mr. Smith's new bank would not hold the money. The Hull public do not think half as much of our team as do outsiders, and the proof of this is that we were one of the best 'drawing' teams in the Second League. How many Second League teams could have attracted 52,000 to Chelsea? A Grimsby man only the other day told me we were the best team to visit Blundell Park last season, yet we are told that a team which for two months was top of the Second Division requires changes. I should like to be in a position to give the cost of each player and the price we could get for him, and the offers we have had. It is an absurd idea that at the end of every season the club should 'sack' the old hands and get a new lot.

Such a policy would soon break the strongest of clubs. I do not doubt the ability of the team to do as well, or even better, than last season. We have improved each season, and our players are now a year older, and have a year's more experience and growth, and will continue to improve. We have the material to form a team for the next six or seven seasons, improving year by year. Of course, we are ever willing and anxious to improve our team, and are willing to spend money to attain that object, so if any of your readers know of a class centre who is at liberty, I should like them to inform me.

There may possibly be other players than those mentioned, and during the practice matches we shall give trials to several outsiders, and also several promising locals. You can say that the directorate are quite satisfied that the present team are quite capable of worthily upholding the honour of the club."

Manager Ambrose Langley – speaking in conversation with a local journalist in August 1908, on players, supporters, and the club's prospects.

The local press published some in-depth interviews not just with players, or the manager, but also certain directors, who it was assumed, had a sporting background of interest to the readership. One of these was Jack Bielby, a man with a long involvement in football at local level, and someone whose energy and persistence helped shape the club.

John Henry Bielby was a founding Tigers director whose reminiscences of playing organised football went back to some of the earliest known games played in the city. Having played the game as a youngster, Bielby then became an administrator of the game he loved, devoting many years to its growth in Hull and East Yorkshire. He is listed in the 1892 Bulmer's trade directory as a bricklayer of 588 Hessle Road and was noted at the time of City's formation as a 'builder'. The construction and design of Hull City's Anlaby Road ground was overseen by him, as was its frequent maintenance thereafter. Perhaps not the most illustrious of the early directors, but his local footballing pedigree was second to none in terms of practical involvement and length of service. He had been a symbolic builder of the club as well as being actively involved in the physical construction of its home.

Talking in 1908, he remembers 27 years previously (1881) when he first played the game, and the lack of local opponents. He also recalls the struggle for local autonomy and consequent recognition by the Football Association, the steady growth of the game in Hull and the very real social barriers occasionally impeding it. He proudly relates the development of the hierarchy of local leagues and even identifies a weakness in City's scouting network:

"I played for the N.E.R. Dairycoates Locos, and at that time there was only three Association clubs in Hull. These were Kingston Amateurs – which was composed of the 'better class' players – Blue Star, whose members were mostly engaged at the Holmes' tannery, and ourselves, who, with the exception of myself and a couple of others, were employed at the loco sheds at Dairycoates. At that time the loco sheds gave employment to a large number of men, but later the N.E.R. removed about 150 to York, where the bulk of the work was taken.

Our team was composed of Balmford (goal), L. Clubley and Aberthernatty (backs), Timmins, F. Miller and G. Hall (halves). Milner, Bielby, R. Lawson, 'Teddy' North, H. Marshall, Bell and Cawood (forwards). Balmford was a clever goalkeeper, who stood well over six feet in height, and could kick the ball the length of the field. L. Clubley, the back, is the well known honorary treasurer of the Hull Rugby F.C., and was a very smart back, and Frank Milner has a son playing in the City Juniors who should make a name for himself. With only two local clubs to play we had to look outside for opponents. Beverley had a couple of good clubs, our other opponents

Mr. J. H. BIELBY
Vice-President of the Club

Photo—Duncan, Hull

being at Sheffield, Long Eaton, Gainsborough, Brigg, Barton, and Grimsby.

Our big rivals, however, were the Blue Star, who first played on the Fountain Road ground, and later on a ground now occupied by the Hull C.C. Little did we think in those days that later a first-class Association club would have their ground within a stone's throw of where we were playing.

I well remember our club winning the Scarborough Cup, or what ought to have been a cup. We had to journey to Kirkbymoorside, Scarborough, Oliver's Mount and Whitby, in the earlier rounds, and in the final met Scarborough St.Mary's, at Scarborough. This match resulted in a drawn game, and the replay, which we won, was played on Beecroft's Farm, Anlaby-road. However, the cup was a bogey, as no trophy was owned by the Scarborough Committee. They gave us £5 instead. As it cost each of our players over £4 apiece expenses during the competition, it was not a very profitable transaction. Football was not then the parlour game it is at the present time. Charging was prevalent, and the poor goalkeeper used to have a rough time. I only kept goal on one occasion, this being in the second half against Grimsby M.S. and I., on the Old Clee Park ground. Our goalkeeper was injured, and I took his place. Allowing 11 goals, I determined that goal-keeping was not my forte. This was a very keen match, and no less than seven of our men came home on crutches or broomsticks.

I was hon. secretary of our club when the first English Cup-tie was played in Hull. It was against Lincoln, in the first round, and I acted as linesman. This match was played on the Hessle Road ground where the Oil Works are now situated. A. Wetherby was the trainer, but the interest in the tie did not equal that experienced in the Tigers' last season.

The N.E.R. Locos, for one season only, amalgamated with the Hull Town A.F.C. I was an apprentice at this time, and well remember attending the joint meeting, which was held at a first-class hotel. We were charged 6d for a glass of lemonade, which did not tempt us to often visit the establishment. The amalgamation was not a success. The Hull Town section was composed of well-to-do persons, while our lot were working lads, so naturally the blend was not satisfactory. It was about this time that the Rovers F.C. was formed, their first ground being at the bottom of Gillett Street.

I think it was in 1889 that I gave up playing, but I never severed my connection with local Association.

The Hull clubs then, and for many years afterwards, were under the jurisdiction of the Scarborough Association, to whom we had to send all moneys, etc, and in return were practically neglected. There were no leagues in my playing days, and the first competition for Saturday football in Hull was the 'Hull Times Challenge Cup', which has proved of the greatest value to local Association football. Later Saturday footballers had the 'Sunlight Cup', which disappeared somewhat mysteriously. The first Saturday League comprised seven clubs, and of the older members of the committee, only Messrs A. Spring, F. Stringer, B. Smith, and myself still take an active part in Association. There was the Gough Cup for Thursday players, and Thursday football owes a lot to the then Rev. Mr Gough, who was a curate at the St. Paul's Church. As the local clubs grew in number and strength it was most inconvenient to have all our business transacted at Scarborough, and the expense to reported players, etc, was too much for many of them to pay. We appealed to the Scarborough Association to allow us to manage – as a local sub-committee our own affairs, but they refused, and we appealed to the Football Association. Messrs A. Spring, C.J. Hampton, and another member attended the conference at York, and, thanks to the work done by Mr Spring, we were granted our request.

The local clubs appreciated Mr Spring's work, and he has since been elected a life member of the East Riding Football Association. We had about 12 Saturday clubs at this time, and several Thursday clubs, and were being reinforced by a large number of new clubs. As their numbers grow, we began agitating for direct affiliation, and a few years ago, after an enquiry held at the Station Hotel, we were granted full power to rule over the whole of the East Riding.

I have been the honorary treasurer of the Association for 17 years, and on only one occasion have I been opposed. From a small beginning (seven clubs), we now have 124 clubs in membership with the East Riding Football Association, and have the following Leagues:- County, Combination (Divisions I and II), Minor, Wolds District, and Mid-week (Divisions I and II); and the East Riding Intermediate, Junior, Mid-week, and Dr. Lilley Challenge Cups. There are, however, two links yet missing, namely one between school and the Minor

League and one between the County and Midland League. It requires someone to interest himself in picking out the best schoolboys, and see that they obtain situations which will allow of them to take part in Saturday football, and not go as errand boys to the grocer's or fishmonger's business. The other link missing between the County and Midland Leagues is most unfortunate. The difference in class of football is enormous, and is the chief reason why the City cannot find local recruits. We (the City) tried to fill in the gap by running a reserve team, but the local clubs rose up in arms against it, not realising that by doing so they were the sufferers. However, our local football is improving so rapidly that the gap will gradually close, and we shall not have to scour the country to secure players for our City teams.

My connections with Hull City are soon told. Along with Messrs J. Barraclough and A. Spring I have sat on the committee since the formation of the club, and have acted as chairman of the Grounds Committee."

This Baines card carries a reference to the 'Hello-Hello chorus that was frequently heard at the Anlaby Road ground.

The 1908/09 season saw the Tigers starting to feel comfortable and settled in their new surroundings. With this familiarity, supporters developed the habit of attending games regularly and gradually found their own preferred part of the ground. In recognition of this, the local press started to detail not only the match incidents but also the lively events off the pitch realising that a rich humorous streak existed among the fans, who needed little encouragement to break into witty or popular songs, especially if it could somehow be linked to events on the pitch.

The first home game against Clapton Orient in early September started as the Tigers 'emerged from the dressing room and the bugle rang out merrily from the popular stand. 'Here we go again', sang out a band of enthusiastic supporters, followed by 'We're pleased to see yer'. For the visit of Bolton on October 3rd, as the Tigers took the lead, reference was made

to the 'Hello-Hello' chorus which greets the goal. Later on 'Sweet Genevieve' and 'Diabolo' were also sung, as well as 'I'll tell Tilly on the telephone'.

With widespread poverty and pitiful living conditions in many parts of the city, Saturday afternoons at Anlaby Road were an opportunity not just to support the Tigers, but to enjoy the company of friends, like-minded souls, workmates, neighbours and football enthusiasts in a lively and exciting atmosphere, far removed (for a few hours at least) from poorly-paid toil or squalid housing.

Against Blackpool on October 17th the strains of 'We parted on the shore', 'Love me, and the world is mine', 'Sweet Genevieve' and other melodies were contributed by fans enjoying the win. Two weeks later against Glossop after a goal-less first half, it was reported that the crowd on the

popular side whiled away the interval with the 'Flip-Flap' and 'Oh, Oh, Antonio'. 'Poor old Carolina Brown' and 'Sweet Genevieve' were forgotten this time. Against Fulham in December 'Oh, Oh, Antonio' or 'Up will go Antonio' as it was also known, was aired, as was 'I am weary' and 'There's no place like home'.

The detailed reporting of the fans' repertoire provides a lively contrast to the photographs of supporters in the ground. Groups of spectators pose impassively or dutifully for the camera of Billy Duncan, their witty and colourful outbursts by definition eluding the visual medium.

The Hull Daily Mail ran a match report after every home game and started to feature a parallel report on the same page describing the occasion and atmosphere at the match. This wealth of detail relating to songs, music and jovial crowd activity at City home games shows an established supporter-culture with accompanying exuberant behaviour. Popular and traditional songs, music hall favourites and the latest musical crazes were all part of the Anlaby Road repertoire.

Left. One local trader who used City to promote his trade was Stewart the tailor, who offered a winter overcoat to any City player who scored two goals or more in a home game that season. The offer also extended to any spectator that the player brought along with him! Numerous City players accomplished the feat although it is not known how many, if any, took advantage of Stewart's offer.

In November T.C. Palmer the 'cash tailor' of Whitefriargate offered 'a unique Hull City badge' to customers placing orders of £2 or more.

Another City personality profiled by the local press was William 'Tim' Wright, the only local player in the Tigers' ranks. The Holderness man was interviewed in October by local football reporter 'Veritas' in an article entitled 'An All-Round Athlete', and like Jack Bielby, he revealed his background in local football circles:

"There is a footballer, if ever there was one'. This was a remark made to the writer by one well qualified to judge and size up a footballer when observing William Wright, popularly known as 'Tim', appear in the Hull City ranks against the Pilgrims a few days ago. Since that occasion the Withernsea captain has become a professional member of the Tigers, and being the first East Riding player to figure in Second Division football for what we may really claim to be his native town, a few particulars relating to this promising player may not be inappropriate on the day of his baptism in League football.

Wright, who was born at Patrington, twenty three years ago, tells me that he doesn't know how he came to be called Tim. It is not related to William, the real handle to his name, but he was called Tim when quite a youngster, and it has stuck to him ever since. He first took an active interest in Soccer football when he was 15 years of age, and since that time has played, more or less, in local senior circles.

'I have never', he says, 'had any football training, but have picked up what I know, and my natural enthusiasm for the game has done the rest, I suppose'.

For two seasons he assisted his native club at Patrington, but mostly he has been associated with the Withernsea Club, of which he was leader up to signing on for the Tigers. The latest addition to the Tigers ranks has generally played outside right, but he has also operated at centre half and centre forward with fair success.

His performances on the running track are better known, perhaps, than his deeds in local football so far, his fine speed having brought him into considerable prominence in the running world.
As a schoolboy he carried off many prizes at local sports, and between the ages of 16 to 21 years he enjoyed much success at all the principal meetings in the district, winning no fewer than fifty first and second prizes. Running under the A.A.A. Rules for the last two seasons, he has won three firsts, namely the 440 yards at Lincoln,1907; 220 yards at Lincoln, 1908; and 220 yards at Castleford, 1908.

Asked what he considered his best performance on the track, Wright referred to his success in winning the half-mile at Patrington in three successive years. This entitled him to the sole possession of the silver challenge cup. He was only 16 years of age the first time he won this event.

He has opposed most of the local cracks, and has generally managed to hold his own with them. Another very creditable performance may be recalled when Wright was at camp with the Yeomanry about two years ago. This was against time, Wright having to walk a mile, run a mile, and ride a horse a mile, the whole distance having to be negotiated in under twenty minutes. 'Clocked' by three independent watches, he succeeded in the remarkable time of 17 minutes 20 seconds, the whole journey being accomplished on a public road.

Wright's versatility in athletic circles is further shown by his performances in the cricket field, he having won the batting average at Patrington for the last three years, his averages being: 1906, 19; 1907, 48; 1908, 28. He is also a fair bowler. Standing 5ft 81/2in, he scales just over 11st.

In football I am convinced that, with average luck, Tim will enhance his reputation in the football world, and I look forward to a new chapter in his pursuit of the inflated bladder being favourably opened to-day at Chesterfield.

Veritas"

City's captain was starting to feature in the local press as the author of articles about the game and about his opinions on topical football subjects. His erudition and experience of the game at a high level were undoubtedly factors which made his views eminently printable. One such article appeared in the Hull Sports Express on Saturday November 14th, and in it Wright gives a comprehensive overview of traditional training methods, details their failings and then outlines what he would suggest as a better system:

"The Training of Footballers – How to Keep in Condition

The one aim and object of the football player, whether amateur or professional is, unquestionably, to keep in proper physical condition throughout the season. A very difficult problem it is – and ever will be – since no hard and fast rules can be possibly laid down.
This surely is obvious, from the well-known fact that each individual is endowed with a physical constitution maybe entirely, or perhaps, only slightly, yet still different from his fellow, and therefore, the treatment accorded to one might not benefit, but even seriously injure another.

This important fact is often, unfortunately, lost sight of, especially in training boys with the result that many a promising youngster has been allowed to do either too much for his strength, or else entirely the wrong thing to do him any good. The old proverb 'One man's meat, another man's poison,' is as true of training as it is of anything else.

Here are a few of the absurd rules I, in common with others, got into my head at school:-

(1) To get up an hour or half-hour before breakfast and do a long fatiguing run in the airiest of costumes. Could anything be more injurious, even to a strong boy! And what madness when practised by a weak one! To take violent exercise without food or anything to support one's strength just at the time when the body physically at its weakest, must surely appeal to anyone who has given the matter a moment's thought, as ridiculous and absurd in the extreme; and yet many boys will cling to this idea of morning exercise as one of the fundamentals of training. As I learnt to my cost after many a bitter experience, it is absolutely the worst thing one can do.

(2) Take an ice-cold bath-preferably when you come back from your run. Here again, the rules of common sense come to our aid in rejecting this also. Not every boy can stand a cold bath in a morning in ordinary mild weather, while to do it in the depth of winter, is little short of lunacy. And even if you discover an individual who can stand it, in taking a cold bath after heated exercise, he is running an enormous risk of catching a chill and putting an end to his football days altogether.

(3) Take as little food as possible. Perhaps I have put this too strongly, but that is what, if my experience of boys goes for anything, the average boy endeavours to do in order to get himself fit instead of cutting off injurious food only, for I will give him credit that he nobly, in most cases denies himself sweet stuff, he promiscuously cuts himself off from the very food which he ought to take, and which would nourish him and keep his muscles in order. For example, many a time I have seen a boy refuse a second helping of meat under the pretext that he was in training for some match, whereas it is meat that builds up the muscles and keeps them in good condition.

One or two more rules I would cite which would show what grievous errors boys fall into for want of good, sound, expert advice – errors all the more dangerous because they often ruin a boy's career at the very outset, or else handicap him through all his life. Why is it that a professional team can always outstay an amateur side? Because they get the pick of the best players you may retort. That is true to a small extent, but it is not the correct answer. It is because the professional is under expert advice. His temperament is studied, and his constitution is carefully analysed. The minutest attention is paid to his condition, and above all, he is set exercise that exactly suits him.

Scarcely any two individuals are treated alike, and they are invariably under medical supervision, and are forced to explicitly obey their instructions.
The amateur, on the other hand, has very seldom the benefit of expert advice, and has to keep himself as best

E.G.D. Wright

as he can, in most cases with the result that he cannot be expected to go the right way to work. He perhaps watches other men, or reads the methods of some celebrated player who advocates this or that policy, that he has found useful. It would be wonderful, would it not, if he did succeed in lighting upon the secret without someone to guide him properly?

But there is one thing that he can surely do, and that is reason out and eliminate such absurd rules as those I have quoted, which I maintain, can do no one any good, and may do positive harm. I hope I shall not offend any of my readers, who still cling to the old ideas instilled into them when boys, by those somewhat outspoken remarks. I know from personal experience how hard ideas picked up and practised in one's boyhood are to eradicate, and habits difficult to break.

After all, it is only experience which can teach a person the proper way for him to train; and if only more attention were paid to physical conditions in our schools and colleges, and boys instructed by experienced persons in the same way that professionals are, the standard of play generally would greatly be improved and a boy would not be allowed to ruin his play and constitution by misplaced keenness. Surely the simple life is the key note to perfect physical condition, and if one keeps to that no one can be wrong. Plenty of good wholesome food and judicious exercise, and above all, the observance of regular hours.

To my mind, the last cannot be beaten in keeping up a good sound wholesome condition. These few simple rules can harm no one, however constituted, and can do an immense amount of good. Give me eleven first-class amateurs who will rigidly obey these rules, and there are few sides, professional or otherwise, who would last better in a strenuous match."

The draw in December for the first round of the FA cup was awaited as always with feverish anticipation by fans and money-conscious directors alike. Neither was to be disappointed with the outcome.

Chelsea had been admitted into Division Two at the same FA meeting as City in 1905. With considerable resources at their disposal, the west London side gained promotion at the second attempt in 1907, watched by huge crowds. They very quickly became a big club in financial terms and this would not have been a point lost on all at Anlaby Road when the draw for the Cup was made in December, pairing the Tigers with the

London side. In view of Chelsea's enormous gates at Stamford Bridge (and the attendant gate receipts), would it not make sense to switch the game from Anlaby Road with a beneficial financial arrangement to City's advantage? City's board, after some deliberation, decided against such a move, opting to play the tie on 16th January 1909 in Hull, much to the satisfaction of their fans.

Although the Tigers had played Tottenham Hotspur in 1907 and Woolwich Arsenal in 1908 in replayed cup-ties at Anlaby Road, both were Thursday afternoon games which meant many fans could not attend even if others enjoyed a weekly half- day holiday on that day. The Chelsea game therefore was the first big home Saturday cup game in their short history that all fans could attend and local press coverage was feverish in anticipation of the tie.

Below; Action from the first home game of the season – Clapton – a 3-2 win on September 5th 1908.

HULL CITY V. CLAPTON ORIENT.

"Hull News" Photo

Constant debate and speculation about the decision to refuse the Chelsea offer was mixed with general excitement ahead of the game.

Workers at the Hull Forge Company were so enthused by the tie that they presented the club with a Good Luck mascot, as reported in the local press. At the home game against Leeds City on January 9th the 'horse shoe mascot' was on show before the game in front of the best stand, according to a local newspaper report on the afternoon's proceedings. It went on to relate how 'During the interval the Forge horseshoe was carried round, the effort of the iron-workers receiving worthy recognition.' Perhaps the picture of the mascot in the local paper helped stimulate sales of the postcard and bring it to the attention of Hull's football public The 'Good Luck Tigers' mascot made by the Hull Forge Company for the Chelsea cup-tie was a measure of how the Cup gripped the imagination of the Hull public (shown right).

In the week leading up to the game, their opponents chose to prepare at the Britannia Hotel in Bridlington, whilst the Tigers based themselves at the Queens Hotel in Withernsea, returning to Hull for a day to visit the Turkish Baths and a visit to see 'The Fair One With the Golden Locks' at the Grand Theatre, according to a local paper which spared its readers no details in the build-up to the game.

As part of the coverage in the days preceding the game, the Hull Daily Mail sent one of their reporters to Withernsea to find out how preparations were progressing. Published on the day before the game, the resulting article gives an account of how the Tigers had trained the previous day. This light-hearted reportage nevertheless provides an insight into the prevalent training methods used by City at the time.

"The regular programme commences at a few minutes to nine. I missed this part of the programme , but understand it is the psychological moment when the physic is ladled out. But I have a strong imagination, and should surmise that Manager Langley stands with a big stick in his hand whilst Trainer Leach, with a big bowl of julap before him, doses each player with a big spoonful as they pass him one by one. I have not heard of any of them, like Oliver Twist, asking for more, but I did once hear a tale connected with a team training on the West Coast. At physic time, the players did their best to 'dodge the dose,' but the management was strict. One morning one of the men got past in safety, but the official in charge knew that he had only distributed 19 instead of 20 doses. At once he pounced upon one of the men who usually tried to give the 'miss,' and, despite strong protestations, he had to receive a second dose! Moral: Don't try and dodge the physic. At nine o'clock, breakfast, which like the rest of the meals, is of a liberal nature, and reflects credit upon the catering of Host Sykes, comes along. Billiards, etc., until nearly eleven

—*Photo by J. Archer, Sharp-street, Hull.*

TIGERS' MASCOT.

The horse-shoe was made at Hull Forge of best iron, and is 18½ inches high, weighs about 11¼lbs. is burnished and silver plated, is mounted on shield 27 inches high with gilded nails. The above is covered with black silk velvet, striped with yellow silk (Tigers' colours), total weight over 14lbs. The mascot was mounted by Mr Stanworth, Waterloo-street, Hull.

o'clock, by which time the whole of the men have to strip and dress in their running attire. A field opposite the Queen's Hotel has been procured for the Tigers, and sprinting exercises are indulged in. There is no need for Manager Langley to use his authority when this task has to be done. Each of the players is so keen that a watch has to be kept upon them lest they overtrain. There might be a tendency on these cold mornings to stick by the fire until the last moment, but 'Here boys!' from the manager is quite enough, and out they go. Ugh, 'tis chilly stepping out of the warm room into the cold, cold world, but this soon passes off. As far as I can judge, 'tis between half and three-quarters of a mile around the field, and the men go at it as though putting in a hundred yards sprint. And let me tell you they can RUN. I have heard people say the Tigers are slow, but don't you believe it. They are jolly fast, much faster than is generally understood. And fit! Why they never turned a hair, and are as fit as the lively flea which lodges at the same summer boarding-house as I did.

Trainer Leach takes them in hand, and gives them a good rub down. Their flesh fairly glows with health, and Leach soon bustles them off with 'You'll do.' By the by, 'tis said that some of the players have an amount of superfluous flesh on them, but this is all rot. Georgie Browell, of whom a spectator on Saturday said, 'What a podge!' has no 'podge' whatsoever. George has a fine chest; in fact, his chest is 'great' and his thighs are equals of many men who display their physiques on the stage, but there is no superfluous flesh. It is all the very best beef.

By the bye, little Jacky Smith is much faster than I thought, and Gilberthorpe can trot it a little. Only little but good, is a good definition of the Tigers' midgets. Temple is continually gaining speed, and it may be information to many to know that in practice Temple is the best shot in team. He may have missed chances in matches, but he is yet very young, and an old head is not always found on young shoulders. Mark my words, Temple will make his mark in football.

Next item is a short rest, followed by a walk. I shone during the rest, and can train during 'resting' time as well as the next man – perhaps better. Seventeen true and loyal Tigers, we commenced our walk up Waxholme-road. Withernsea thought there must have been a wreck somewhere, but could not make out whether we were the survivors or the lifeboat crew! Frock coats and top hats were not worn, appearances being sacrificed for warmth and comfort. The sweet shops did a roaring trade, for the Tiger has a very sweet tooth in his head. Unfortunately, rain commenced to fall whilst we were strolling along the splendidly-paved Waxholme-road, and it was decided to return. More eating and more rests, the 'Mail' representative again shining, but I must admit the Tigers have got rare appetites.

I forget how many stones (or is it tons?) of beef they devour in a week, but I hear that several butchers will shortly be in a position to retire. The afternoon was devoted to golf.

Withernsea has only been talking about building a golf course for about ten years, so it is not to be expected that it has one as yet, but we still live in hopes. There are, however, the sands on which to play, and armed with a driver, two cleeks, a mashie and five balls, we hied ourselves to the sands. There are no bunkers, but any amount of gravel and stones. A good whack, and the ball requires a lot of finding. I have heard golf described as a game where a man hits a ball and spends the rest of the day looking for it. Such is golf on the Withernsea Sands. I think it is in the Hull Golf Club's club-house where there is a picture of an irate Colonel attempting to find his ball amongst a host of white stones similar in size and shape to missing sphere and we had many similar examples. And the golf! Oh dear! It was simply marvellous. Tons and tons of sand were hurled towards heaven. Where bunkers were not they were dug, and the hitherto smooth sands looked more like a series of pits. At times the Tigers hit the balls, and at others failed. They never bothered about the 'stance' or 'keep your eye on the ball.' The 'follow through' was all right in theory, but not a success in practice, still a few of the drives would not have disgraced Ray. 'Pitching' was no use to the Tigers. All they wanted was a good, hard, clout. Browell hit one ball and declared it had gone into the next parish, but it was found peacefully reposing under the shadow of a breakwater some few yards away! Another ball hack – I mean Browell – his broke in twain, so mighty was the swipe. Little Jacky Smith almost hit the ball 90 yards. I say almost – but unfortunately he missed the ball. Manager Langley was kept busily employed looking for lost balls, and Trainer Leach served as fore-caddie. There were no greens to play to and at times the balls were whizzing about in all directions.

Owing to the professional's stock of balls running out, the game had to be abandoned, and at five o'clock, the Tigers attacked the meal ready laid for them. After tea, the great billiard handicap was entered upon. There were 16 entries and many of the matches produced exciting struggles.

THE HANDICAP ; Stanley Smith (scr.) Langley (20), Roughley (25), Leach (30), Gordon (30), Robinson (30), McQuillan (30), Nevins (35), Jack Smith (40), G. Browell (45), Taylor (45), Temple (50), Pace (50), Gilberthorpe (50), Andy Browell (60)."

The minutiae of the billiard scoring would have sated the appetite of even the most avid City follower, and the account of the day as a whole shows a happy and relaxed group making themselves ready for the big game ahead – with no detail omitted.

Preparations continued in Hull for the tie, a rally stand being erected on the unoccupied portion of the best stand to make room for a few more spectators in what was expected to be a 20,000 crowd. The big day arrived at a wintry Anlaby Road. 'Athleo' describes the scenes:

"The gates were opened at one, and long before the advertised time of the kick-off there was a large crowd on the popular side of the ground. Colours and favours were in great evidence, and a great din was created by the miniature megaphones and the shouting of the Hull supporters. The ground was in a heavy condition, and sand had been liberally distributed round the goals and on other parts. A cold, bleak wind was blowing and the lot of the waiting spectators was far from an enviable one. The period of waiting was relieved by selections by the St. Vincent's Boys' Band."

The Hull photographer Frank Overton positioned himself at the covered North stand end (possibly because it afforded some degree of protection from the elements?) and took this action picture of Tigers goalkeeper Teddy Roughley going full length to deny Chelsea's Hilsdon a goal, losing his cap in the process. This picture was then featured in a local newspaper and the incident mentioned in the match report as a highlight of the game. Overton was not known as a prolific photographer of the Tigers and this action shot is a rarity. He chose to annotate the picture with 'Chelsea v Hull City' despite the game having been played at Anlaby Road.

Splendid Save. Teddy Roughley goes full length to deny Chelsea.

HULL CITY V CHELSEA.

(Photo by F. Overton, Hull)

ONE OF ROUGHLEY'S BRILLIANT SAVES FROM HILSDON

CHELSEA V HULL CITY SPLENDID SAVE BY ROUGHLEY

A further flavour of the afternoon is given by the following account in the Hull Daily Mail of City's equaliser, which makes reference to the recent earthquake in Sicily:

> "Shades of Messina! What has happened? It isn't an earthquake, it's an air-quake. There's no doubt about it. It's enough to revivify the corpses in the Spring-bank Cemetery. It could only mean one thing. City had equalised. The shouting, the bell-ringing, the yelling, were all eloquent testimony to the delight of the home partisans, and the smiles on nearly every face would have done old Scrooge a world of good. It must have been worth the extra money to have experienced such a feeling of delight. The day will long be remembered if only for one thing, and that, the terrible weather. Another storm in the second half causes a general rush from the open to the stands, where all empty places were speedily filled."

Vague allusions to 'sly winks' were made in the local press after the game about the convenience of the draw from the City point of view, in that they would probably pick up the not inconsiderable sum of at least £500 from the replay to add to the receipts they banked from this game.

The attendance in the grim conditions was considered an excellent one, and only two ties out of the thirty two bettered it. 'The record of £775 will long stand as the largest amount taken at any football match at the Third Port', remarked one paper. 'All things considered, it is doubtful if under the prevailing weather, they would have benefited much more had they consented to Chelsea's invitation to play the tie at Stamford Bridge. We question it very much indeed, and the City officials are to be commended upon their action in declining to yield to the Stamford Bridge money bags.' City went out at Stamford Bridge in the replay. Chelsea returned to their base in Bridlington, The Tigers to the Queens Hotel in Withernsea to prepare for the second game.

The replay on a midweek afternoon in west London drew some 25,000 fans – the two biggest crowds the Tigers attracted that season, keeping the bank manager happy. The disappointment of honourable principled defeat being sweetened by the ample economic compensation of a lucrative replay.

Block: City Eng. Co., Hull.

HULL CITY V. CHELSEA.
THE RE-PLAYED CUP-TIE MATCH AT STAMFORD BRIDGE YESTERDAY.
A SCRAMBLE IN FRONT OF THE HULL CITY GOAL.

City went out at Stamford Bridge in the replay. Here Teddy Roughley plucks the ball out of the air as Chelsea press.

The Tiger (listening to its own record): "Not so bad for me—I got £700 for making that record. I'm quite a Marie Lloyd."

The fourth place finish was an improvement on the previous season and the club's best in their brief history, beating the 5th place obtained in 1905/6. It was their fourth consecutive top-ten finish, which was helping to establish some very solid foundations for the club. The gap between second place and the Tigers was seven points, however, a considerable distance. Losing four out of the first five games was not the ideal start, but a good run of four wins in the next five repaired the damage slightly. Jackie Smith, the goal-scoring hero of the previous season missed some fourteen games during the course of the season because of injury and his absence was never adequately filled.

Having lost some seven games by the halfway stage of a 38-game-season, City were never serious contenders for promotion. The defence that had shown itself to be so porous the previous season had improved markedly. In 1907/8 the Tigers leaked some 62 goals, this season it was down to 39, but unfortunately the goals scored were also down by ten, to 63. A general tightening-up improved the position in the league table, but could not eradicate the inconsistency or the runs of defeats which punctuated the season.

Despite plenty of goals in the New Year, another spell of poor results leading up to Easter (5 defeats in 6 games) put paid to any lingering hopes of promotion, just as a winning run was required, in the home straight. Constant team changes, whether brought about by injury, loss or form or unavailability, hampered Ambrose Langley's attempt to find or select his preferred starting XI. A slight feeling of underachievement was discernible at the end of the season. Given luck with injuries and a little more consistency, promotion would surely be in sight next season?

The Chelsea cup-ties had filled the coffers in a satisfactory way but against that the cost of buying forward Wally Smith for £750 from Leicester in March had to be offset.

In a newspaper article, Smith was profiled at length:

"Although comparatively a newcomer to the Anlaby-road, 'Walley' Smith, the Tigers' smart inside left, has earned for himself a warm corner in the hearts of Hull City supporters. 'Walley' is probably one of the most popular of the players, at any rate amongst the supporters.

A good sportsman, he has high ideals as to how the game should be conducted, and, what probably means a great deal more, of how a player should conduct himself. During his sojourn at Hull, 'Walley' has played some very good games. 'Walley' is a player whom to know is to respect. He is not of that ultra-robust character one has to learned to look upon almost as inseparably from Hull City players. When he first came to Hull he was not in the best of health, and by arrangement with the directors he resided for some

Forward Wally Smith arrived from Leicester Fosse for £750 in March 1909, and soon began to score for the Tigers. Never as prolific as team mate Jacky, his versatility in playing in other positions was a valuable asset to manager Langley. His previous spell at Bradford City would have brought him to the attention of John Baines, the football shield producer based in that city. He was also photographed in his training kit in the north stand goal at Anlaby Road (shown opposite).

time at Withernsea, and is now a great deal stronger. He is a tricky, scientific forward, and plays a clean, clever and gentlemanly game. He is superior to the general class of Second Division forwards. It is a somewhat curious fact that 'Walley' enjoys the distinction of being the only Yorkshireman in the Hull City team, he being a native of Allerton, near Bradford.

After playing with a number of junior clubs, he threw in his lot with Northampton. He remained with that club one season, and then went to Bradford, where he remained three and a half years. For Bradford he played inside right and centre forward, and during his connection with the club scored some 65 goals. As a centre, he found the net 23 times. When 'Walley' left Bradford, he was subjected to a great amount of criticism, and great indignation was felt by 'Walley' and his

Wally Smith

If he would not try for his old club, a director of a new one could have no guarantee that he would try for them, and it would therefore be extremely injudicious for a player not to give his best at all times. The most consistent player that ever breathed had his off day. This controversy took place just prior to Smith's transfer to Leicester. On that occasion the 'Fossils' paid the big transfer fee of £800. This was at the beginning of last season. It is now a somewhat open secret that the only reason the Fossils parted with him was on account of financial difficulties, and their consequent inability to retain him. He only stayed at Leicester for the very short period of six weeks. Walley states that he was very comfortable during his brief sojourn there. From Leicester he came to Hull, at one of the highest transfer fees ever paid by the directors. The amount was never officially announced, but it is generally understood that a guess at £500 would be very near the mark.

In the opinion of the majority of Tiger supporters, it has been money well-spent, and expenditure which no one will begrudge. If a change were necessary-and as a Tiger supporter I earnestly hope it will not be – the management would have little difficulty in getting a little more than their money back. As is, of course, well-known, Walley has been put in a new position in the Hull team – inside left. Personally, (and I am not alone in this view) I incline to the opinion that it would have been a wise policy to have tried him at centre. However, that is a matter on which opinions will of necessity differ. He has shaped very well with the Tigers, and has given general satisfaction. 'Walley' stands 5ft. 10 ins., and weighs 11st 7lb."

All that remained was for the players to enjoy a foreign tour once more to conclude their season's endeavours. Following the previous year's end-of-season trip to the Low Countries, a more ambitious tour was organised to Scandinavia. Arriving at Gothenburg on May 15th, City thrashed Southampton 5-0 later that same day. Writing of the game, a nameless Hull Daily News correspondent relates:

…When the Football Association gave the Hull City Club permission to play on the Continent, Mr. Wall, the F.A. secretary, expressed a wish that the boys should play their best and treat the trip entirely as a holiday. Well, I am sure the players in this match have done their utmost to carry out the F.A. wish. Who said a football strike amongst the Tigers against the F.A.? No, they are far and away a too happy family for that.

The Southampton team are a good side and play excellent football, but they could not do anything against eleven 'mad' Tigers. The crew of the s.s. Rollo from Captain Wood to the firemen, were watching the match, and it was quite exhilarating to hear that familiar cry

club-mates at the allegation made in letters to a certain journal that he deliberately went off form to 'get his papers'. These letters were not published and "Walley" published a challenge to anyone to bring any tithe of proof of the allegation. But this was not accepted. Smith does not think any player would adopt such 'gutter' principles. To do so a player would be fighting against his own interests.

'Now Tigers!' and 'Let's have another one, Tigers!' One man called to Roughley, 'Are you cold, Rough?' Geordie's goal was greeted with cries of 'Well played, Bovril!'

All our boys played well, and it is impossible to pick out anybody for special mention. The Tigers say that it is the splendid training they received on the s.s. Rollo that made them fit, and they hope they will be sent on the s.s. Rollo to train for cup-ties next season instead of Withernsea.

The Gothenburg officials are awfully pleased with our display and we are now firm favourites with them. The Gothenburg chairman said 'he could quite understand us getting such a great quantity of people to our matches. The Hull players are so young and they play such fine football, and it is the best game he has witnessed.' In fact he was so pleased that he tried to open negotiations with Director Stringer for the Tigers to return here in the early autumn. Mr. Langley says 'No, not until electric railways or flying machines run across the North Sea.'

After the game, the team relaxed by attending a concert given by 'one of the crack Swedish military bands' who acknowledged the Tigers' presence by playing several English tunes before concluding with the (British) National Anthem, which was sung lustily by the City contingent.

"The whole audience out of compliment to the boys stood up during the playing, and were greatly interested in the three hearty Tiger cheers that were given for His Majesty the King. Afterwards the natives cheered our boys. There seems to be the very best feeling between the two countries, and I am sure that football will further cement that feeling. After the concert Mr Stringer had an interview with the conductor, and the latter had promised the Tigers a fine selection of English music for next Sunday, in the evening, upon our return from Stockholm."

City's Arthur Temple had requested the band play 'Oh, Antonio!' but they claimed to have left the music at home and were unable to oblige him.

Time in the capital was spent at the National Museum, art galleries and the zoo (amongst other activities). During the Stockholm sojourn, City also managed to beat the local club 2-0 and lose to the touring West Brom side 1-2. It was reported that the players would receive medals as a souvenir of their visit to the Swedish Capital, and the directors and manager would receive badges.

More medals were collected back in Gothenburg at the end of the week, as the Tigers' players had been promised, for beating Southampton in the first game on the tour. Having beaten the local Orgryte team 6-0 on the same ground as the Southampton victory a week earlier, City's players duly accepted their promised mementos.

" ... 'Davy' Gordon responded on behalf of the team, and thanked the Gothenburg club for their kindness. The medals, he said, would always be a souvenir of an enjoyable visit to this city. The medals are of silver, the size of a five-shilling piece, and have the Swedish ribbons on, after the style of the soldiers' medals in England.

We spent the evening at a cafe, where we heard a fine musical programme. Before we had been in the place five minutes, the band (evidently in our honour) struck up our National Anthem, which we again lustily sang. The greatest items of the evening were those between the selections of the band, which were English choruses heartily sung by the Tigers. The Swedes in the cafe thoroughly enjoyed it and repeatedly shouted 'Hoch, hoch, hoch,' which is the equivalent to 'encore.' Viewing the sunset from the cafe window was simply magnificent, and to anybody with an artistic eye, was most enchanting. We shall most certainly revisit this cafe before we leave this historical city.

A cinematograph syndicate have been this last week showing very good pictures of our match with Southampton. All the Tigers visited the hall last night, and were very interested to see themselves playing football. The whole show was as good, or better than anything we have seen in Hull, the pictures being so clear and distinct. After the pictures we passed the evening at the pleasure gardens of Lorensburg, where a very fine military band was playing. There were various forms of amusement such as skittle alleys and shooting galleries &c. There was also going on at the same time the annual poultry show and there were some exceptional fine birds."

The pleasant routine of playing matches and sightseeing continued, with well-documented socialising in the evenings. On Monday May 24th, after a miserable day of incessant rain, the City party found themselves invited to visit the British Sailors' Institute in Gothenburg.

"The Tigers very soon made themselves at home, and being joined by the crew of the s.s. Orlando, settled themselves down to a very good impromptu concert. Amongst those present were Miss Cundale and Mrs Dickmann (who are the pioneers of the institute, or in other words, the friends of British sailors in this port), Mr and Mrs Coodly and their daughter and two sons, the officers of the s.s. Orlando, and many others.

The proceedings opened with Director Stringer being pressed into the services of chairman, Mrs Dickmann presided at the piano, and at this lady's special wish the concert was opened with due loyalty, the whole company singing 'God Save The King.' Our genial and ever-ready vocalist, G.Browell, was No.1 on the programme, and he very ably rendered the White-Eyed Kaffir's famous song. 'The Blind Boy.' A comic song, entitled 'An Irishman in France,' sung by Mr Walker, a fireman on the s.s. Orlando, came next, and he put a lot of work into his song, which proved a great success. Leach asked for 'Love me in December.' Roughley (all goalkeepers are quick) replied 'I don't mind if I do, Bill, if you will make it worth my while.' A duet followed by the famous duettists, the brothers Geordie and Andy Browell, entitled 'Our hands are clasped.' Mrs Dickmann, who has a very fine voice then gave us 'Fiddle and I.'

The Tigers Glee party, whose leader is G. Browell, and the accompanist Tim Wright, then obliged with selections as follows: 'If I should plant a tiny seed of love,' 'Sandy MacNab,' 'Suffering Suffragette,' 'O Antonio' (Arthur Temple got his wish), 'Has anyone seen a German Band,' &c, Mr Temple (second officer of the s.s.Orlando) sang 'The Veteran.' Trainer Leach quite came out of his shell and gave us the patriotic 'Ould Ireland.' Bill was received with great cheers. Manager Langley was asked to oblige, but he said he would if he could, but was unable. Then came an interval for a very nice supper, and the Tigers had their first good cup of tea since leaving the s.s. Rollo."

The second half started with Director Stringer making a speech in which he promised the seventy-two-year-old Miss Cundale a photograph of the Tigers as a memento of the occasion, and wished her many more birthdays. She in turn thanked him and wished City well in their game the next day, hoping to see them again next year. The music started again and amongst other performances, Geordie Browell sang 'The Anchor's Weighed' and concluded with 'I can hear the angels calling,' and as an encore gave the assembly 'The Wandering Boy.'

"The party, after singing 'Auld Lang Syne,' broke up and returned to the hotel, only to find the popular chairman and secretary of the West Bromwich Albion club waiting for them, they having just arrived from Stockholm. Tomorrow we have an invitation to go over a brewery in Gothenburg, which we have accepted. The attack upon the brewery commences at 10 a.m."

The players and management arrived back in Hull, having avenged their earlier defeat to West Brom, on Sunday May 30th after a fortnight away, having set sail from Gothenburg at 12.15pm local time.

"Miss Cundale and Mrs Dickmann (Sailors' Institute) came to say good-bye to us. Two American friends we met in the Gardens during the week were also there. There were crowds of people seeing relatives off to America, via Hull, and some of the sights were pathetic. The great Swedish custom is to decorate their departing relatives with wreaths and bouquets of flowers of every description, and some had most beautiful roses. Just as the Calypso moved off two of the girls from our hotel rushed up, only to be too late, so they threw seventeen flowers in the water for us. The boys were very glad to be on their homeward journey, and kept the crowd alive with songs.

When we were on the boat the chairman of the Gothenburg Club presented Directors Stringer and Glossop and Manager Langley with badges as a souvenir of the trip. He also informed them that the Tigers have left the best impression of English football of the three clubs visiting there this season.

Now, a few words as to the voyage. We had a capital lunch shortly after we sailed, and to which the Tigers did justice. About 4p.m. the Rollo was sighted, and we passed her within a few hundred yards, and gave three cheers, to which they replied. Captain Chambers very kindly signalled, saying 'Tigers all well.' The Rollo was rolling, and we all smiled to ourselves. One of the party remarked, 'Fancy giving that three cheers, when she nearly killed us a fortnight since!'

Friday night came and everyone fit. During the morning, from 2 o'clock until about 5 o'clock, we were in fog. Saturday, 5.30 a.m., brought Jack Smith fully dressed on deck feeling fit, and from that time until 8.a.m the Tigers gradually appeared on deck all well. Breakfast time came, and out of seventeen entries there were fourteen starters, and one of the absent ones was the great Jacky! He was found in his bunk, having undressed again, holding a book. He said it was quiet there, and wanted to finish his book, and that he was not hungry .Well, Tigers can swallow a lot of things, but Jacky Smith's excuse would not go down. Andy Browell and Tim Wright were the other non-starters.

Eventually all three came on deck, and the morning was passed away with games and card playing, &c, For the luncheon stakes all seventeen went to the post, and all finished the course going strong. The afternoon was simply glorious, and the Tigers slept in the sunshine and had sea water baths. For the dinner handicap (7.30) all started, but Andy soon dropped out, being followed at once by Director Stringer (who was, however, in a nervous breakdown, and he was put to bed, and there he stayed until 11.30 p.m.). Jacky Smith got two laps (I mean two courses), and he then gave up. Wally Smith kept up bravely, and just managed to stay the course. All bar Director Stringer were all right when on deck.

After dinner the Tigers gave their usual concert and, all feeling well, struck up the song 'The little ship upon the sea.' About 11.30 p.m. Spurn lights were seen, and with that most of the Tigers turned in. Manager Langley refused to go to bed, as he said he would be in his own bed by 3 a.m. The s.s. Calpyso was docked in the Albert Dock this morning at 3.10 o'clock, and thus Captain Chambers had brought the precious Tigers safely back. Jacky Smith, followed by Martin and Mr Langley, was first on land at 3.24 a.m., those three preferring to walk home to waiting until six for cabs,&c.

The Tigers are always up to date, and Director Glossop and Temple opened a shaving salon at 4.30 a.m., as the Tigers had been talking about shaves and how they could get them. Trade proved very brisk after Director Stringer had had three days' growth taken off successfully by Mr Glossop. McQuillan was the next and Temple wielded the razor manfully over him. Musgrave was the only unfortunate one of seven or eight to get a slight cut, and it was account of a new razor being tried. Mr Glossop shaved one side, and then Temple finished him with a little nick on the lip. The Tigers had breakfast about six, and were pleased to see Mr Haller waltz into the saloon to welcome them back. Then the party gradually melted away, until next August, all being fit, and having enjoyed a real good trip and holiday."

With all playing engagements over for another season, thoughts turned to the topics to be heard at the AGM on June 12th. The club's recent progress and direction for the next season would have been in the minds of shareholders as they assembled to hear the directors' views.

It was thought that Gordon Wright's days with club were over, as the amateur was leaving his teaching post at Hymers College after three years there, to study mining engineering at Kensington. It was hoped that maybe he could turn out for the club when City were playing in the south. In the course of the AGM at the Grosvenor Hotel, Alwyn Smith referred to the winger's presence in glowing terms declaring that in his opinion the team 'seemed to play with far greater confidence' when Wright was on the pitch. The men tried hard but it seemed that when he was out of the team there was something lacking, and the players seemed to feel it. They would not only miss his services as a player, but his influence with the players on and off the field.

Ernest Morison moved a hearty vote of thanks to Wright for his services in the past season. Wright himself was present at the meeting and responded by saying he would like to say a word about the players. He was afraid, supposing the directors of Hull City had elected not to try for the First Division, that they would have to get a very different set of players. The players in the teams he had played with in Hull City had always been keen on the First Division, and were always trying to get into it. He was afraid if they had been told it was not exactly policy to get into the First Division, there would have been a mutiny among the players. He continued that he got a good deal of nonsense talked to him,

usually when on his holidays, and by certain gentlemen. People said to him 'Are Hull City going to get into the First Division?' He always replied 'I don't care what Hull City are going to do, but the team I am captain of are always trying to get into the First Division.'

Contrary to opinions believing Wright's days at City were over, the Tigers' captain would again lead them the following season and demonstrate his continuing commitment to the cause.

City were by now firmly established is a featured football club in the world of the cigarette card producers. This rare early Murray Cigarettes Football Colours card, issued in 1908, features a simple black and amber flag.

GROSVENOR HOTEL,
HULL.

THE MOST MODERN HOTEL IN THE CITY

1909 – 10

PLAY UP, TIGERS!
HEADQUARTERS:
GROSVENOR HOTEL,
CARR-LANE.

The best place for Football Teas, Smokers,
Banquets, etc.

DAILY LUNCH, 12.30 till 2.30   Three Courses
of the Best for 1s 6d.

CHOPS and STEAKS from 1s.

HULL CITY A.F.C. SEPT. 1, 1909.

"We are bound, sooner or later, to reap the reward of careful management. We must make a special effort this season, and I can answer for the players themselves that we shall not spare ourselves, but set the First Division as the ONE AND ONLY goal to be reached this season. Not that we have never made the effort before, but we have not heretofore been much disappointed on not obtaining our desires. We have done well enough for a young team in such good company and our places in the League table for the past five seasons, in fact ever since the club was formed, have given much cause for congratulation. But this time I fancy, if we do not succeed, we shall experience much of the feeling that the poor West Bromwich players must have felt when they were ousted with such cruel luck from promotion last year."

Gordon Wright, Tigers' captain, September 1909.

City started their season on Thursday 2nd September at Barnsley. Unusually, Duncan has dated the exact day of the postcard shown above – as the day preceding the Barnsley trip. It is interesting to note that there are two Browell brothers, three Smiths, two Wrights and two Gordons, all in the same picture. The location is one that Duncan will come to favour in future years – the cricket ground backing onto West Park, with its trees visible behind the players. This picturesque setting provided a pleasant and almost rural backdrop in late summer, when the team group picture was traditionally taken.

E.G.D. Wright, the famous amateur, teacher, and later mining student is shown in a studio photo cameo to the top right of the group; presumably his busy schedule necessitated his absence on this day, as with so many City team photographs, and Duncan, not wishing to have an incomplete group lacking its most well-known player, inserts a previous studio portrait of the absent star. The captain missed the opening games of the season and his absences were a fact of life for the club, who learned to adapt to these competing activities.

'TIGERS' IN TRAINING.

EXCLUSIVE "DAILY NEWS" PHOTOGRAPH.

1. Stanley and Jack Smith sprinting: 2. George Browell shooting; 3. Stephenson and D. W. Taylor (full back from Newcastle East End); 4. A. Browell on the defence. 5. Nevins, Roughley, and Storey in the goal mouth.

The excursion to Barnsley the next day proved to be a fruitful one, as the Tigers recorded a 2-1 win. The season had started well and pre-season optimism was proving to be well founded. In an article published in the week before the Barnsley game, the Hull Daily Mail reviewed City's prospects for the season:

"DIVISION 1
ARE HULL CITY AMBITIOUS?
THE TEAM'S RIVALS

The Tigers will need a lot of shaking off this season. Rarely has a club [had] at its command so promising a string of juniors as Hull City have this season secured. Their performances in the trial matches have been such as to make one feel great confidence as to the result of the coming season. The older hands, also, have lost none of their old cunning and ability, and the directors have plenty from whom to pick and choose. The club has an able and hard-working board of directors, and a staff of conscientious officials, and everything promises to go merrily as marriage bells. It is thought that that hero of the Tigers, Gordon Wright, will be able to assist City in, at any rate, a large proportion of their matches. This is a matter for congratulation, for although there may be a number of sound players who, if necessity should arise, could be placed in Mr Wright's place, it is certain that none would be so brilliant or so reliable. He and that other very fine winger, Stan. Smith, earn the envious regard of all the clubs visited by the Tigers. In common with all well-wishers of City, we earnestly hope the services of these two brilliant men will long be retained. The two other Smiths are men who need reckoning with. 'Wallie' has become firmly enshrined in the hearts of the club spectators as a steady, reliable and clever forward, while Jacky's exhibitions in the trials have shown much improvement. It is to be hoped that he will come out of last season's temporary cloud and regain his brilliance of a couple of seasons ago. If so, the Hull attack is likely to prove a

TERROR TO ALL COMERS.

Temple shows very pretty football, and if his form of Thursday last continues, methinks the directors will be ill-advised if he is not included at centre. One of the goals he scored on that occasion was as pretty an effort as any ever witnessed on the Anlaby-road ground. Gilberthorpe has not yet recovered from his injury sustained last Saturday. It appears that his knee is sprained and has swollen considerably. He will be in the doctor's hands for the next three weeks. As with the forwards, so it is with the defence. There is a rare basket to choose from, and to get the pick of that basket will be no easy matter. In Roughley and Storrey, we have a couple of custodians extremely hard to beat – as would-be net finders will speedily find. Of the backs, Nevins has 'bucked up' considerably, while a likely recruit has been discovered in Taylor. McQuillan and Stephenson are also still proving sound defenders. With such halves at our disposal as Andy Browell, Gordon, Tim Wright, George Browell, to say nothing of such 'nippers' as Stott, Wylde, and the old Midland League warhorses, Morrison and Martin, we should have no apprehension as to the effectiveness of this line. If anything, we are likely to be

At any rate, this line will without doubt, be strong, and would be hard to better. It must be borne in mind that the men have considerably improved from 12 months ago. Wally Smith has made the forwards more effective, while Jacky Smith and Temple have made great strides. Musgrave and Townend are two likely juniors also in this line. Altogether, the team is stronger and cleverer than before, and is likely to make a name. The way they pulled themselves together last year after the unfortunate Christmas matches was a revelation, and their progress was practically one of unabashed victory until they came to a 'stone wall' at West Bromwich. From the beginning of the year to March 13th, the team did not lose a single match, earned 15 points out of a possible 16, and scored 22 goals to 5. With a team who can perform feats of this character it would be

UTTER FOOLISHNESS

to interfere. The position of the club ever since its formation has been one to be proud of, for with one exception they have always occupied

OUR TIGER CARTOONS: SEASON 1909-10.
"ATHLEO": PUSS! PUSS! PUSS!
PA STRIPES: PIP! PIP! HOW'S BARNSLEY FOR A START?

The local newspapers shared the conviction that promotion was a real possibility for Ambrose Langley's team, and the win at Barnsley in the first game did nothing to dispel this.

the leading position of the Yorkshire clubs. This exception refers to two seasons ago, when Bradford City won promotion. Will it be Hull City's turn this year? In spite of all that has been said to the contrary, readers may rest assured that, if the players are capable of doing it, the team will be carried up. The players are not of the calibre to be deterred from doing their best by any question of policy, and the directors are too true sportsmen to request them to hold back, whatever the prospects of a First Division team in Hull may be – and some of them have such views. The Tigers are out for promotion if it can be secured. Of their prospects it would at this early date be absurd to speak. It is likely that one of the most interesting matches of the coming season, and, incidentally one of the hardest, will be that with Manchester City. The team did poorly last season, but it is certain the Mancunians will spare no effort to retrieve their lost position. Hull City open their season on Thursday at Barnsley, and good luck to them. Four points should have accrued by Saturday night next."

JACKY SMITH.
THE MAN WHO DID THE "HAT TRICK" ON SATURDAY.

As the fans had hoped, the Tigers started off their campaign with a 2-1 win at Barnsley (who were to lose to Newcastle United after a replay in the season's Cup Final). They followed that up two days later with a 3-1 win against Leeds City as Jacky Smith scored a hat trick in front of 10,000 supporters. Another away win on the following Monday at Burnley by a single goal made it six points out of six – and three wins in five days. After a draw at Molineux in which Jacky Smith and Joe Smith scored a goal apiece, City crushed Gainsborough Trinity by five goals to one at Anlaby Road, with Jacky Smith (2), Wally Smith (2) and Gordon Wright scoring.

Home gates were now around 10,000, a healthy increase from the previous season. The home game against Gainsborough Trinity sees mention of a vocal element of the crowd dubbed 'the City Glee Party' by the reporter for their musical contribution as the Tigers race to a convincing 5-1 victory. For the visit to Grimsby:

HUMBERSIDE DERBY.

HULL CITY FIRST PAST THE POST

What Does the City Captain Think?

◆

I HAVE

NOTHING

AT ALL

TO SAY.

Wright's terse seven-word comment appeared after the 0-0 draw at home to Lincoln.

WHY THE TIGERS FAILED.

◆

We had our nerves quite upset when that early penalty was given against G. Browell. Whether the referee's decision was right or wrong, a lead of a goal to a side like Manchester City under the circumstances was a tremendous handicap to us.

We certainly were presented with a few chances of scoring, but if every opportunity materialised we should be as certain of First Division honours as we are of death. Manchester City, however, got the glory, and we do not begrudge them their victory.

Whilst our defeat was a sad blow to the team, we believe our supporters recognise that we fought an uphill game under conditions that after all were perhaps undeserving. By no means, however, are we downhearted.

Ernest Gordon D. Wright

'A large number of Hull supporters, probably 1,500, travelled. On the 11.50 boat there were about 600, and about 800 on the 12.40, while stragglers came in by later trains. The ground began to fill early, and the tedium of waiting was relieved by music supplied by the boys of the Newland Orphan Homes, whose band and vocal selections were much appreciated.

The bell which is so often heard ringing at Anlaby-road had been brought over for the occasion, and kept time merrily with the band. There was a demonstration and counter demonstration by adherents of the respective teams as they trooped on to the field, and the Tigers were encouraged by hearty cheers and cries of 'Now City!"

OUR ILLUSTRATION SHOWS LYALL, OF MANCHESTER CITY, FISTING OUT A SHOT FROM ONE OF THE HULL CITY PLAYERS

Tigers attack the Manchester City goal in vain.

The short trip over the Humber to Grimsby held no fear for City as the winning form continued. Grimsby were beaten 3-2 by goals from Jacky Smith (his seventh in six games), Wally Smith and Andy Browell. Eleven points out of 12, and only two of those games being played at home. Such a blistering start must have exceeded the hopes of all but the most optimistic Tigers followers.

The goals were being scored in abundance (even if only one clean sheet had been kept at the other end) and the large crowds were becoming accustomed to convincing victories. More importantly, City headed the league table. The month of September had proved very fruitful for the club but their next opponents – relegated Manchester City – would present a more realistic yardstick against which to measure their merits as genuine promotion candidates.

The highest league gate yet recorded in Hull attended the game on October 2nd. An expectant home crowd witnessed a scrappy and hard-fought game, with City lacking their usual clinical finishing. Geordie Browell had a penalty harshly awarded against him after only nine minutes as he tangled with Lot Jones and the Manchester player came into contact with the City man's outstretched leg. The goal rocked City and steadied the visitors, who then restricted City to sporadic innocuous shots which failed to trouble the Manchester goalkeeper. On the rare occasions City threatened, a massed rank of blue shirts

WHY DERBY PREVAILED.

We caught Derby quite on the top of their form, and it was another instance of a side laying themselves out for a team occupying a threatening position. We certainly had our chances of scoring, but our opponents were always a winning combination. Their forwards were fast and clever, and in several instances there was little wonder our defence was unreliable.

We were severely handicapped by Walden's injury, but we were never allowed to get into our accustomed stride. We got not the slightest encouragement from a fearfully one-sided crowd, some of whom urged their players, in very forcible language, to do the most despicable things towards us. I am happy to think our Hull spectators belong to an entirely different class.

E. Gordon D. Wright

CITY CAPTAIN'S EULOGY.

Our victory over Birmingham was a splendid one, because it showed our men up in their truest light. The Hull public have enjoyed a glimpse of the form we have frequently displayed away from home, and what was most satisfactory of all was the correctness of our aim at goal.

The whole team was imbued with one idea, and that to sling the ball about, thus keeping our front line continually engaged. Birmingham played good football, but they caught us on the top of our form, and I trust the excellence of the same may be long maintained.

Our spectators must have had a very enjoyable time; I'm sure we had.

E. Gordon D. Wright

materialised to protect their goal. This degree of organisation and teamwork was at a level above that encountered by City thus far, and they lacked the composure and precision to break it down. Manchester City had adapted to the occasion more pragmatically and played a typical second division game – complete with robust methods when needed. Their forwards threatened whenever an opening appeared and their shooting was invariably dangerous. The visitors increased their lead thus wrapping up the victory, although City's response was a late penalty converted by Jacky Smith, which prompted a brief siege of the Manchester goal. Alas their goalkeeper Lyall held firm and marshalled his defenders to extinguish any hopes of an equaliser.

The unbeaten record had gone, the home record also and City had been stopped in their tracks by a team intent on regaining their First Division status. The following Saturday at Leicester Fosse was a chance to resume the winning habit. Arthur Temple scored the only goal as City's away record was lost in a 3-1 defeat.

Another victory against Barnsley was obtained two days later, Alf Toward netting the only goal. The following Saturday on October 16th, City could only share a goal-less draw with lowly Lincoln City – a result which alarmed their captain. Gordon Wright had written two weeks earlier in his weekly newspaper column: 'If we don't win, we might as well pack up our things and enter the Midland League' (the league in which City

Reserves played). Unhappily for the normally measured and astute Tigers' skipper, his words demonstrated the unpredictable nature of football – or his side's inconsistency. The head of steam built up in September was rapidly being dispersed, this time against a team with a notoriously weak defence. City's forwards struck the bar and the post but otherwise the Lincoln goalkeeper was equal to anything that City's out-of-sorts attack could muster. Toward looked out of his depth, Jacky Smith had to go off injured and the Tigers generally lacked guile and imagination in attack.

The same result attended City's game at Clapton the following Saturday before the Tigers crashed on October 30th at home to Blackpool, Jacky Smith scoring the goal in a 2-1 defeat. October had yielded three defeats, two draws and just one win. The torrent of goals had dried up to a trickle (only four in six games), whilst the porous defence continued September's form. City had lost their momentum and place among the league leaders. November arrived with a welcome victory at Bradford on the 6th (new boy George Walden scoring the only goal) but a hammering at Derby by four unanswered goals demonstrated that the problems were getting worse, not better. In the first minute John McQuillan deflected a shot past Teddy Roughley, who seemed to have had the ball covered. City fought back to keep in the game until five minutes before the interval when George Walden had to go off. City missed three good chances and lived to regret it.

No substitutes were allowed and the dazed Londoner resumed after half-time as a mere passenger in the game. A second soft goal (the ball was adjudged to have crossed the line as it struck the post and Roughley gathered it to kick clear – neither referee nor linesmen being in any position to judge the ball's position) made City's task extremely difficult. By now Derby were brimming with confidence and sensed City's spirit

OLDHAM ATHLETIC RECEIVED THEIR XMAS BOX LAST SATURDAY

J SMITHS HAT TRICK

The 4-0 win on December 18th against Oldham was a pre-Christmas boost.

HOW NEVINS SCORED HIS GREAT GOAL LAST SATURDAY.
(It is only a slight exaggeration, too.)

THE RIVAL FISHERMEN
OR THE CATCH OF THE (NEW) YEAR.

With the first team winning at West Brom, Tommy Nevins' goal for the Reserves at Anlaby Road was deemed to be of such high quality that a cartoon depicting it was published in a local paper.

ebbing away in front of a partisan crowd. Two further goals were added and City were well beaten by one of the division's strongest sides in front of a 10,000 crowd. A home draw with Stockport on the 20th was followed by a 2-1 defeat to conclude another miserable month – a solitary victory, a draw and two defeats. October and November had yielded just eight points out of a possible 20, after September's 11 out of 12.

In the next game City scored seven without reply against Birmingham City. They followed that up with a two-nil victory at West Bromwich before returning to Hull to vanquish Oldham by a 4-0 score-line. Three victories, 13 goals scored, and none conceded – the complete opposite of their games in the previous two months when the defence leaked goals and the attack was badly out of form. The form shown in September was now evident again and City started to climb the table. It was suggested by some observers that City had at last started to show some of their away form at home. Or as the Hull Daily News reporter 'The Prodigal' observed: 'When the Tigers are caught on form, somebody has to look out for squalls. Birmingham, West Bromwich, and Oldham Athletic now know what Tigeritis is.'

Full back Tommy Nevins scored a remarkable goal for the Reserves at Anlaby Road while the Tigers were playing at West Bromwich, prompting the cartoon shown above, which depicts the conclusion after the full-

back had dribbled from his own penalty area to the other end of the pitch, and hammered a fierce shot into Huddersfield net.

Some 25,000 people turned up at Craven Cottage on Christmas Day to see Fulham beat City 3-1 (Jacky Smith getting a consolation goal – his sixth goal in four December games). Forty-eight hours later City avenged that defeat by inflicting a 3-2 scoreline on the London side in front of a new record Anlaby Road league crowd of 16,000. Morale was good as the goals flowed freely once more. On New Year's Day, Grimsby visited the Tigers and were thrashed 5-1 in front of a modest 8,000 crowd, the prolific scoring of Jacky Smith was now being supplemented by Wally Smith, Arthur Temple, Joe Smith and Gordon Wright. The Tigers' directors had kept faith with their forwards through their loss of form and were now being repaid with an abundance of goals.

A game in West Yorkshire proved to be another day out for the Anlaby Road crowd for "Leeds is a favourite rendezvous for Hull, and it was not surprising to find a large number of trippers accompanying the Tigers. These made their presence very evident when the visitors entered the field. The welcome accorded them was much more boisterous than that given the home team."

Following the draw at Leeds on 8th January, the City party headed directly to Worthing to prepare for the Cup-tie against Chelsea the following Saturday. The Sussex resort was becoming a home from home for the Tigers as they prepared for their fifth Cup game in London in as many years. The now familiar routine of long walks on the beach or along the seafront during the day was augmented by billiards and local music hall or theatre visits in the evening, to tone the players and keep them occupied. As well as trainer Leach and manager Ambrose Langley, local journalists and City Directors would also accompany the players to complete the entourage.

The financial rewards of the Cup and its unique profile ensured that no club took it lightly or played at anything below their best. Supporters expected and demanded performances of a level appropriate to the nation's favourite and most highly regarded competition. Supporters, too, made the now familiar cup excursion to the capital and to West London. The Tigers' enterprising start would have lifted their hearts, as City took the game to their First Division counterparts. Disappointingly for them, the home side took the lead on the half hour when Teddy Roughley could only turn a corner from Chelsea's Williams straight into his own net, as the greasy ball somehow eluded his grasp compounded by the presence of two City defenders disturbing his field of vision. At the other end the normally deadly Jacky Smith seemed overeager and snatched at a couple of headers, when he had ample time to chest the ball down and shoot. Worse was to follow a minute after the break as the Pensioners scored their second – a seemingly offside effort that saw Brawn race from an offside position to shoot past Roughley. Temple scored for City after a move started by Andy Browell, which involved Stanley and Jacky Smith, whose shot was parried by Chelsea's Whitley. The ball was not cleared properly and Arthur Temple planted it safely in the net. Wally Smith was stretchered off unconscious 15 minutes from the end after being on the receiving end of Whitley's elbow, and although the Tigers were numerically disadvantaged, they continued to press and create real chances. Jacky Smith was again wasteful towards the end when his normally reliable goal-scoring touch appeared to desert him. Overanxiety appeared to affect him at the crucial moments.

Observers reckoned that the result was a travesty, as the Tigers easily held their own in midfield and Chelsea's forwards got little change out of the City defence, the goals being isolated attacks with a hint of fortune or illegality about them. City seemed the more likely to score for most of the match, but composure and luck deserted them when it mattered. The tie was watched by some 38,000 fans – easily the highest attendance of the round, and receipts were £1,017. City's share of this was some £400 – a tidy sum and some consolation for their brief presence in the competition, despite the lingering feeling that their exit was premature and ill-deserved.

A modest draw with Wolves the following Saturday in front of a disappointing 6,000 crowd set the Tigers up for perhaps their biggest challenge in the League campaign with promotion-chasing Manchester

ROOM FOR TWO ONLY.

"SPORTS EXPRESS" TEDDY BEAR: Remember you've got to go through that door, so get a move on!

"BUCK UP, TIGERS!

Unless that beast soon mends his ways,
He'll be "tailed" off in the race,
For the road is growing steeper,
And he's not yet got a "place",
It's just four weeks ago to-day
Since he came in a winner,
And if he doesn't hurry up
We shall all be crying "Sinner!"

The longer he stays fooling round,
His chance is growing harder,
So "Buck Up, Tigers!" is the cry,
We want a well-filled larder!
Don't at the entrance archly gaze,
Just make a desperate dash;
Don't heed the foes in front of you,
All three may yet come crash.

Though the pathway's getting smaller,
Don't give up or lose your heart;
Nor let the narrow entrance door
Cause your nerves to jump and start;
Show once more the real Tiger-
Make your way again in front;
Don't be content to amble on,
But join briskly in the hunt.

Convince that bold Mancunian
That you don't intend to fail,
A proceeding that will force you
To kind of twist that gay Ram's tail.
Don't let the Fossils worry you,
Nor of Glossop pay much heed;
It's the first pair who're your rivals,
So away, and get up speed!

JINGLE"

City at their Hyde Road ground. The away game at Manchester on February 12th had been designated as 'the official outing' for travelling City fans that season. "A large number of Tigerites" made the journey over the Pennines to the Hyde Road ground; 'Athleo' of the Hull Daily Mail relates the day:

> "Some enthusiasts had travelled on the 8.20 G.C. train but the majority left Paragon Station by the special which went out at 9.10, and by which the team also travelled ... The Hull contingent was further strengthened by the trippers, who travelled by the H & B special which arrived at Central Station a little after 12.30. The kick off was timed for 3.15, but before three o'clock there was a large number on the ground, and the amber and black colours were in evidence in all portions. On the popular side were a number of familiar 'Spion Koppers,' who had brought their bells along with them ... The threepenny standers, Spion Koppers and even the aristocrats of the 'bob' stand have invaded Cottonopolis. Market-street and Piccadilly will be studies in black and amber tonight."

Writing in the same paper, 'Nimrod' decided that:

> "The selection of Manchester for the official outing is not half a bad 'un. There's one or two things to see, plenty of places to rid you of your surplus wealth, a 'panto' or two, Belle Vue, the perennial fountain of ink, the River Irwell, and it isn't such a far cry from Hull."

The travelling contingent's support went unrewarded as Manchester beat the Tigers by three unanswered goals in front of 28,000 spectators on a gluepot of a pitch bereft of grass.

The Mancunians were considered to be the best side in the division and outplayed City for periods in the game in a way no other side had done. They scored after 38 minutes through Holford, and thereafter, the Tigers barely got a look-in. Like the game in Hull in October, it was often fast and furious. Wally Smith had to leave the field injured and Manchester City's Dorsett was sent off seven minutes from time, having badly fouled the Tigers man on two occasions. The home side's nimble fleet-footedness was often too slick for

SECOND LEAGUE.

POSITIONS UP TO DATE.

	P.	W.	L.	D.	Goals. F.	Goals. A.	Pts.
Derby County	24	16	4	4	56	30	36
Manchester City	23	15	4	4	54	24	34
Leicester Fosse	24	16	8	0	59	36	32
Glossop	24	14	6	4	47	30	32
Hull City	25	12	7	6	48	33	30
Fulham	25	11	6	8	36	23	30
Wolverhampton Wan	26	13	10	3	53	50	29
Oldham Athletic	22	9	7	6	31	29	24
Barnsley	23	11	9	3	47	31	25
West Bromwich Albion	24	12	11	1	38	32	25
Bradford	24	11	11	2	38	36	24
Blackpool	25	8	10	7	30	37	23
Burnley	23	9	10	4	35	34	22
Stockport County	24	6	11	7	25	28	19
Clapton Orient	24	7	13	4	23	38	18
Lincoln City	24	5	11	8	28	47	18
Leeds City	25	7	14	4	30	53	18
Gainsborough Trinity	24	7	13	4	24	50	18
Birmingham	25	4	14	7	28	51	15
Grimsby Town	24	3	17	4	20	57	10

PROMOTION, AHOY!

For the third time in our history we have won four matches straight off the reel, but for the first time on earth we are going ot win promotion. We got a couple of points to the contribution on Saturday, and we might have obtained more goals had we set our stall out in the second half as attractively as we did in the first part.

Our defence was admirable in every way, and whilst we might have kept the ball more on the floor than we did, it was not always easy to intend a thing and do it. The best schemes oft gang agley. We have a momentous meeting against the Derby Rams next Saturday, and another very awkward hurdle against the Burnley Cottonspinners on Easter Monday; so altogether, my lads, with a long strong pull!

David Gordon.

DAVID GORDON STILL HOPEFUL.

The Tigers have not played on such a treacherous surface before this season as that at Hyde-road on Saturday. Indeed, I only ever remember being on one other, worse ground. That also at Manchester, when we met the United in our first year of League football. Manchester City fairly revelled in the mud, but they are a very sound side, and I am not surprised that their form is arousing expectations at Hyde-road. Though we played fairly spirited football at times, it always appeared as if the Manchester representatives were holding the whip hand. The Tigers never gave up trying, and had our efforts been rewarded we should have scored a couple of goals.

Owing to other mishaps in leading places we are still where we were in the League, with all the stiff away fixtures now fulfilled. I am still hopeful.

David Gordon.

THE GRATITUDE OF GORDON.

Superior combination sums up our hard-earned victory at Blackpool. Both sides were energetic to a degree, but I think we gave a better display of football, as we have come to know it, than did our opponents. We had a terrific quarter of an hour towards the end of the game, but getting goals was like getting blood out of a stone.

Our defence was grand during that bombardment; at the same time the firing of the opposition was often as crooked as a dog's hind leg. For this we were very grateful in our pursuit of promotion. We're going up into the top League, and no swank either?

David Gordon.

GORDON WRIGHT'S RETURN.

It was quite a treat to get back into harness, and join the boys in their upward journey towards the First League. I wasn't satisfied with the game as an educative process, but the two points gained largely extinguishes any shortcomings on that score.

Although Wally Smith's hat trick was the full extent of our shooting, we should not have belied our superiority had we doubled the total. Clapton at the same time missed two lovely chances. They had plenty to provide in midfield, but they were very lean near goal. I hope we shall keep up our reputation at Blackpool next Saturday, and make the promotion race still more engaging.

Gordon Wright.

More post-match analysis from Davy Gordon and Gordon Wright as the promotion struggle neared its conclusion.

Davy Gordon and George Browell in the Tigers midfield. Up front, Jacky Smith's threat was nullified by the imposing Eadie who dominated the Tigers' leading scorer. The supply of passes from Nevins and McQuillan to the forwards was a small percentage of its normal rate, as the full-backs struggled to contain the skilful Manchester wingers. The home crowd – used to First Division football in their city every week – derided Tommy Nevins for his lack of footballing skills and his inability to create play for his own forwards. It was a sobering excursion for the travelling fans, as for a second time that season they saw their side beaten by a superior and more sophisticated opponent.

After the Manchester City game City were in 5th place in the table with 30 points from 25 games. Derby led with 36 points from 24 games, followed by Manchester City with 34 from 23. They had played one game more than three of the teams above them, and two games more than Manchester City, in a 38-game-season. Any further slip-ups would almost certainly spell the end of City's hopes.

After the setback at Hyde Road, the Tigers bounced back in the best possible way with a 3-1 win at Lincoln, the side against whom City had drawn in October in such disappointing fashion. Another Jacky Smith hat-trick against Clapton restored momentum as the Londoners were sent packing on March 5th. Two successive 2-1 wins followed at Blackpool at home to Bradford (Park Avenue) before Derby at Hull on Easter Saturday.

The hungry Tiger devours the West Bromwich Throstle in the final home game.

GORDON STILL HOPEFUL.

Half a loaf is better than none, so I must pretend to be content with the point we got against Derby. We were so infinitely superior to our opponents that we not only ought to have got the big loaf but the very bakehouse itself. How we failed to score quite half-a-dozen goals, goodness only knows, and Derby can thank their lucky stars they got off so cheaply.

The other point would have been so delightfully acceptable just now, but we haven't given up trying. Lots of things will happen before another fortnight is over, and mark my words if we don't yet make the front men gallop. The promotionists cannot be named safely even now.

David Gordon.

GORDON ON THE VALUE OF GOALS.

It was like playing on the Fish-Dock on Saturday, and if we didn't do all we intended to do against Glossop, I hope our supporters will give us credit for our intentions. We meant it all through, and whilst meaning it, we got four goals, and it's these that count in the end.

Glossop played a nice game at times, but there was no sting in their efforts. Whilst our defence was a bit shaky at times, I don't think there was anything to grumble at. We shall make up for it against Leicester on Thursday. We must make the most of the short time left to us now in this desperate struggle for promotion.

David Gordon

Derby had stayed the course as promotion-contenders and City would not have forgotten the manner and style of the 4-0 defeat at the Baseball Ground in November. Here was an ideal opportunity to right a wrong, inflict a blow on a rival, and maintain the gathering momentum of their promotion bid.

Fifteen thousand spectators packed into the cramped confines of the Anlaby Road ground to see the Tigers dominate the Rams for at least 80 of the 90 minutes. Wally Smith was given a great chance and Jacky Smith got two, but none were taken. Given the importance of the game and the relative simplicity of the chances, such wastefulness was both astonishing and frustrating. Not for the first time this season, City's attackers were afflicted with a crippling nervousness and inexplicable loss of poise. The sense of a precious point lost to an undeserving rival was palpable, as was the suspicion that the point might weigh very heavily at the end of the season, given the narrow margin for failure that would determine City's fate.

City dominated Derby to the same extent that Derby had done against them, except that Derby had four goals to show for it – City were unable to muster one. 'Not a single man in the visiting attacking party ever threatened a moment's danger' – reported the Hull Daily News, concluding that: 'Hull City deserved to win, and win comfortably, too, as they were so immeasurably superior to the opposition.'

Just as after the Manchester City disappointment, the Tigers responded with a string of wins. As the games ran out, City chose the final quarter of the season to put together their best run of victories – seven of them, one after another. They scored 22 goals in those seven games, conceding seven times. Fourteen points out of 14; after the Manchester City game in February, City had now taken 23 points out of 24. The gloom after that defeat had long since been dispelled and only the lapse against Derby blotted a brilliant record. The Tigers thrashed West Bromwich Albion 5-1 in their final home game

Since the Fulham game on Christmas Day, which marked the beginning of the second half of the season, City had lost only twice and drawn three times in 18 games. This was form that easily matched that of any of the other challengers, whose faltering steps combined to make the final fixture against direct rivals Oldham a decisive one for the whole season. For City a point would suffice, for Oldham a win would see them leap-frog the Tigers into the second promotion place. The Lancashire side's momentum coming into the final stages was equal to that of the Tigers, emerging from deep in the trailing pack to take their place among the main contenders. From being bottom of the table in the early part of the season and having been thrashed 4-0 by City in December, the Lancashire club had recovered to lose only twice in the final 22 games. Before the game, they trailed second-placed City by two points, who in turn were one point behind leaders Manchester City. The vital game was previewed:

"The match sees the close of most successful season in the history of the Hull City Club. The minds of all local sportsmen will be centred on the match at Oldham, where the Tigers and Oldham fight out the question of promotion to the First Division of the League.
If the City win or draw then they achieve their ambition, and First Division football will be witnessed at Anlaby-rd next September.
If they lose and Derby County win at West Bromwich, they (Derby) join Manchester City in their upward flight.

The Management of the City Club have left no stone unturned, and considered no reasonable expense in their endeavour to further the intention of their players to seek higher game. A large amount of money has been expended in special training to make sure the men take the field fit.

HULL'S HOPE.

"SPORTS EXPRESS" TEDDY BEAR: Go it, Davy, never mind the shadows on the wall.

FISHERMEN DISCUSS PROMOTION FOR THE TIGERS,

A group of Hull fishermen discussing the chances of promotion for Hull City, snapped on a trawler in St Andrew's Dock.

Promotion fever affected the entire City and the Fish Dock was no exception.

HULL CITY'S MOMENTOUS MATCH

ANDY BROWELL.

J. McQUILLAN.

WALLY SMITH.

A. TEMPLE.

SOME PROMINENT PLAYERS.

The local press printed photographer Duncan's studio portraits, as the fervour grew in the days leading up to the game.

Unfortunately McQuillan, who has played most consistently and well throughout the season, will be an absentee through injury and ill-health. Nevins, however, has returned to the ranks, and will operate at left back. It is anticipated the team will be;

Roughley
Dan Gordon and Nevins,
G. Browell, A. Browell and Davy Gordon,
Joe Smith, Temple, Jack Smith, W. Smith and Neve."

A local journalist, caught up in the frenzy of anticipation gripping the city, saw fit to exhort the Tigers in verse:

"Forward, Tigers! No more halting!
Be the first to break the tape!
Let us deck ourselves in colours;
We are sick of dismal drape.
Set us shouting madly, gladly,
Cheering our young City team!
Let us harmonise proud music
In a mad, ecstatic dream!"

A damp Lancashire afternoon and muddy field greeted the Tigers and their followers on that late April day. A local newspaper detailed the goings-on at Oldham:

"A large number of Hullites travelled here to see this important match. There must have been at least a couple of thousand Tigers' supporters who availed themselves of the fast excursion. Twenty minutes before the start of the match the number of spectators on the ground was estimated at about 40,000, and enthusiasts were still pouring in. A posse of mounted police was maintaining order, though the crowd was a very orderly one. I learn the Hull team have definitely decided to journey home by the train leaving Oldham at 6.50, due at Paragon station at 10.12. It is to be hoped that on arrival their reception will be one of the heartiest, whether they have gained First Division honours or not. The teams played as selected. The old bell from Spion Kop at Anlaby-road was early in evidence. There were many humorous sights, and one Oldham Athletic enthusiast paraded with a parasol of the club's colours. The period of waiting was whiled away by strains of music to the accompaniment of the bell from Hull. Rain had fallen heavily in the morning, reducing the pitch to a quagmire. City emerged first, led out by captain Davy Gordon. A mighty cheer greeted their entry, showing the strength of the Tigers supporters was very great. Pandemonium appeared to be let loose when Oldham turned out some three minutes later. The ground was packed to its utmost capacity, and many found 'accommodation' on the roofs of the stands."

DAVIE G.: "HOOTS MON, DINNA FASH YERSELS, IT'S A BRAW BRECHT NICHT, THE NOO!"

Davy Gordon was a particular favourite of local cartoonists and became subject of many promotion-related cartoons.

Jack McQuillan

The climax and decisive match of the whole season went to the home side as Oldham ran out 3-0 winners. A bitterly disappointing outcome, and one which must have been very difficult to stomach for the club and its fans after the increasing optimism of the run-up to the game. This unforeseen defeat and its implications, were pondered at length in local papers in the days after the game, and the city itself had suffered a body blow. Promotion would have had immense benefits to the prestige of the city and the standing of the football club. The opportunity to establish the football club as the city's premier sporting outfit in only its sixth season of existence had also been lost. A remarkably detached and sanguine overview of the season and the Oldham result was offered on the Monday after the game. The Hull Daily Mail considered the situation as follows:

"After all has been said and done, it was perhaps a blessing in disguise that Hull City should fail to achieve promotion at the last hurdle. Sound, convincing, and even brilliant as some of their games this season, have been, there is no denying the fact that the present side, as a whole, is some way removed from First Division football as it is known to-day. In their present sphere they are pretty nearly 'cocks of the walk,' and their existence, during their five years' occupancy of the Second League, has indeed been a glorious one, and one which the most optimistic individual, at the beginning, never anticipated they would attain. Excellent management has been the cause of these five years' successes, and from that standpoint commiseration is demanded at having lost the honours in the expiring moments of the season. Since there was a chance of gaining the first League the whole of the players have had one set purpose in view. To them, therefore, the failure to ascend has been very disappointing. To be beaten on goal average and at the last kick of the season may be disheartening in many degrees, but the way is left open for another keen encounter next season with the opportunity of getting the side more up to date for the larger experience that looms beyond. There are positions that need strengthening, as the directors well know, and these may be dealt with during the course of another season.

Hull City were fearfully handicapped by reason of the ankle-deep slush in which they had to play, but more so because of the absence of McQuillan. The forwards could not trip over the ground in their usually fast and fascinating way, and when the attack is so shackled, defence has to a great extent, to make up for the drawback. Hull's defence, however, did not make up for the forwards' deficiency, and the introduction of Nevins at left back, where he is never at home, proved the main stake in the Tigers' defeat. Nevins has never been more easily beatable than in this match, and Broad the clever Oldham right-winger, had the hitherto irrepressible Tommy at his mercy on every occasion. Nevins would have given Broad the go by on a dry turf but that's not the point now – it was a question of superior brain-power. Still the Hull City management had to do the best they could with the material at their disposal, and in this instance it was a case of 'Hobson's Choice.'

The unfortunate absence of McQuillan and the disgraceful condition of the ground may be honestly mentioned as the main causes of Hull City's failure at the last opportunity. It's no use deploring the loss of the point against Derby County at Anlaby-road on Easter Saturday; the bare fact remains that the Oldham match ought to have given the Tigers promotion, and with it gold watches and chains which the players were promised if the distinction were achieved. From a football point of view, Hull City were quite on a par with their opponents, whose goals were all scored as the result of sudden breakaways, after being penned up by the Tigers.

On returning to the Paragon Station on Saturday night the Hull City players and directors retired to the Station Hotel, where Davy Gordon was presented by Director E. Morison with a silver rose bowl as a memento of the eminently successful season which had attended the Tigers first eleven. The Hull captain, in acknowledgement, said he and his team were exceedingly disappointed at just failing by a hair's breadth to reach the First Division, but he thought the honour was only deferred for a season. The players would now be relieved from the severe tension which the position had entailed, but they would return next September to their work invigorated for the task which would be set before them, and which they meant to accomplish a year hence. It was not a funeral meeting by any means, and instead of finger biscuits champagne prevailed."

This resolve in the face of crushing disappointment was understandable. To miss out by such a narrow margin on the last day of the season would have induced the players and directors to believe that promotion was within their collective grasp, and had temporarily eluded them. Dropped points and missed goals were rued, but in the final analysis long-term deficiencies were more indicative as to reasons for the failure to come up. The Tigers won 11 out of their final 13 games, but the damage had been done with only two wins in 10 games in October and November. An early cup exit away at Chelsea would have saved the players' reserves of energy for the run in.

The final league table had City level on points with Oldham on 53 points from 38 games, but Oldham's goal average was 2.03 to City's 1.74 (Oldham goals 79 for 39 against, City 80 for – but crucially 46 against). To be denied by fractions and averages only augmented the regret and feelings of 'if only', but at least the directors now knew that if the attack could not be strengthened, then the defence needed reinforcing. To add insult to injury, the scorer of the second goal for Oldham was Alf Toward who had played and scored for City earlier in the season. Derby's failure to beat West Brom elsewhere meant that Oldham slipped into second place behind Manchester City

The inquest in the aftermath of the defeat made mention of the pitiful state of the pitch (which was deemed to be to Oldham's advantage), and the enforced changes to City's defence in the absence of Jack McQuillan.

At the club's annual meeting on June 17th at the Grosvenor Hotel, the intense disappointment had evaporated somewhat and the focus had shifted to the positive aspects of the season. Chairman Alwyn Smith claimed, to general laughter, that he knew City were beaten as soon as he saw the Oldham pitch which 'comprised four green corners and pea soup in the centre,' and that the Tigers were used to playing on hard ground. He also stated the directors' opinion that Tigers would have won 'but for the ground'. Smith then went on to remind the assembled shareholders of the steady progress which had been made in the last five seasons – in the first year, they were fifth, in the second ninth, in the third eighth, in the fourth year fourth, and in the fifth year third – surely first place could not be too far in the future?

The last-gasp failure at Oldham had been digested and, at least publicly, the reason for it was ascribed to the state of the pitch, and not to any shortcomings of the players or the club. Given that the directors themselves were involved in selecting the team, this perhaps comes as no real surprise. A united and optimistic front was presented at the meeting, which then proceeded to take its course in the usual fashion. It was announced that the club had made a profit of £34 7s despite its exit from the Cup at the first time of asking – thus proving that the club was capable of making a profit purely from League games, and also thus disproving the suspicions of some that this was not possible.

An England Amateur International game against Sweden was held at Anlaby Road which helped swell the club coffers, and raised the profile of the Tigers and their ground.

Hull Working-Men's Football Hospital Cup.

To be competed for annually by Hull City and a League club. Sketch of the approved design for the cup on plinth of fumed oak. It stands 3ft. 9in. high over all, weighs about 280oz., and will cost £75. The cup is of pure silver, richly chased, with enamelled pictures of the Hull Royal Infirmary on the body of the cup, and pictures of the Children's Hospital and Dispensary on the base. The cover of the cup is finished with a modelled figure of a footballer. Messrs W. Elvin and Sons, Savile-street, are supplying the cup.

HULL CITY A.F.C.

For the annual team group photograph in 1910 Duncan chooses an almost identical location and format to the previous year's. There are now four Smiths, three Browells, two Wrights and two Gordons on City's books. Gordon Wright once again appears in the same studio cameo shot in the upper left part of the picture. The disappointing end to the previous season will still be fresh in the memory of many of these players, who will no doubt be doubly determined to ensure that in their fifth season in the league, the club ascends to the First Division.

The Tigers began their pre-season training in customary fashion. Sprints and ball practice in the morning, followed by bowls or cricket matches in the afternoon, with a Whites versus Stripes warm-up game the week before the start of the season; the gate receipts for which, were distributed to local charities.

Some new faces had appeared on the training ground and in the warm-up game. James Mackintosh is described as: 'only 23 years of age, standing 5ft 9in and turns the scale at 12st 6lb. A stiff-built sturdy-looking player, seen at his best either at right back or centre half'. He started his career at Petershall before moving on to Third Lanark, Aberdeen and Celtic.

Edwin Arthur Smith – known to his colleagues as 'Ted' – joined the list of Smiths at the club, and like many of them was also a forward. He had undergone seven years of army training and this no doubt contributed to his rambunctious bustling style. A Midlander, who had played for Brierley Hill Alliance, he was reputed to be a noted goal-scorer in the Birmingham and District League.

John Houghton had been signed towards the end of the previous season – yet another recruit from Tyneside. The 21 year old Wallsend youngster was a central defender with 'huge limbs and weighing 12st 8lb'. His previous teams were Wallsend Elm Club and then Wallsend Park Villa. The rich seam of talent that the Tigers had discovered in the Newcastle area was still providing new young prospects.

Nicholson – more usually Nick – Hendry joined City after two seasons at Darlington in the North-Eastern League, having previously played for Middlesbrough reserves as a goalkeeper.

Cricket was a regular component of City's pre-season programmes. Here, Manager Langley comes out to bat with Wally Smith.

In spite of this crop of new talent the club was still inviting any promising local footballers to participate in a trial game before the professionals' match on the 27th August, through Jack Haller's message in the local press on the 19th August: '... all players wishing to take part should communicate with the secretary, Mr. J.F. Haller, 26 Scale Lane, on or before Tuesday next, giving full particulars as to height, age, position on field, and last club represented.' Whether this is testimony to the strength of amateur football in the area at the time, or an indication of lack of finances on the club's part is not recorded.

The reports of the practice game naturally enough focused on the performance of the new recruits, and John Houghton made a favourable impression with his intelligent use of the ball as well as his imposing physique. But another player also took the eye – young 'Tom' Browell, the younger brother of George and Andy, who had recently been signed by the Tigers. Playing in the practice game on the left wing, Tom Browell:

> "... showed himself to have a knowledge of the game far beyond his years. He was clever and tricky to a degree, and his goal was capitally placed, he planting it just where Hendry was unable to get to the ball. If ever a youth had a promising future Tom Browell has. The crowd instantly made him a great favourite and with ordinary luck he will be a greater one."

Another journalist wrote of his admirable command of the ball and the neatness of his passes, adding:

> "... he is only 17 years of age at the present he can only be described as a big boy. And he is a big boy, too, weighing 10 stones 7lbs, and standing 5ft 9ins in height. He was born at Walbottle, and as centre forward and outside left played for Newburn in the Northern Alliance, with which club he secured a medal as runners-up in the

John Houghton started to appear in the Tigers defence in 1910.

Alliance. He then assisted Sheldon Athletic, a North-Eastern League team, as centre forward, scoring four goals in the four matches he played in. Sheldon Athletic were very desirous of retaining his services, but as he was so young, his family did not like his making the long journeys from home, so that they decided he should join his brothers in Hull and along with young Gordon, the City Club hold a retainer upon his services. Evidently D.Gordon and G.Browell must have a high opinion of Hull and the City Club when they persuade their brothers to join them. There is a marked resemblance in the play of 'Tom' to 'Andy' Browell. Neither of them can be described as graceful runners.

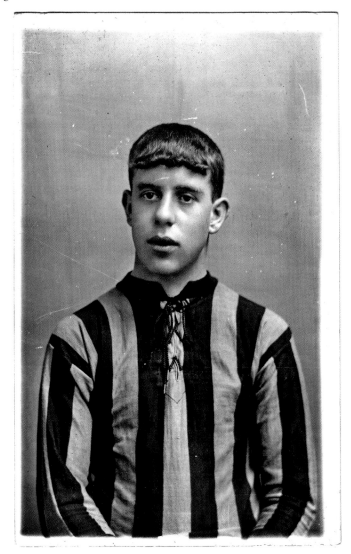

Tommy Browell

Their knees look as if they were about to knock together, but bless you they don't, although their opponents sometimes wish they would. There appears to be some misapprehension as to the ages of the Browell family. I actually heard George Browell described as the old Browell. Yet George himself is only 24 years of age. Andy or Aunty Browell, will celebrate his 21st birthday on the occasion of the Fulham match on September 17th, celebrate it, I hope, at the expense of Fulham. There should be years and years of service in the Browells for Hull City, and George ought to qualify for at least another benefit. (Intriguingly, one newspaper reported that Tom had a younger brother who was being nursed for football fame and it was understood that 'he promises to cap the lot of a very useful football family.' This sibling unfortunately does not join the Tigers."

The same journalist later wrote of:

"... an overgrown boy, with loose legs, the knees apparently not being able to be kept under sufficient control, he gives the impression of awkwardness but once give him the ball and those same legs develop an unexpected power, and can juggle with the ball in a manner which is perplexing to the opposition and the admiration of the spectators."

City opened their season with a tame draw at home to West Bromwich, new man Edwin Smith making his debut at centre forward, and last season's top scorer, Jacky Smith, found himself in the outside-right position, hardly a ringing endorsement for his efforts a few months earlier. City seemed to lack cohesion and the players appeared unfamiliar with their roles. Indeed the directors' team selection raised a few eyebrows. The opening seven games yielded but two wins and the goals scored were nowhere near as abundant as in the previous season's confident start. Edwin Smith played in only the opening game before making way for Jacky Smith again. Tom Browell had four starts on the right wing before he was given a run out at centre-forward (in place of Jacky Smith) against Stockport on October 22nd, seizing his opportunity and scoring a hat trick. He scored another goal the next Saturday at Derby, followed by another hat-trick in the home game against Barnsley, making it seven goals in three games for the young winger-turned-centre forward.

This startling goal-scoring form was a revelation, and the directors' selection problems took on a different complexion. A promising young winger had been an immediate success as a striker, an untried young centre forward had yet to make an impression and the established goal-scorer was going through a lean period, with one goal in the opening seven games. The directors sensationally sold Jacky Smith to First Division Sheffield United after the 2-0 win at Leicester on 12th November, to relatively little reaction from fans. Perhaps the Tigers' lukewarm season and Smith's indifferent form had convinced many fans that changes were inevitable, and the sparkling form of Tom Browell had demonstrated

ON THE SCENT AGAIN.

Davy Gordon leads the Tigers, one of whom has the face of Tom Browell, on the Road To Promotion. Despite the youngster's goals, such early season optimism was not to last

Tommy Browell

to the directors that he was their new main forward. Smith had been bought for around £10 and re-sold some five years later for a sum in the region of £500. Whether this sale was shrewd dealing by the directors or enforced selling to reduce debts was open to debate. Much depended on Tom Browell's continued goal-scoring, as the focus of attention shifted onto the young player's exploits. The arrival of Browell in the team sparked City into a run of four straight wins and a draw. Then followed three defeats which served to remind the club that the underlying problems remained. The Tigers continued their schizophrenic course with five consecutive wins, which took them to just over the halfway point of the season. Browell had scored 15 goals in his 12 games in the number nine shirt, statistics which would have come to the attention of clubs in the First Division seeking to recruit promising young talent.

"A native of Walbottle, a Tyneside Colliery village, Browell stands 5ft 8in. He is 10st 7lb – a player on the light side – but is quite a wizard with the ball, three goals in a match being not an unusual feat with him. He is always extremely dangerous when he has the ball at his toe, for he shoots at every opportunity, without hesitation, whilst on the run. He is the type of player who ought to do even better in First than Second Division football. He is but 19, and the youngest of the trio of Browells."

The club's ambitions remained what they had been since their election to the league, and the businessmen who made up the board of directors continued to work towards their goal of first division football. Alwyn Smith's financial expertise, Ernest Morison's advertising flair and journalistic experience worked in tandem with the attributes of the other directors such as Jack Bielby, whose construction expertise had proved so useful in building and maintaining the Anlaby Road ground, and Jack Haller, the energetic and versatile secretary. All local men and all with a background in either playing or administration roles in local sport. Aside from these qualities, they were all well ensconced in the business and commercial life of the city, with its network of local politicians, masons, J.P.s and other valuable social contacts.

TOMMY BROWELL (HULL CITY).
Oh, Tommy, Tommy Browell,
Your hat trick it was grand,
You're a credit to the family,
And to all your native land.
May your luck be never failing,
May your aim be ever true,
As the Tigers' centre forward,
You have shown what you can do.—"Mac."

WAISTELL'S (CHAMPIONSHIP) OVERCOATS.

WEAR AT
WAISTELLS v. HULL CITY
OVERCOATS MATCHES

41 Whitefriargate, and other Branches.

Waistell's was another local shop keen to be associated with the increasingly popular local team, and used the City name in their advertising.

One City director who maintained a low public profile however, was James Barraclough. One of the original founders of the club, he kept his place in the directorate for many years whilst never rising to public prominence as some of his peers did. The reasons for Barraclough's involvement with the Tigers are not apparent from a brief scrutiny of his circumstances. Unlike the other founders, Barraclough was neither from Hull nor resident in the city. He had been born in 1863, the eldest of ten children, and at the time of City's formation in 1904, aged 41 years, he lived at 52 Holydyke, Waterside, Barton upon Humber.

'Big Jim' Barraclough was an ambitious and enterprising young man who gradually built up the family business of owning and running small cargo

boats, the ships in question being the sloops which ferried goods between the inland Humber ports. His occupation had been variously given as 'mariner', 'mariner-riverman' and 'Seas mariner' in the census returns. Realising the commercial opportunity of Barton's proximity to the South Yorkshire coalfields, he used his water transport to became a coal factor, and the steady profits allowed him gradually to increase his fleet of barges. Barraclough maintained a company office at Imperial Chambers, Bowlalley Lane in Hull's Old Town, with its concentration of the city's most important economic activity and businessmen, and would

Jack Barraclough

no doubt be familiar with the commute to and from work using the ferry service across the Humber. His base in Hull allowed him to expand his commercial activities and interests to encompass a wide range of business outlets. As well as owning sloops, he was also to become vice-chairman of the Hull Coal Exporters Association, and governing director of James Barraclough and Co Ltd, (a lightering, forwarding and brick-manufacturing firm). Other posts he held were chairman of the directors of the Keel and Lighter Owners Mutual Insurance Society Ltd, director of the Grimsby Express Packet Co, director of W. Dealsdale and Co Ltd, and director of the Barton Electric Supply Co Ltd.

Barraclough was also a member of the Company of Arts and Feltmakers, which enabled him to become a Freeman of the city of London. He became a Justice of the Peace in 1924 and was a member of the St. Matthew's Lodge of Freemasons. Whether he was a passionate soccer enthusiast or a shrewd investor seeking a return (or both) is not documented, but his long association with the club tends to suggest the former at least as much as the latter.

HULL CITY FOOTBALLERS BACK AT WITHERNSEA.

A snapshot of the Tigers on the Promenade at Withernsea, where they are staying until to-morrow, when the match with Bristol is re-played

The City players on the seafront at a breezy Withernsea before the Bristol Rovers game.

The FA found City being drawn away at Bristol Rovers where they shared a scoreless draw. The replay was won at Anlaby Road the following Thursday but only after a single goal in extra time from full-back John McQuillan. The games were scrappy and undistinguished, the Tigers making hard work of seeing off the West Country side. The opponents in the next round were Oldham Athletic – no City fan needed reminding of who the Lancashire club were and what they represented. The players too would need no incentive to raise their game against the (now) First Division club, who so narrowly and dramatically beat the Tigers to the second promotion spot the previous April.

Oldham drew a healthy 17,000 crowd (paying £707) to the cramped Anlaby Road enclosure – more than double the normal gate. An Arthur Temple goal was enough to see the Tigers through on the day and gain

Hull pressing round the Oldham goal.

their £5 per man win bonus. The total receipts for the three cup games played so far were £1,368 – a very welcome and substantial addition to the club's coffers, and seen in those terms, the Cup campaign was already judged a success.

The pace of Arthur Temple, Tim Wright and Stanley Smith caused Oldham problems throughout, the only goal coming from a teasing cross by Gordon Wright which created uncertainty among the Oldham defence.

Tom Browell tussled for the ball with Oldham's Hamilton, and Arthur Temple lunged in to stab the ball into the corner of the net before Oldham's defenders could react.

Gordon Wright did not always round his full back but the quality of his centring was always of a very high standard so that the onrushing trio of speedy inside forwards were fed a constant supply of accurate and well-judged passes. Behind them the half-backs were expertly marshalled by Davy Gordon,

WRIGHT'S COMMENDATION.

I was delighted with the convincing game that our men played, and the victory was even more deserving than the single goal indicates. The game was fast, but not furious, and, for a Cup-tie, was exceedingly pleasant. Although our opponents often gave promise of doing something out of the common, our defenders had them quickly weighed up, and checkmated efforts that only flattered to deceive. Oldham will now have time and opportunity to attend to their own none too secure position in the First League, whilst we endeavour to forge ahead in the most popular competition in the feotball world.

E. Gordon D. Wright

Gordon Wright's view on the Oldham victory.

and the Nevins-McQuillan partnership at full-back was unyielding to the demoralised Oldham attackers, who had so exposed City's shaky rearguard the previous April.

City's happy knack of drawing money-spinning illustrious opponents continued as Newcastle United's name was matched with the Tigers. This tie would have delighted everyone involved with the Tigers – a guaranteed bumper pay day generated by the St James Park gate receipts, a chance to play a new opponent – one renowned nationally as one of the leading sides in the country – and a trip to one of the more famous football venues of the age. Newcastle had won the Cup the previous season, and the League three times in the previous six seasons, so this was about as good a draw as City could have hoped to get.

The by now familiar Hull City cup-tie build-up began; the mobilisation of fans by special rail excursions, the daily newspaper updates from the team hotel and the growing anticipation before the big game on the Saturday. 'No fewer than 17 saloons attached to the first train leaving for the North' were reported in the local press in the build-up to the game, this eventually increasing to 25 including the 'ordinary saloons'. Some 1,500 travelling fans journeyed on this unusually large train. 'The utmost enthusiasm prevails in football circles in Hull, and the Tigers have never previously commanded such a large following as is likely to be seen round the enclosure at the Cupholders' rendezvous St James' Park', reported the Hull Daily News.

One unexpected outcome of the intense pre-match newspaper focus was a communication issued from their hotel by the 12 City players in response to rumours of unhappiness in their ranks. It read:

> "We, the undersigned players, were very much surprised to read the statement that there is discontent or bad feeling between the players and the directors. This reply, coming from us, should be satisfactory. There is not a word of truth in the rumours that have been circulated. We are all on the best of terms, and always have been. We think it unfair to put these rumours about, especially in face of what we think the greatest of all matches in our careers. Our supporters can take it we are in good health and spirits, and hopeful of either winning or being able to make a draw.
> – E.Roughley; T. Nevins, J. McQuillan, W.Wright, A.Browell, David Gordon, Joe Smith, W.Smith, A.Temple. E. Neve, T.Browell and George Browell."

The game itself began badly for the Tigers. Newcastle captain Colin Veitch demonstrated his pedigree by putting in a low drive from 30 yards, cleverly threaded between City's defenders and past a flat-footed Teddy Roughley, as the Tigers seemed overawed by the occasion. With the wind

HULL CITY'S FINE FIGHT IN THE NORTH.

Before 50,000 spectators the Hull club put up a great fight against Newcastle United in the third round of the English Cup at St James' Park, Newcastle, on Saturday. Up to the moment the whistle put an end to the contest the result was uncertain. In our picture the Newcastle goalkeeper is watching a shot from Tom Browell which just skimmed the crossbar, nearly equalising, ten minutes before time.—(" News.")

Action from the game at Newcastle as Tom Browell threatens the home side's goal. His shot hits the top of the crossbar ten minutes from time and the Tigers are out.

at their backs, the First Division side increased their advantage as Albert Shepherd added a second, expertly guiding home a precision centre, making the ball curl just inside the post at the last instant. No fault could be attached to Roughley this time – it was confident First Division quality that was almost impossible to stop. Shepherd then added a significant and controversial third – seemingly three yards offside. The Newcastle man was fed by Sandy Higgins, and went on to net what turned out to be the winning goal.

Hull City are now at Withernsea training for Saturday's Cup-tie. In picture are seen (left to right), A. Nevins, Tim Wright, and T. Browell.

City in training for the Newcastle game.

Stanley Smith got a goal back before the interval and then another one in the second period. Wally Smith had a goal disallowed for offside, Tom Browell handled right in front of the home goalkeeper and Gordon Wright badly missed a glorious opportunity with only one opponent to beat. The famous winger looked out of sorts all afternoon and was an

inexplicably weak link in City's attack. Very little of note came from City's left flank, as time after time moves petered out due to his lack of control, and he wasted several corner kicks as the ball sailed harmlessly out for a goal kick. Given his experience as an international, and his quality, it was a desperately poor display from the one player whose skills might have caused the home side some anxiety.

A draw seemed a fair result, and reflected the balance of the chances created, even if Newcastle's play was more sophisticated and fluent. City's hustling style of play handicapped Newcastle to an extent but never completely stifled the intricate First Division 'combination' work. City stormed forward in the final 15 minutes in search of what had seemed an unlikely equaliser. Had they attacked with such purpose and energy earlier in the match, they would have surely got the goal they needed. The attendance of 46,351 produced receipts of £1,698, meaning that City's receipts from the Cup totalled £3,066 10s – a massive factor in the financial balance at the end of the year, and an extremely positive outcome for the directorate. The player who made the pass for Newcastle's winner – Higgins – related to a Hull journalist how his team mates sympathised with the Hull City players, yet for their own sakes and the sake of the club were overjoyed at the piece of good fortune which enabled them to enter the next round. 'Tim' Wright reflecting later on the goal said: 'I stood struck dumb with dismay and disappointment and shall always remember the incident.'

Gordon Wright continued to play for the England Amateur team as well as captain the Tigers. In the 1910/11 season he made only ten league appearances for City. Despite this, he remained a popular and talismanic leader of the club. Discussing his role with City, local journalist 'Saturn' wrote in November:

> "With the 'Tigers', the captaincy of Mr Wright has been an unqualified success, and I ascribe much of the success of the team to his example and influence. There is another view we must take. The inclusion of a good amateur in the team makes a vast difference to the takings on the best stand, and in these days of commercialism

A CUP-TIE CARTOON.
"Tommy" Browell and Colin Veitch: Hull City think they will "do something with Newcastle" yet.

Colin Veitch and Tommy Browell in a pre-match cartoon.

the receipts are the most important item of the day ...

The public still have a great admiration for the sportsman who plays the game for the game's sake, and one who is willing to join and assist a professional club, and, on the field, not post [sic] as an amateur, but as one of the team. On and off the field, Mr Wright was one of the 'Tigers,' and it is this true British sportsmanship which has made the names of Lord Hawke [the Yorkshire cricketer] and Mr. C.C. Lempriere [the Hull rugby player], and Mr Wright beloved by the British public. They stand for all that is good and clean in sport, and long may the day be distant when we fail to admire the best side of football."

On the 17th April Wright lined up at the Houten Stadion in Amsterdam as part of the England side who defeated Holland 1-0. He is seen in the postcard shown below as the fourth player in from the right, his hands clasped nonchalantly behind his back looking at the camera.

Wright must have impressed the selectors with his form, as he was picked on no fewer than seven occasions in 1911 to represent his country. This faded team group of the England Amateur team also dates from 1911. In a studio in an unidentified town, the following players line up to get their picture taken:

Wright had also toured abroad with the Corinthians earlier in his City career, visiting the USA, Canada, Holland and Germany, and would be a member of the 1912 Great Britain Olympic squad which won the Gold. The only game Wright played in was the semi-final against Finland in Stockholm, which was won 4-0.

THE HOSPITAL CUP

In an era when sickness and ill health were worrying and potentially expensive problems for a large majority of the population, it was not uncommon for football teams to compete against each other for trophies, with any funds raised being donated to benevolent causes connected with hospitals and to assist in care of the sick.

City had been invited to contest the Norwich Hospital Cup a few months earlier, and a meeting was held in Hull in late August 1910 to investigate setting up a similar event locally. At a joint committee of the Working-men's Committees of the Infirmary, Dispensary and Children's Hospital the decision was taken to go ahead, the cup to be called The Hull Working-men's Hospital Cup. The meeting was attended by directors of City, Hull and Rovers but the rugby clubs 'could not see their way clear to subscribe to the cup', according to the words of Mr J. Burrows, the secretary of the movement, having said it would be too expensive. City's chairman Alwyn D. Smith stepped in at this point and pledged support for the initiative.

He said he would like the working-men of Hull to provide the cup themselves, and Hull City would find an opposing team to play for it. He suggested that they should not ask anybody but working-men for donations towards the cup, and Hull City would be prepared to make up the shortfall, even if the men only collected £10 towards a £50 cup.

Standing from left are A.E. Knight (Portsmouth), P. Healey (Bishop Auckland) – reserve, A.E. Barclay (Ilford) – reserve, G.W. Webb (West Ham), E.G.D. Wright (Hull City), F.V. Monk (Southampton), J. Dines (Ilford), P.I. Lloyd (Wednesbury Amateurs).
Seated are R.G. Brebner (Darlington), S.J. Hoad (Blackpool), V.J. Woodward (Chelsea, captain), G. Hoare (Woolwich), H.C. Littlewort (Glossop).

THE HOSPITAL CUP ARRIVES.

Directors Bielby, Glossop, and Spring: Now, my bonny, blue-eyed darling, whatever has happened at Newcastle, we have still another pot to keep the fun alive. Wot!

The men responsible for raising the funds for the Cup in cartoon form – these included City directors Jack Bielby, Alfred Bulay Glossop and Alfred Spring. Bulay Glossop was associated with the club for many years, even if not always as an official director. He was a familiar figure in the East Riding and hunted with the Holderness pack. It is likely that the social circles in which he moved were relatively wealthy and not as concentrated in the commercial life of Hull's Old Town, as those of his associates among the City directorate.

The Hull Hospitals charity cup was competed for at the end of each season by the Tigers and invited guest opponents at Anlaby Road, the winners also receiving a set of gold medals. The cost of the trophy had been paid for by subscriptions organised by the Hull Working-Men's Hospital Committee. Having conceived the idea of the fund-raising match, gathered donations and commissioned a trophy to be made, there still remained the task of publicising the game. A few years earlier, City's directors had employed sandwich board men to walk around displaying news of match arrangements for the Manchester City friendly in 1905, and advertising games in the local press was a long-established

HULL WORKING MEN'S HOSPITAL CUP COMMITTEE.

Back row: Mr B. Smith (East Riding County F.A.), Mr A. E. Spring (Hull City F.C.), Mr E. C. Crabbe (Infirmary Committee), Mr A. B. Glossop (Hull City F.C.), Mr E. Rudd (Infirmary Committee), Mr T. Featherstone (Victoria Hospital Committee).
Front row: Mr H. Hings (Dispensary Committee) Hon. Treasurer; Mr J. T. Wells (Dispensary Committee), Vice-President; Mr J. H. Bielby (Hull City F.C.), President; Councillor H. Dean (Victoria Hospital Committee), Secretary.
The Hospital Cup, which is shown in the centre of the group, is to be competed for annually at Hull by the Hull City team and another first-class team the proceeds to be devoted to the local medical charities.

(Photo: W. H. Duncan, Hull)

method of publicity. The postcard above shows a group using innovative means of drawing the public's attention to the game, in the streets of Hull. The gleaming cup is paraded on a rully flanked by two men wearing the shirts of the two competing teams, together with a large board advertising details of the game. A vendor or distributor of postcards of the trophy can be seen to the left of the rully and a bowler-hatted man seated on it appears to be holding a collection-box for money.

Judging by the small crowd gathered around, the spectacle appears to be enthusing local inhabitants and passers-by, and succeeding in its aim. The presence of photographer William Duncan (or one of his employees) to record the scene suggests he was supportive of the cause, and the cards of the trophy shown on the photograph are also taken by him.

The opponents in the inaugural game were Sheffield Wednesday on April 27th 1911 with a six o'clock kick-off to allow those who had been working to attend. In spite of this, a modest crowd of only some 5,000 or so attended the game, which started in a downpour. The Tigers ran out 3-1 winners against their more illustrious First Division opponents.

Shown on the left is a postcard of the 'Hull Hospital Charity Cup' and the handwriting in the margin of the card reads 'Played April 27th 1911 first competition Hull City 3 Sheffield Wednesday 1'. On the reverse the card, which has been franked at 10.30pm that evening, the sender declared:

> "... you will see by the photo on the other side that this is the Hull Hospital Cup which is played tonight at 6pm.
> I am very disappointed I shall not be there to see it played for.
> Sheffield Wed are coming down for the occasion so it should be a good match.
> The Cup stands between 3 & 4 foot high so it will take a lot of stealing if anyone was so inclined."

The final league-placing of fifth was ultimately deemed to be disappointing. The last league game of the season saw Lincoln defeated at Anlaby Road and also the debut of ex-Sheffield Wednesday right-winger Harry Chapman, described as 'a whole-hearted, always-keep-smiling player' as well as a very good footballer. Signed for £200, he made an impressive debut for his new club that promised much for the following season.

After the failure by the narrowest of margins in 1909/10, this league-placing represented a slight decline, and for supporters, a frustrating inconsistency, particularly at Anlaby Road. Ten league games were drawn, and the extra ten points that the wins would have provided, would have seen City win the league by a single point. City's total of 16 draws was the highest in the division. If the first half of the season had been a topsy-turvy tale of victories and defeats punctuated by goals from Tommy Browell, the second half of the season was remarkable for the drawn games.

After New Year, the Tigers won only three times in 17 games and lost the same total. 'Boy' Browell scored only once more, to finish the season with 16 goals from 32 games – a more than respectable total for such an inexperienced player. As it was, the Tigers finished seven points behind second-placed Bolton and never really closed the gap to make promotion a genuine prospect.

The Hull Hospitals Cup in all its glory.
Postcards of it were sold to raise funds.

The Tigers were always strongly placed and supporters became accustomed to seeing them in pursuit of the leading teams, but the winning formula seemed to desert them all too often. A Press comment – 'Many harsh words have been used between Spion Kop and the tram terminus' – aptly renders the disappointment supporters must have felt on leaving the ground and returning into town after yet another drawn game.

On the financial side, the Cup run enabled the club to make a 'handsome profit' together with the £300 taken for the sale of Jackie Smith, although it was not lost on anyone that the receipts from the league games alone were insufficient to enable the club to break even.

The dependency on the little coloured balls was a gamble that had hitherto helped City to return a healthy balance sheet, but sooner or later this risky strategy was bound to fail. To finish the season, the Tigers undertook a short expenses-paid trip to Belgium to play Southern League Swindon Town.

May 9th; The Hull Daily News reported:

"The Hull City team, returned from the Continent this morning, arriving on board the Jervaulx Abbey, at the Riverside Quay, at eleven o'clock. The players were naturally jubilant over their success at Brussels, where, on Sunday, they beat Swindon, the Southern League club, by one goal to nil, and won an elegant cup presented by the Brussels Racing Club. The Tigers have now won three cups, namely, the Norwich Hospital Cup, the Hull Hospital Cup, and the Brussels trophy.

The players, who were accompanied by Directors F.J. Stringer and J.W. Locking, Manager A. Langley and Trainer W. Leach, were welcomed by a large crowd of admirers on disembarking, and were heartily congratulated upon their victory. The party had a highly enjoyable week-end, and coupled with the success achieved at Brussels, the little holiday has proved one of the best in the history of the club.

A 'News' reporter chatted with several of the party when they stepped ashore. The directors told our representative that the tour had been a splendid one, and that the 'boys' played a sterling game against the Southern Leaguers, fully deserving their victory.

Manager Langley paid a tribute to the capital form shown by the team, and added that the passages had proved excellent. Both on the outward and return voyages the weather was ideal. The sea was like a mill pond, and he was glad to say that not one of the party had any need to feel a desire to be 'alone.'

'It was a very even match,' said Davie Gordon, the captain. 'Swindon were without Fleming, their international, but with that exception they had a full team. Our boys played a romping game, and so did the Swindon fellows. They are a very sporting side, and I am pleased to say there was not the slightest ill-feeling displayed. It was a very gentlemanly match. One of the best I have played in. The spectators, numbering about 8,000, were very fair in their opinions, and very appreciative. Geo. Rushton, the ex-Hull City forward, was played for Swindon, and it was rather singular that he should come into severe collision with Roughley, who sustained a rather big bruise on his chest. It was towards the finish of the game and Ted was running out to clear.

He played to the finish, and is now about all right again …'

'And who scored for the City?' asked our representative.

'Chapman, the new player, did the trick,' replied Gordon. 'Temple put in a long drive, and Chapman, who was well up towards goal, caught the ball and placed it safely past Skiller.'

Davie added that the rest of the time had been spent in sightseeing, and that they had the company of the Swindon players – it was a pleasure too. Other players of the team spoke in similar terms of their experiences.

'Laugh,' said Houghton, 'I never laughed so much in all my life as I did at some of the 'foreigners'.'

'Yes,' said Nevins, 'I wasn't half glad when we met an Englishman. The jabber of the 'foreigners' was tiring.'

The 'News' man was shown one of the medals Tommy Nevins (who was, of course, the 'smiler' of old throughout the weekend) producing his from a small round box. 'We thought,' he said, 'they were pills when they were handed to us in these boxes.' The medals are of a pretty design, and bear the letters B.R.C. (Brussels Racing Club).

'You should hear Davie make a speech,' said Wally Smith. 'He is a real orator now; we have won three cups you know.'

'And,' said several of the players, in a chorus, 'Davie is a jolly good captain, too.'

The Cup arrived by rail at Paragon station this afternoon and was met by some of the officials and players. It was stated that the original cup was burnt in a Brussels fire. The trophy obtained by the Tigers is, therefore a new one. The making of a box for it prevented the Tigers bringing the prize on the ship.

The Hull players who took part in the match were:- Roughley, Nevins, McQuillan, Tim Wright, Houghton, D.Gordon, Townend, Chapman, Temple, Wally Smith, and Neve."

"Teddy" in the Tigers' Goal.

HULL CITY A.F.C. 1911 - 12 COPYRIGHT

The traditional pre-season squad picture has a backdrop of the covered terrace of the railway end or the north stand. Photographer Duncan has blacked out the faces of some curious fans in the background to the right of the group, around Leach the trainer, although one or two faces have been left visible. The injury-prone Wally Smith sits in his everyday attire in front of trainer Bill Leach wearing his usual flat cap.

"READY FOR THE FRAY – HULL CITY'S PROSPECTS
Monday August 21, 1911.

The season is knocking at the door, and before it is opened there may be a few more capable reserves secured by the Tigers' management. None of those who 'sought ambition' in the practice match can hope to depose any of the regular first teamers for some time to come, but with proper tuition and extended opportunities there is the making of several useful players in two or three cases. The Tigers' strength, as in past seasons, seems to lay in the half-back line, Tim Wright, McIntosh, A. Browell, Houghton, and David Gordon being a very powerful quintette from which the team selectors will have much difficulty in appointing the required trio.

Barring illnesses, transfers, &c., the forward line looks like being delegated to Stanley Smith, Chapman, T. Browell, Wally Smith, and Neve, and this combination is the most likely one to provide that element of First Division football, which appears to be desired at Anlaby-road. There are other good forwards to be considered, namely, Temple, Ted Smith, Townend, and Pearce, and in certain circumstances the two first named would almost always command respect and attention from the other side. The positions of goalkeeper and the two full backs are easily determined, and Roughley, Nevins, and McQuillan will operate constantly under all ordinary conditions.

Business is really meant once more at Anlaby-road, and considering the cost of running the show, something tangible ought to result. The right spirit is abroad, and this can be very largely augmented if the team show their determination by successes in the early matches. Public support will not be wanting in the maintenance of a victorious team, and therein lies the whole situation. Whether E.G.D. Wright will assist the Tigers remains to be seen. At the present time he is pursuing the practical part of the Cornwall tin miner.

'Prodigal'"

HULL CITY WIN THEIR FIRST HOME MATCH.

Our pictures show incidents in Saturday's match, when Hull City beat Glossop by two goals to nil. On the left Roughley fisting out, and on the right an exciting moment near the Hull goal. ("News" Photographs.)

Action from the first home game of the season with Glossop

This somewhat unusual reason for the absence of the Tigers' captain gave some indication of the difficult juggling act he performed in dividing his energies between studying and playing. As if missing pre-season training were not enough, Wright's desire to pursue all aspects of his mining studies meant that his match-day preparation for games could be unorthodox.

Having recently spent time underground in Cornwall, he augmented his tin mine experience with a trip down a coal mine on the morning of an away game. On the occasion of City's game at Barnsley on September 23rd, Wright, accompanied by director Ernest Morison, took the 7am Hull and Barnsley Railway service from Cannon Street station to Cudworth. A 'pleasant walk' led the men to the Grimethorpe Colliery and the offices of the pit-manager. Having surrendered any tobacco or matches and having been kitted out with safety lamps, they made the descent some 1,200 ft down the shaft to watch the miners at work with their picks, so that Wright could observe their operations. After their ascent, the two men enjoyed an excellent lunch provided by their hosts at the mine before making their way to Oakwell where Wright helped the Tigers to a 2-1 win.

It was the third successive win of the season for City, who after a disappointing defeat at Blackpool in the first game, had beaten Glossop and Burnley at Anlaby Road to build a solid foundation to the season. After Barnsley, it was Bradford's turn to be beaten as another free-scoring home display pushed the Tigers up the table. Fulham were then beaten in London by a solitary Arthur Temple goal. The run of wins petered-out and successive draws at home to Derby and away at Stockport followed.

CITY PLAYERS WATCHING COLLEAGUES AT PRACTICE.

Mr A. Langley, the Hull City F.C. manager, and Charley Best, the new recruit from Eston United, and W. Smith, watching other members of the team training at Anlaby road

Manager Ambrose Langley watches pre season training together with Charlie Best and Wally Smith

Tommy Browell threatening the Bradford goal in September

Arthur Temple had the unfortunate distinction of missing late penalties in both of these games, before a Tommy Browell hat-trick at a mid-week game at Gainsborough on October 25th enabled City to go to the top of the Second Division.

An unusual but regular visitor to the Anlaby Road ground, was this bulldog.

It was reported afterwards that:

"We are getting the real sign now that Hull City DO intend to play a great part in the fight for the Championship of the Second Division this time. I never remember seeing so many directors of affairs at Anlaby-rd present at an out-of-town match as was the case at Gainsborough."

A win at home to Leeds the following Saturday in front of 12,000 continued their success, before they suffered a defeat, as heavy as it was unexpected, on November 4th. This 8-0 defeat at Molineux was by some measure the worst in the Tigers' history. The fact that it occurred after a nine-game run which had lifted them to the top of the table was all the more baffling. The disastrous result didn't seem to affect Tommy Browell too much. The following Saturday he reaffirmed his credentials as one of the country's hottest goal-scoring prospects as he helped himself to four unanswered goals against Leicester Fosse. City had responded in the best way possible to the ignominious defeat in the Black Country.

Grimsby were the next team to be beaten, by a single Harry Chapman goal in front of 15,000 at Anlaby Road. A trip the following week to the City Ground in Nottingham would have been one to savour for the travelling Tigers fans, who had designated the game as their annual outing. Over 1,000 fans made the trip by train in anticipation of a good day out and another away victory. A description of the match recounts that:

"... there was a frolicsome crowd of City supporters on the Forest's grounds by two o'clock, and they passed the time away in the usual manner by singing and bell ringing. One enthusiastic excursionist provided an exhibition on the touch line with a toy tiger, which occupied a prominent position during the match near the touch line."

In the week before the next home game against Chelsea on December 9th, a whist drive and dance took place at the Newington Hall on Albert Avenue to raise funds for three players who had completed five years

service with the club: John McQuillan, Edwin Neve and Teddy Roughley. In the absence of organised commercial activities by their clubs, footballers relied on the benevolence of supporters and people connected with the club to generate money. In the case of this trio, it was an enthusiastic

More colourful crowd scenes as a fan releases a pigeon at the Burnley game.

ladies committee who organised the event. They sold over 300 tickets and the evening was so well attended that another similar event was planned to allow more people to participate. Most of the players – as well as the three beneficiaries – attended the whist drive and dance for which two City directors. Messrs Locking and (the now) Councillor Spring acted as M.C.s, and Manager Ambrose Langley also attended. The directors' wives were involved in the organisation of the event and Mrs J Spring acted as both chairwoman and honorary secretary of the event. The gate receipts after expenses for the Chelsea game, which attracted 13,000 spectators, were also distributed to the three men.

A section of the crowd at the Chelsea game.

The game against the polished London side was decided by a solitary Tom Browell goal and the Hull Daily Mail's 'Nimrod' recounted the more colourful aspects of the afternoon the following Monday. Of the crowd he wrote:

'The twopenny standers and the Spion Koppers, the ex-office boy and the 'horny handed son of toil,' and other swanks who are in such affluent 'circs' that they can afford to plunge every week, quite recognised what a load of responsibility rested upon them, and had got their throats lubricated for the occasion. Great had been the run on chlorate of potash, tannin, glycerine and other specialities calculated to produce those gentle whispers which are wafted over St. Matthew's steeple when one of the Tigers rattles the rigging.

Then Tom, Dick and Harry had another duty almost as important as the one mentioned. They were bound to turn up and help to swell the 'gate,' every mother's son of 'em that possibly could. If anyone doubted that McQuillan, Roughley and Neve were the idols of the crowd, they should have been at the Anlaby-rd crossing at 2.15 o'clock post meridian. The sight of the teaming mass of humanity would have set all his doubts at rest. All sorts and conditions of individuals laid themselves out to signify their appreciation of the yeoman service rendered by the afore-said three stalwarts in a substantial way. Whatever the reward may be, I can testify that it will be well deserved.

I have seen the beneficiaries in the bulk of their matches home and away, and I know that the club has never been blessed with more loyal and more enthusiastic workmen."

If the attendance was slightly below that which had been anticipated, the sense of occasion was nevertheless undiminished as the presence of an early cinema cameraman attested. The same correspondent continued:

"During the interval the bioscope operator [was] very busy, to the great delight of the Spion Koppers who stood on tip-toes and craned their necks to get in the picture. Everybody seemed animated with a desire to have their photos 'took' and reproduced on the screen at – but no, wild horses shall not force me to give a gratuitous 'ad'. The aristocrats on the best stand had their turn and it was only right that the dead beats. I might mention by the way that the music on this occasion was provided by Wilson's Band, and that there was no call for the choral society. That was why the rain kept off."

Tom Browell's second-half winner evoked this response:

"Gee whizz! What on earth has happened? Only Tommy Browell scored a goal! What a whisper! What a rising! What a handshaking! Tommy needed to be pretty strong to stand it. No wonder the cornet broke into melody. And after this the Tigers woke up. In response to the prayers of the people they went at it hammer and tongs!"

Whilst McQuillan and Roughley had established themselves as first team regulars, the other member of the trio – outside-left Edwin Neve – found himself second choice to captain Gordon Wright. The Tigers' illustrious amateur was often plagued by an injured knee and when he was fit, he

Teddy Roughley pictured here in his goal-keeping jersey. 1911 was the first year in which goal-keepers could were a different coloured jersey to those of their team mates.

sometimes had other playing obligations for the England amateur team or the Corinthians. The initial phase of his Tigers' career coincided with his time at Hymers College in the city, but his enrolment at the London School of Mining in South Kensington necessitated his living in the capital. This meant that Neve played regularly and often on the left flank for City. After the win against Chelsea,

City then lost their third game of the season at Clapton – again an eyebrow-raising heavy defeat as the Tigers conceded four goals without reply.

The Christmas period saw City play Bristol at home on the 23rd and then Birmingham on Christmas Day, winning both games, 3-0 and 4-0 respectively. Then 24 hours after the free-scoring win against the Midlands club, the Tigers went down 5-1 against the same team on their St. Andrews ground. These freakish extremes must have concerned all those connected with the club, as the defeats were some of the heaviest in their short history and seemed to occur without warning. At least the goals were consistent at the other end of the pitch as City continued to notch up impressive quantities of goals among the occasional heavy defeats, with young Tom Browell leading the attack by example.

After the Birmingham win on Christmas Day, which marked the completion of the first half of the 38-game season, Browell had scored no less than 16 goals in 19 games. The promotion bid relied on the frequent goals of this teenager who had been in league football for little over a year, as the Tigers were tucked in at third place behind Derby and Burnley.

As well as the photograph seen on page 118 Duncan also took a smaller team group this season, in what was probably the area immediately in front of the Circle pavilion; there is no indication of the occasion or of any match taking place. This line up took the field on Christmas Day 1911 against Birmingham City – the last time Tommy Browell (third from left, seated) would play in front of the Anlaby Road crowd. A notable absentee is Gordon Wright – his place taken on this occasion (and on many others) by Edwin Neve (back row, second from right).

Given that this line-up only played together on one occasion at Anlaby Road, it seems possible that Duncan may have combined a visit to record this Christmas line-up with a chance to photograph the crowds, and then sell the resulting efforts in his shop window on Anlaby Road.

Matters came to a head when Hull City unexpectedly sold Tom Browell for £1,600 in late December 1911. With no inkling in the press – and by luck or design coinciding with the festive season – there was outrage among supporters who felt that the club was selling its best chance of promotion, and was thus guilty of a lack of ambition. The club had only recently declared its intention not to entertain any offers for its first-team players. Despite this, Browell's sale was sanctioned by the club and the opportune timing of the news hinted at the directors anticipation of the angry reaction of the fans. Better to announce it when attention was distracted and try to minimise criticism. In this they were only partially successful, as disillusioned and aggrieved fans soon began to question the methods and strategy of those running the club.

T. BROWELL'S GOOD-BYE.

MANY FRIENDS WITNESS TOM BROWELL'S DEPARTURE.

A large crowd gathered at the Paragon Station, Hull, yesterday afternoon, to say au revoir to Tom Browell, who was leaving for Liverpool en route for Everton.

There were a host of friends present, including the majority of the City players, and many other well-known sporting faces were also to be seen.

After much handshaking, a ring of colleagues was formed with the youthful centre in the middle, whilst "Auld Lang Syne" was lustily voiced

Browell, as the train moved out told a "News" man that he was very sorry indeed, to leave so many friends, but he wished them, and Hull City, every success for the future.

His brother and sister, along with his enthusiastic supporters, sang "He's a jolly good fellow" with much fervour after the photographers had done their work.

A pleasing presentation took place at the Hippodrome on Saturday evening, when Tom Browell, who has been transferred from Hull City to Everton, was the recipient of a handsome suit-case as a parting gift from several friends.

Mr Charles Owen, the manager of the Hippodrome, in making the presentation, remarked that he was going to probably the wealthiest club in England, and wished him every success in his new sphere.

The recipient remarked that although he was sorry to leave his colleagues, he thought he was bettering himself, and expressed the hope that he would soon be meeting his old comrades in higher circles.

The young Browell when approached by a local journalist for his thoughts on the transfer, said he: 'was sorry to leave his old club, but he must look after himself, and he would have a better chance in the First Division club'. The newspaper cutting shown here relates the departure of Boy Browell – from the presentation of a suitcase by his team mates at a local theatre the night before, to the touching and public farewell at Paragon Station, as he is seen off with suitably appropriate choruses.

Chairman Alwyn D Smith, speaking at his Hessle home on the morning of the game at Anlaby Road against Blackpool, remarked that it had been the policy of the management not to discuss matters of this kind in public, but he realised that this might be a case where supporters could be taken into the club's confidence:

"I need hardly assure them that I have the interests of the club at heart, ... and, of course, we had no intention of throwing Browell away. But bearing in mind the last offer, we could do nothing else but part with him. We had been asked time after time by several clubs if we would let him go, and we told all of them that we would consider it. Everton offered us a large sum first, and they subsequently so increased it that we could not refuse it.

But for that we had not the least idea of parting with Browell. We had been in communication with Everton some little time, and yesterday following a further letter to Mr Haller, their representative came over to Hull, and made such an offer that I could not say 'no'. The club could not throw such a chance away. You will realise what it was when I say that I shall never receive such again."

Smith refused to reveal the exact sum received saying that Everton did not wish the amount to be known but it was well over a thousand pounds. When asked about the effect Browell's departure would have on the team, he replied:

"Yes, I think we can spare Browell. Best will take his place, and, I have confidence, will serve the club well. It is not as if we had no one to put in young Browell's place. We would not have done so had it been so. But in letting Browell go we had to think of the future of the club, and here was our chance. We never dreamed of having such an offer."

Of the future, the chairman said emphatically:

"I want to say that the club is thoroughly in earnest in striving to get into the First Division. We intend to keep in that course to attain that end. But it's no use trying to run before we can walk, so to speak. If we were to get into the First Division, prove to be financially unsound, and in a miserable state and then drop back, what would our supporters say then? We think we have a very good chance now, but in the First Division especially, if you have not got the money, and don't get it, you are absolutely out of it. The right way is to consolidate your financial position as we are doing. I feel sure our supporters will realise that in connection with the Browell transfer."

He also stated:

"I didn't let young Browell go with my eyes shut, you will realise. It was altogether in the interests of the club. I am very pleased the players we bring out should make a name, but I cannot part with other players. We had no desire to part with Browell, but after we had talked it over the offer was one we could not refuse. We would not think of it at first, and asked an amount that seemed quite out of the question."

Tommy 'Boy' Browell.

The question of the reaction of supporters to the transfer was then addressed and he stated promptly that the club had done the deal for the best, and that they would not mind. Personally he should not care about it because he was convinced he had done the best for the club:

"I have great faith in my team and the players.
I believe they are quite good enough under favourable circumstances, to carry us through."

When the issue of replacements was raised, Smith pointed out that it was no use getting tenth-rate men or signing on men offered them who were only half as good as those they had, and concluded:

"You can put it in that we are just as keen on the First Division, and just as anxious as at any part of the season, and we are going to get there if we can."

Seemingly unnoticed in the furore, City also transferred Ted Smith to Crystal Palace. The Press had been asked as a favour not to publish the information until Saturday 30th December (the day of the Blackpool game). This they had done and were given to understand that no other transfers were under consideration. Indignation and a sense of betrayal thus came across in media treatment of the unexpected Browell transfer. This would only fuel supporters' disappointment at the development. Gates had been good as the public backed the team at the turnstiles and the timing of Browell's exit was damaging to prospects. Browell had in fact been transferred to enable him to play for his new club in time to be eligible for the English Cup starting in January. Ted Smith meanwhile scored a hat-trick on his debut for Crystal Palace at West Ham and another the following week on his home debut, finishing the season with spectacular statistics of 20 goals in 25 games, going on to become one of the all-time leading goal-scorers for the London club.

Newcomer Charlie Best was left to assume goal-scoring duties, and was reckoned to be an inside rather than a centre forward. 'We were years trying to find a good centre-forward, and the club said they would give £1,000 for a good one, and now we have found it, they open a shop' – was the alleged comment of one spectator outside Anlaby Road before the Blackpool game, summing up the bemused anger of supporters, perplexed at the simultaneous sale of their match-winner, and his potential replacement.

The typical cartoon of the era, shown below, cleverly depicts the event as seen by Hull's other two sports clubs and their possible gain from the furore at Anlaby Road. The Robin and the Airlie Bird mull over the pickings to be had, as disaffected supporters consider switching allegiances. The Tiger finds himself in the grip of an angry elephant (City's support) who threatens to shake him to such an extent that he loses his bag of gate takings.

THE ROBIN: "I don't think he means to throw him up this time?"
THE AIRLIE BIRD: "No, just give him a bit of a shaking. Still, the Tiger might drop that bag, then we should stand a chance of picking a bit of it up."

HULL CITY A.F.C.

Sir,—Excuse my trespassing on your valuable space, but as a strong supporter of the Hull City Football Club both out and home, I think the time has arrived when the Hull City Directors should try to acquire new players and not keep on telling us that they mean promotion, when such is not their intention and never has been since the club got admitted to the Second League.

It is all right for our esteemed captain to say that letter writers do more harm than good, but after exhibitions that have been given lately I think it high time the directors should realise the need of new players, and not keep playing the same team week after week who are at sixes and sevens, and not stick in the same old place, namely, hovering round the top of the Second League.

There they are, a splendid chance of gaining promotion, and the directors won't move a peg to try to get there.

Now, Hull City Directors, while you have the chance, grasp it, and don't for Heaven's sake let sentiment stand in the way of gaining the coveted goal, but from now till the end of the season send your best team on the field, acquire new players, and I am certain that next September would see the dawn of the First Division football in Hull, and then the directors would find out that the public of Hull would rally round them and give them their whole-hearted support. With this I conclude, with best wishes for the future success of the Hull City Football Club. —I am, Sir, etc.,

AMBER AND BLACK.
February 2nd, 1912.

The Browell brothers; Andy, George (seated), and Tom.

"WALLY" SMITH & HULL CITY.

REPLY TO "MAIL" CRITIC.

TO THE EDITOR   THE "DAILY MAIL."

Sir—In reference to "Saturn's" criticisms in last night's "Mail" with regard to the position I occupied during the second half of the match at Burnley on Saturday, I think it is only fair to Davy Gordon (who was captain on that day) and myself to state that in consequence of injuries during the game the team was reshuffled several times, with the result that I occupied three different positions. Under these circumstances, "Saturn's" remark, "Goodness knows what use he" (that is myself) "was when stood in a position between the halves and backs," is distinctly unfair and ungenerous.

It is not often that a player is called upon to occupy so many positions in the course of one match, and the inference to be drawn from "Saturn's" criticism is neither just to myself nor Davy Gordon who as captain, ordered the successive changes.—I am, Sir, etc.,

WALLY SMITH (Hull City).
Hull, January 23rd, 1912.

City's 'Wally' Smith takes the unusual step of defending himself – and his captain – in this right-to-reply letter to the Hull Daily Mail in January 1912.

The Browell transfer effectively fractured the season, and a large fault-line appeared – results before the transfer on one side, and results after on the other. A school of thought considered that the Tigers' league position was falsely high and that many displays were distinctly average. The lack of talent in the reserves meant that a couple of injuries had a serious impact upon the quality of the team, as inferior players were called into the fray. Some also believed that Browell's replacement – Charlie Best – would score goals in the same abundant quantities, reckoning that what he lacked in Browell's ability to lay the ball off cleverly, he compensated for in his superior speed.

It soon became clear that this optimism was misplaced. Writing of the transfer and its aftermath in The Hull News, the journalist 'Prodigal' reflects upon the state of the club's finances and how it affects the viability of a concrete promotion bid:

"… Other really tempting offers have been made for City players, but until the directors consider the time opportune, always having in mind a capable substitute for the position, the City supporters can rest assured that the directors will not betray the confidence which has been reposed in them. I do not blame the Hull City officials the least but in carrying on the club on business lines, provided they are content to remain in the Second Division, and that is where I honestly believe they will stop for several years to come. I admit that business ability must be more essential to the successful working of a first League club than it is in the maintaining of a Second Division organisation, but the crux of the question is this: Is there a sufficient following in Hull to perpetually maintain a First League club?

When that is answered to the complete satisfaction of the Hull City directors, then we may expect to talk seriously about promotion and all the vicissitudes such distinction entails. The retort may be, 'Nothing venture, nothing have.'

Again, that is a matter for the directors. Personally, I honestly wish we had a First Division team in Hull, but this could not be established without considerably curtailing the financial resources of the two Rugby clubs. Whilst many may preach the doctrine of a 'survival of the fittest,' my own policy is 'live and let live,' and especially when it comes to sport."

The Tigers finished the year with a convincing 3-0 win over Blackpool, Andy Browell stepping into the goal-scoring breach vacated by young Tom, as he netted two goals.

In the first half of the season, City had been outstanding at Anlaby Road: out of ten games, nine had been won and just a solitary draw against Derby spoiled their record. Away from home the Tigers were much less predictable, with four defeats, two draws and three wins, conceding three or more goals in all of their losses. A little strengthening of the squad would see them climb even higher but the loss of their better players would see them tumble down the table. An away draw at Glossop on the 6th January kept the promotion bid on track before the English Cup provided a distraction with a trip to Oldham. Vice-captain Davy Gordon said of the game:

> "We shall go prepared for a very stubborn opposition in what is likely to be a most strenuous tussle. I must confess that I did not like the appearance of the draw from our standpoint when the news arrived that we had to visit Oldham, but circumstances have altered very much since then. With the right spirit animating the Tigers and given decent conditions underfoot, I don't think we shall come back defeated.
>
> It is gratifying to hear that the Oldham ground has been re-turfed and properly drained since we last figured at Boundary Park. That was at the end of the season before last, when victory carried the 'Latics' in the First Division on goal average at our expense.
>
> We were beaten solely by the wretched conditions that day, and we had a weak team out into the bargain, more than one of our players being unsound in limb. I confidently think we shall put up a big struggle this time, and if we are beaten it will be by a superior team."

Despite the fee received for Tommy Browell, the crucial importance of the Cup in providing funds to balance the books would have been on the minds of the directors as the Oldham tie approached. The loss of £410 on the previous season came on the back of a very lucrative cup run – the competition was fundamental to financial well-being for many clubs.

Having prepared at Hornsea, the City party made their way to Oldham on the 10.05 a.m. train out of Paragon. Travelling supporters could also choose a Hull & Barnsley special excursion from Cannon Street at 8.30 arriving at Oldham at 11.20, and giving free onward passage to Manchester Victoria and back. Return from Manchester Victoria was at 11p.m. allowing travellers to celebrate the victory or drown their sorrows until the late evening. The N.E.R ran two trains returning direct from Oldham at 7.12 and 7.30, the fare on all of these trains being 3s 9d.

City started badly at Oldham as the rampant home side besieged Teddy Roughley's goal, hitting the bar once and the posts twice in the opening quarter of an hour. Oldham looked a vastly different proposition from the side beaten by the Tigers the season before and their form belied their lowly position in the First Division. Oldham also rattled the woodwork

New signing Charlie Best.

three more times in the second half, and had a shot that trickled along Teddy Roughley's goal line. They dominated the Tigers throughout and at times it seemed that another of the season's heavy defeats was inevitable. City survived until the interval, but finally succumbed after as the home side, playing down the slope, took the lead. The visitors, although outplayed, never gave up hope as long as the margin was only one goal. Their tight and cautious play prevented them from feeding their wide men, who were easily contained by the Oldham full-backs, and it was left to a piece of individual brilliance by Browell's replacement Charlie Best, ten minutes before the end to keep the Tigers in the competition. According to one eye witness:

'The Hull centre forward was put in possession just outside the half-way line, and with indomitable pluck and determination this player dashed down the middle with the ball at his toes. Several times he was severely threatened with dispossession, but he controlled the ball magnificently, and rushing between the backs at the last hurdle, he swiftly banged the ball low into the corner of the net. It was a great triumph for this very promising player.'

It was back to Hornsea to prepare for the replay on the Tuesday, after their customary trip to the Turkish Baths on the Sunday morning.

The atmosphere at Anlaby Road on the day of the game was hampered by the poor weather, a bitingly cold wind and fine drizzle restricting the gate on a midweek afternoon to some 13,000 spectators. The game was markedly different from the match at Oldham the previous Saturday. It was City who dominated the possession this time, pinning Oldham in their own half for long periods and rendering Roughley, who had been overworked at Boundary Park, a virtual onlooker. For all the Tigers' possession, they lacked the penetration to create real opportunities. In front of goal they were hesitant and ponderous, the inevitable questions about how Tom Browell might have fared being asked. Best was industrious and inventive but was surrounded by colleagues who lacked the spark and self-belief to trouble the visitors. As the game headed towards extra time, Oldham won a free kick on the touchline in the Tigers' half. With three minutes left, McQuillan and Nevins were sucked into the play near the corner flag as the right flank of Oldham's forwards, supported by their right half-back, tussled for possession. Woodger, for the visitors, drifted to the far post unattended and unmarked, and waited for the inevitable centre, which duly came. The Oldham attacker didn't even have to step to meet the ball, guiding his header cleverly past Roughley who had failed to cut out the centre.

Oldham, who ought to have won the first game by a large margin, thus triumphed in the replay despite being a distant second best on the day. Observers considered the outcome a just one and that greater injustice prevailed at Oldham than at Anlaby Road. For the Tigers this result was a severe blow as receipts of £722 for the two games meant that less than £300 would find its way into the club's coffers. The league position was still such that a push for promotion was not impossible, but a lack of belief, and doubts about the club's ability to sustain the efforts needed, meant that it was now an uphill struggle.

The journey from Paragon Station to Liverpool by Tom Browell was repeated by centre-half brother Andy some two months later, accompanied later by Joe 'Stanley' Smith. As they said goodbye to friends and admirers, they spoke briefly to a local journalist of their move. Both players had wanted to move and, although sorry to leave their

friends, felt they would be more comfortable at Everton – which undoubtedly they would be, given Everton's status as an established First Division club. Andy Browell revealed that he had received over £200 (approximately a year's wages) as his part of the deal and that this was more than he would have received had he waited for his benefit. Smith on the other hand, reckoned that he would receive around £100.

Everton officials had come over to Hull the previous Wednesday, and they took Browell to the Station Hotel where he signed the necessary papers. Smith was caught when he was getting on the train to Withernsea, and in his own words he 'seized the pen and signed quick, before anyone could change their minds'. One of the pair told an Everton official: 'We have been playing in the Reserves, not being good enough for the first team.' To which the reply was: 'Never mind you are quite good enough for us!'

The Everton officials declared themselves delighted with their earlier purchase of Tom Browell and said they were willing to buy all players of a similar calibre that the Tigers could produce.

This latest development seems to present the players as being motivated by greed and whilst the relatively low wages of a footballer at the time, meant that a move to a bigger club would be more rewarding financially and in terms of status, there also appears to be a degree of rancour in their departure. Whether this was due to perceived injustices on the part of the two players or general disillusionment with the Anlaby Road club (or both) is open to speculation. That City had yet again sold some of their better players was not open to speculation, but an incontrovertible fact. Similar to some of the smaller clubs in the Second Division, such as Gainsborough Trinity or Stockport County, they were in danger of becoming a mere nursery club. Despite protestations to the contrary, it was strongly rumoured that the boardroom was divided on this policy of selling prized playing-assets. But by now there were not many attractive assets left to sell.

Reflecting on these developments in the local press, one journalist with the nom de plume 'Saturn' wrote of the air of resignation among fans at the news of the Andy Browell / Joe Smith transfer when compared to the furore which greeted Tom Browell's sale, and questioned the club's policies saying:

"... there are a few thousand supporters who put their hands into their pockets equally as deep as do the majority of the directors, and whose interest in the club is equally as sincere, who do not think things are in the least satisfactory. A journalistic colleague – probably the leading writer on Association football in the county, says in regard to the transfers:- When a club like Hull City gets rid of four such excellent players, whatever the transfer fees may have been, it is not difficult to find a reasonable cause for disquiet among its supporters, and it is pretty certain that further agitation will arise in the Third Port, to discover a substantial cause for these transfers."

Another journalist 'The General' is quoted thus:-

"Hull City must be feeling the effect of transferring their players to Everton, for yesterday the team gave one of their poorest displays seen at Leicester this season. I should imagine Hull City have not much thought of securing promotion."

'Saturn' finishes his article in a bitter vein, rounding on the writer of the article in the club's programme for patronising the supporters with pleas for any criticism of the club's policies to cease. He writes:

"I am sorry that my journalistic friends have not yet had the opportunity of receiving 'official advice.' The 'programme' states 'The unthoughtful allegation that either the players or directors do not seek promotion is an unfair aspersion which we ought not to hear again.' Upon my word, what a (sic) amusing little print!

So now kind reader, I must ask you all to desist from criticising the club, or its methods. We have really nothing whatever to do with it. All we have to do is plank down our money and give three cheers for the Club and its Management. It is a bit hard I know, but I should not like to be a party towards getting the readers of the 'Mail' into trouble with the Powers that be! (Ahem!)."

Whilst the Tigers were going down 3-0 at Leicester, their travelling fans were still faithfully following their team with five saloons on the early train out of Cannon Street – 'chartered by various departments of Reckitt's and some recreation clubs, were included in the train, and I should think some 300 enthusiasts undertook the journey.'

North Easterner Billy McDonald signed for City in February, his right flank skills quickly making an impression at Anlaby Road, where he soon found himself involved in first team action.

Once in Leicester:

" ... the miniature stuffed tiger, most erroneously asserted to be a 'mascot' (a deal of luck it brought) was paraded through the principal thoroughfares, and yellow and black colours were freely displayed. During the game those three hundred trippers were vocally a match for any three thousand Leicester supporters."

The affair was disastrous for all connected with the Tigers. A possible promotion attempt fizzled out. Morale was low and the players unsettled.

Gates declined as disillusioned fans lost faith, and any local newspapers that had carried fans' letters of protest and critical cartoons, were banned from the Anlaby Road press-box. A palpable cynicism and bitterness soured the rest of the season and set a precedent for future events. Despite the board's protestations about good business for the club and an almost record fee being received, the supporters and local press cared only about on-field matters. The damage had been done and the hitherto positive and benevolent relationship between club, supporters and local press had been harmed. For supporters of a relatively new club such as the Tigers, the event served as a loss of collective innocence, as financial reality and economic prudence triumphed over ambition and hope.

AMATEUR INTERNATIONAL MATCH IN HULL.

Gordon Wright was selected to play for the amateur international game at Hull against Holland on the 18th March. Bill Leach was England's trainer and is seen standing on the far left.

A photo gallery, including a youthful mascot, from the Wolves game on March 9th.

The Tiger Comes Back To His Form.

THE TIGER: "Now, my lads, you'd better get that lesson into your heads quickly, or I shall make it warm for you top ones.

An unexpected win at promotion chasing Derby County prompted this cartoon, in which the Tiger admonishes Chelsea, Derby and Clapton Orient amongst others, to beware of City.

On April 13th, the Tigers visited Chelsea in front of 30,000 people at Stamford Bridge. This was by some margin the biggest crowd at a City game that season, and an indicator of the size of one of the biggest opponents in the division and the money they could generate at the turnstiles. A goal 12 minutes from time sank the Tigers who had mounted a steadfast rearguard throughout the game – something they had not always done away from Anlaby Road. The London press were generous in their praise of the visitors' defence:

"It was magnificent" ... "Roughley, McQuillan, Houghton and McIntosh, Hull City's goalkeeper, backs and centre half back respectively, played the game of their lives at Stamford Bridge, and stormed as was their citadel for, to write mildly, three-fifths of this match, they conceded only one goal, and that twelve minutes from time.

... I have seen many exciting matches, but I have seldom seen a crowd so worked up as were the many thousands who viewed this game. They did so want a goal, and it was so long in coming – quarter-time, half-time, three-quarter-time – and then a goal! What a mouthful the assembled thousands made of it, to be sure! Again and again they shouted 'goal', and, indeed, they continued shouting it to the end, when there was tremendous cheering for every one of the victorious side, and not a little applause for these gallant Hull defenders. You have heard of matches being bought and sold, eh? Perhaps there have been such transactions; but this 90 minutes' struggle was as tough a show as I have ever witnessed. The men might have been playing for all they hold dearest. It was thrust hard and thrust again from start to finish. Good men all."

One of the more unusual recruits to the Tigers ranks was well-known local rugby star Harry Taylor, who had played and captained Hull, Yorkshire, the Northern Union League and England (all in the same year – 1908), who is pictured below (left) in a cap and representative shirt. The card has no publisher's name but contemporary newspapers carried the picture, attributing it to Walter Hancock, an Anlaby Road photographer.

In making the five minute journey from Airlie Street to City's ground in October 1911, he not only crossed over Anlaby Road but over codes as well. From being a captain and full-back for Hull, he joined City, initially as a reserve goalkeeper, turning out for them in the Midlands League. As the photographic postcard by Richard Garside below (right) shows, Taylor was no stranger to the round ball game. He is shown as a player (middle row, third from left, white shirt) in an unidentified game with an impressive number of local dignitaries in attendance.

On April 23rd 1912, City's trainer Bill Leach, an instantly recognisable figure with his moustache and flat cap since the club's beginnings in 1904, died of liver cancer at his home, 8 Chatham Street off Albert Avenue. Leach was the archetypal trainer in appearance as well as background. His skills lay not in medicine, science or the coaching of football, but in enabling the club's players to run faster and longer. With his towel draped over his forearm, and in his shirtsleeves, he presented himself as a typical trainer of the Edwardian period. He was one of the last remaining connections with the team of the 'friendly season' of 1904/5 and had a background in athletics, having been a long-distance runner in his day. He had been the trainer of A.E. Duffey, the English Amateur 100 Yards Champion from 1900-1903, and had also been associated with W.G. George, the long-distance champion of the 1880s. In his footballing years, he had been attached to Derby County, Newcastle United, Barnsley and Luton Town as trainer.

The ever-versatile player, captain and occasional joiner, Davy Gordon had deputised for him as trainer during his illness but a more permanent appointment would be needed for the new season. Gordon and goalkeeper Teddy Roughley both lived in nearby Brougham Street, and would no doubt have paid their final respects to their dying trainer, reflecting not only the close ties among the club's staff but also the physical closeness typical of the period when most people lived very

HARRY TAYLOR'S FIRST GAME FOR HULL CITY.

Harry Taylor, the old Hull F.C. back, made his debut in Association football yesterday, when he played in goal for Hull City Reserves against Huddersfield Town Reserves. Our photographs show (1) Taylor saving (2) coming on the field; (3) saving a high shot; and (4) a "snap" in his new colours. ("News.")

Harry Taylor's debut for the City Reserves.

near to their place of work. Several City players had lodgings in the Chatham Street area, and manager Ambrose Langley living in De La Pole Avenue – the street parallel to Albert Avenue.

Step forward Harry Taylor – outstanding local sportsman of impeccable credentials and character. If Leach had been a prize-winning sprinter in his youth, Taylor had leadership qualities, proven at the highest level in his sport as well as experience of physical conditioning in team sports at an international level. His convictions as a teetotaller (although not his liking for tobacco) may have proved useful in an era when players who socialised among supporters were frequently plied with free alcoholic drinks – well-meaning but misguided generosity.

Pre-cup tie stays at seaside resorts were as much about 'protecting' players from this supporter 'generosity' as they were about enjoying the sea air.

The postcard shown top-right portrays Harry Taylor sitting in front of Hull Cricket Club's pavilion smoking his pipe; no doubt engrossed in a City training session on the cricket pitch.

"Instead of finishing at the top of the League table, we have to be content with position number six. To state the cause of this fall from grace is unnecessary, as the facts have been fully discussed in the 'Mail' and 'Times,' and the opinion we gave at the end of December has been fully justified by events. Throughout, the 'Mail' has taken a strong stand in an effort to get first Division football in Hull, and whilst these efforts have been strongly resented in certain quarters, the end has proved conclusively that the 'Mail' was in the right, and had

these opinions and suggestions been followed out, the probabilities are that we should at the present time have gained the First League. From Everton alone a sum of £3,100 has been received for the transfers of Tom and Andy Browell, and Stanley Smith, and further sums were obtained for Ted Smith, Waldon, and Pearce. The balance at the end of the season will amount to about £1,400. Although the balance appears satisfactory, it must be remembered that it has been obtained at the expense of parting with the club's chief assets – their leading players. Those who have seen the team play during the past month know that it is an absolute impossibility for the Tigers to open the season with the present material. To expect to build up a team on the remarkably small outlay they have made in the past is futile. Manager Langley, successful as he has been in the past, is only human, and the probabilities are that before we get a team equal in merit to the one which made such strong running during the early part of the season, the balance at the bank – and perhaps more – will have to be expended."

The Hull Daily Mail's unequivocal and damning verdict on the season contrasted with the more pragmatically diplomatic and measured words of captain Gordon Wright, who wrote:

"Another season has ended, and we shall have to wait for a lapse of four months before the next will be upon us. The performances of the Tigers have, on the whole, been disappointing, but, considering the changes which have taken place in the team, our final result has been far more satisfactory than at first sight might seem apparent. As a whole, however, we must admit that we have been disappointing, but some of the victories that have been gained cannot but add to the lustre already acquired by the club. The old fault that we have never yet been able to eradicate has cost us more than I care personally to think about. I refer to the nine points dropped at home. In the 'Sports Express' recently I stated how necessary it was to acquire the maximum number of points at home if ultimate success was to be gained, and as I look back on the past season this fact is once again vividly brought home. Despite defeats away from Anlaby-road, if we had only remained undefeated on our own pastures we might have attained the summit of our ambition.

As regards the personnel of our team I need not here recapitulate the great and sweeping changes that have been made. Enough has been written and said about their advisability, and everyone has their own opinion on the subject. We may miss one of two of our old familiar faces on the field next season, and new reputations have to be made by the new men. One has been firmly established this past season. I refer to Tim Wright, who has shown consistent good form at right half during the whole time. He has improved beyond all expectation, and at the present rate should develop into one of the best half-backs in the Second Division. His passing and heading improve almost every match, while there are few halves, if any, playing now who can beat him for speed.

Jack Houghton, too, is making great strides as a back. Originally a half, he has taken kindly to his new position, and like Tim Wright his speed will stand him in good stead against fast wing forwards.

Of the new men, McDonald seems to have the makings of a worthy successor to Joe Smith, while Shaw is very promising and Stevens should develop into a good centre forward. Of the older members of the team I need make no comment here. One and all have rendered yeoman service to the club, and their reputations are too firmly

established to be further enhanced by any words from me. I never wish to play with a nicer, more willing team of players, who are all out for victory every time.

Before closing, I should like to say how grieved I was to hear of the death of poor 'Bill' Leach, our trainer. Leach was a most conscientious and hardworking trainer, and the club will have difficulty in finding a successor anything like his equal."

The club embarked on two post-season tours in 1912, the first to Belgium to play Tottenham Hotspur on May 12th, and another later that month to Norway to play a series of friendlies against local sides. The game in Brussels was for the Belgian Charity Cup or the Coupe De Decker as it was also known. The match itself was played in very hot conditions on a rock-hard pitch. Despite these testing circumstances, City won 2-0 against their First Division opponents. The Cup itself had to remain in Belgium, as City had experienced problems with the Customs when they brought the Cup back to Brussels and had no wish to go through the same problems the following year.

'Have you got the cup?' asked secretary Jack Haller as the Rotterdam steamer pulled alongside Hull's Riverside Quay on the Monday morning after the previous day's game. Fred Stringer, the City director who had accompanied the team responded 'No, thank you' and would have no doubt explained the full circumstances later.

HULL FOOTBALLERS WIN BELGIAN CUP.

The Hull City team arriving at the Hull Riverside Quay yesterday by the s.s. Rievaulx Abbey on their return from Belgium, where they won the Dedecker Cup, which is played for annually in Belgium by English teams. Hull City's opponents were Tottenham Hotspur.—(" News.")

The cup had been brought back to Hull the previous year after victory over Swindon in Brussels and was described as 'a handsome piece of silverware modelled in the shape of an urn'. Because of customs regulations regarding duty payable on silverware, lengthy discussions ensued in Rotterdam and then again on the Belgian border, as diligent officials enquired about the cup. After eventually convincing them that the cup was purely a sports trophy, Ambrose Langley was seemingly allowed to continue into Belgium with the cup alone – as the rest of the City party had travelled on ahead with Davy Gordon and Harry Taylor in charge. Langley commented 'If we win this cup again, I shall leave the blessed thing behind' – which he did.

The players did not return empty-handed however, and displayed their gold medals to a crowd of admirers as they landed on the quay. The unusual medals were 'of exquisite design, representing a seal on the back of which is a footballer, a connection which is not quite clear, unless both are supposed to be slippery customers in their natural environment.' They had been congratulated by Belgian officials on their slightly unexpected win and were invited back to defend the trophy the following year against Belgian opponents.

The game itself had been a poor one on a narrow and bumpy pitch, with a lively ball, which invited miskicks. Charlie Best put City in front before the interval as he converted during a scramble in front of the Spurs goal. New signing Stanley Fazackerley increased the lead early in the second half with a glorious oblique shot from 12 yards after clever work by Herbert Goode. There was no further score as the teams tired in the hostile conditions, both sets of players being happy to seek the shelter of the pavilion after 90 minutes under the scorching sun.

After a few days rest back in Hull, there then followed a four-day voyage to Norway for the Norwegian trip. The first game on the 28th May saw a crushing 16-1 victory for the Tigers against a team drawn from Trondheim and District. Aside from the disparity in abilities, it was another unusual playing experience for the team on a pitch that was flooded in winter and used as a skating rink. It was said to be comparable to a school playground in Hull with the advantage of being relatively stone-free, unlike the Swedish pitches of previous tours.

The Norwegians gave their visitors a friendly welcome in the official programme which was loosely translated as follows:

"A hearty welcome is hereby given by Nordenfjeldske Fotballforbund on behalf of all our players to our guests, the members of Hull City Football Club, who so readily accepted our invitation to come over and show us how football has to be played properly.

We hope the visit will greatly assist us in our endeavours to make this excellent game as popular in our country as it has been for generations in the land of its birth, namely, England. We wish you all an enjoyable stay at this old historic place, Trondhjem, and hope, when leaving us, you will only take back with you pleasant and happy memories of this short sojourn here."

The game kicked off at the unusual time of 9 p.m. in front of a crowd of 5,000 curious locals, and a handful of enthusiastic followers in their newly-acquired black and amber rosettes from the S.S. Oslo (the ship on which the Tigers party had sailed). The Tigers won the toss and made the hosts play into the still bright Nordic sun. Fazackerley put City ahead after six minutes, then scored again on 12. The half time score was 6-0; Roughley, in City's goal, had kicked the ball on only two occasions. Fazackerley had scored all six. The second half continued in the same vein with monotonous scoring from City, interrupted only by a fine oblique shot into Teddy Roughley's goal by Tellefsen for the home side.

City manager Ambrose Langley refereed the game combining this role with some coaching of the Norwegians on the pitch. Fazackerley finished with 11 goals to his name and this feat marked him out as a very promising new acquisition. Patsy O'Connell too, took the eye, being described as a 'nailing good player, who will also do the Tigers a lot of good next season.'

The second game was against Kirkbrage FC. It was another 9 p.m. kick-off, this time on a cold and dull Scandinavian evening. It was another one-sided victory, with Fazackerley netting four times in a 15-1 victory. A third game against Trondheim and District finished 9-0 in the Tigers' favour (Fazackerley scoring four times).

The group then journeyed to Sweden to play two games against a Gothenburg XI . The narrower victories obtained reflected the superior prowess of the Swedes compared to their Norwegian counterparts. The Tigers final game was to have been played against an unofficial Swedish national side (as a warm-up game for the 1912 Stockholm Olympics) but some Stockholm-based players were unable to get to Gothenburg, so the fixture was rearranged against a Gothenburg XI. All matches having been played and many sights having been seen, the tourists began their return voyage to Hull. Before they did so, a small leaving ceremony was observed. To thank director Fred Stringer for having arranged and organised this long and enjoyable tour, the players bought a massive silver ink stand for him, which Ambrose Langley presented on their behalf, saying:

"I have pleasure in performing this pleasing duty on behalf of the party. Personally I have never had a finer trip in the whole of my life, and I think I am voicing the opinion of every one of us.

No one knows more than I do the amount of work and trouble Mr. Stringer has been put to, and to work up a seventeen days' tour for a party of this size, and for it to go through without a single hitch, speaks volumes for his organising abilities."

The party left Gothenburg for home after their long tour, eating sleeping and resting, with manager Langley throwing his by now habitual message in a bottle into the sea.

At the A.G.M. held in the restaurant of the Imperial Hotel on June 20th 1912, chairman Alwyn D. Smith announced a profit of some £707, and gave a comprehensive review of items on the balance sheet in front of a moderate attendance of shareholders. Addressing the team's league position, he stated that failure to win promotion was not entirely due to the players themselves not being good enough but to the large number of injured players such as James McIntosh, who was unavailable for most of the season. Smith stopped short of pinpointing a lack of strength in depth in the squad, although this may well have been in the minds of some in the room. He then continued to thank the generosity of

spectators which enabled the club to support local charities so generously and the £30 or so pounds collected for 'deserving objects' in connection with the Titanic disaster brought the overall total to roughly £280. Brief mention was made of the honour of hosting the England versus Holland amateur international game, and the news signings of Fazackerley, O'Connell and Good. Sadness on the passing of Bill Leach was expressed as was pride in the selection of Gordon Wright for England for the 1912 Olympics in Stockholm. The minutiae of the balance sheet were pored over and explained in detail, depreciation of playing assets and stands were clarified and eventually it was moved to adopt the report and balance sheet. Councillor James Spring seconded, and the adoption was agreed unanimously.

Mr Lofthouse, the auditor moved a vote a appreciation of the directors, Dr. Lilley, J.P., the club's honorary doctor and Gordon Wright. As far as he was concerned they had done their duty and if the team had not got into the First League – 'the directors could not be blamed for that.' Doubtless some in the room and outside may have seen things differently, but the meeting moved swiftly on as the vote of thanks was seconded. There was no discussion of the Browell transfer. After the obligatory thanks, nominations and re-appointments, the club's honorary solicitor Mr M.V. Gosschalk said that the chairman was the best they could possibly have and moved a vote of thanks, adding that his (Smith's) task had not been so easy during the past year as it should have been, but no doubt he had done his duty and done it well. Gosschalk then added that he hoped the Press would do their best to assist their chairman in the interest of sport during the coming season.

In reply Smith thanked them and said he had done his best, and if his best had not been right, he was very sorry. If his best and his views were not the same as other people's he was very sorry. It had been a pleasure putting in the time but one could not please everybody.

The Anlaby Road ground hosted various local cup finals and representative games between amateur sides, such as this team of Corn Merchants in their unusual collection of football jerseys, cricket blazers and rugby shirts.

1912 – 13

By 1912-13 the standard location for the traditional pre-season squad photograph by Duncan was West Park. The Duncan souvenir postcard shown below was available in two versions, one marked 'copyright' and the other not.

No Gordon Wright (as usual) and no more Browells. Two new forwards to strengthen the attack – Sammy Stevens and Stan Fazackerley – had been acquired in the second half of the previous season following the shock departure of Tommy Browell. In this group Fazackerley is standing directly behind manager Langley and in front of Sammy Stevens on the back row. Manager Langley has abandoned his boater and standoffish stance, taking his place seated in the middle of the front row. Harry Chapman sits to his left, and would see his career ended by injury a few weeks after this photo was taken. Goalkeeper Teddy Roughley has opted for head- wear on the middle row. The respected former Hull FC player, Harry Taylor, appears on the extreme left of the same row, having taken on the role of trainer following the death of Bill Leach.

After the depressing exit of some of the club's best players in the second half of the 1911/12 season, genuine optimism was in short supply as the start of the new season approached and , instead, the possible merits of the new recruits were the object of journalistic scrutiny.
Reflecting in August on the season ahead, one local journalist enthused

"At no time in the history of Hull City has the season been ushered in with more promise of class football, and with less expectation of the kick-and-rush policy being pursued. The style of play will be in keeping with the quality of the crowd, and that is saying a good deal."

Gordon Wright also focused on the changes in the summer months in a newspaper column in early September, returning also to a familiar theme – the need for the public of Hull to support the club:

"Several well-known faces will be absent from our ranks, and much as we deplore the departure of old and valued servants, the infusion of new blood, and especially young blood, cannot but make our prospects exceedingly rosy.

The great thing is to secure the effective blending together of the elements of our new team, and to inspire them with that spirit of good-fellowship and camaraderie without which a team would invariably fail, however good individually they might be. So long as there is harmony between the members of the team, and between the team and the directors, promotion is assuredly half won, and,

Bert Goode was signed from Aston Villa in the close season and scored on his debut

at any rate, failure will be less pronounced. So long, then, as the above questions are satisfactorily settled the only other factor of success, other, of course, than the great essential – good football – is that of public support.

I am greatly hoping for increased support this coming season, and I am beginning to think that the public are at last realising that if they keep away because their favourites are losing, they are only making matters infinitely worse; even, in some instances depriving the club of any chance of mending matters. The public supply the money that keeps the clubs going, and the cutting off of revenue by keeping away from home matches can do no possible good."

After the first home game against Blackpool, another local journalist, 'Nimrod' of the Hull Daily Mail, was much less enthusiastic about the club's prospects and despite the 4-1 win, the tone of his article mirrored the pessimistic mood of the end of the previous season:

HULL FOOTBALLERS IN TRAINING.

The Hull City players are now to be seen training every morning at the Anlaby road ground. Our photographs, taken yesterday, show physical exercises (1) and (3) Simmons, Wright, Gordon, and Nevins; (2) Hendry keeping goal (4) Temple, Best, Good, McDonald, McQuillan, Potts, and Roughley.

The Tigers are put through their paces in August 1912

"Since the Tigers were included in the Second League I don't think they have had such a limited number of players to draw upon as is the case now. Neither does the quality seem to be up the standard demanded by the public. I am basing this speculation on the work in the practice games. I may turn out to be wrong. City enthusiasts will hope so. I think a wager that Hull City will not earn promotion this trip would be a safe bit of business.

... It is the forward line that is the source of the worry. Wright and Best we know, but what of Goode, Stevens and 'Fazzy'? Will they turn out trump cards? The first-named impressed me very favourably in practice, and was responsible for a few items which were stamped with the hallmark of 'class.' The other two were not so convincing, and did not strike me as being above the average. It may be true that

A goal for Hull City against Blackpool.

A goal for Hull City against Blackpool in the first home game of the season.

they have youth on their side, and that they may develop, but there is such a thing as the steed starving while the grass is growing."

Given the scoring feats of Fazackerley during the course of the season to come, such pessimistic views thankfully proved to be inaccurate. Sammy Stevens, too, would turn out to be a very useful player and goal-scorer. Charlie Best was also proving to be a valuable attacker.

OH! JUST A FEW ALTERATIONS AND IMPROVEMENTS. I HAD A FEW OF THESE POINTS TAKEN AWAY LAST SEASON BUT I DONT MEAN TO THIS.

ANLABY ROAD

WHATS YER GIME?

CLAPTON ENT

City's indifferent home record in 1911-12 is referred to in this cartoon published before the Clapton game.

Tigers fans celebrate a goal against Clapton.

His winning goal against Nottingham Forest on 5th October in front of 15,000 fans took City to the top of table, and he earned praise for his opportunism and hunger in fashioning the winner from a seemingly hopeless position, as visiting goal-keeper Hanna's fatal lack of concentration allowed Best to score. Gordon Wright, too, earned praise as the City captain was forced to endure a meagre supply of passes out to the wing from his inside players, which when they did arrive, were rarely in front of him, and did not allow him to run onto them at speed. Despite this, his consistently accurate crossing in the final quarter of the game – often in the face of unscrupulous tackling – was a constant threat to the Nottingham side and allowed City to snatch the points.

As part of the deal that took Tommy Browell to Goodison Park, City played Everton in a friendly on the afternoon of Thursday October 10th. A healthy crowd of 10,000 attended and were understandably disappointed that Everton had not brought their first team, but only one regular – Browell himself. The other two former Tigers had failed to establish themselves in their new surroundings and were not picked for the game. City also fielded a weakened team, opting to rest many regulars such as McQuillan and Nevins, Tim and Gordon Wright, and Sammy Stevens. If the paying public felt cheated about the nature of the game, they could have had no complaints about the quality of the goal-scoring skills on view. The 4-7 score line included no less than five goals by Tom Browell, each unstoppable and expertly-taken. If Browell had left City with some raw edges, these had evidently been smoothed; Browell's play now encompassed slick passing, which also created opportunities. According to one report of the game:

"It was obvious that Browell yesterday stood out in a class by himself. Whereas the other forwards – both Everton and City – were attempting to drive the ball into the net by sheer force and speed, Browell used his brains, and placed the ball where the goalkeeper could not get to it."

Fazackerley confirmed his growing reputation as a goal-getter for City by scoring three times in what was a very tamely-contested game, and the main beneficiaries were the Tigers' coffers – swelled by the gate receipts.

City v. Birmingham.

In the absence of Bailey in the Birmingham goal, Police-constable Crosswaite acted as substitute, and, despite Gordon Wright's centres, the home centre was unable to score.

Cartoonist R.W. Lawson makes light of City's failure to beat Birmingham City, who were without a proper goalkeeper.

City were defeated in the league for the first time by Birmingham City on October 19th. Despite the by now mandatory goal by Fazackerley, Birmingham were able to come away from Anlaby Road with a 2-1 victory. Birmingham played without their first-choice goalkeeper, Bailey, and his replacement Crosthwaite – a police officer by profession, was able to keep the Tigers at bay.

Another emerging talent was Sammy Stevens. On November 2nd in a home game with Leeds City, he scored four goals in an emphatic 6-2 victory, this despite the Tigers being handicapped by an injury to forward Charlie Best who tore the lateral ligament of his knee after only ten minutes. Stevens also had one disallowed, and shaved the bar or post on three other occasions.

The previous week City had lost heavily at Huddersfield by five goals to two, and they confirmed their utter unpredictability by putting the Loinenders to the sword with Gordon Wright at his very best on the wing, supplying an endless array of crosses and through-balls. Wright was sometimes subdued if the ball was not supplied to him, but given ample possession by Stevens and McDonald, his speed and precise crosses were deadly. The Tigers were cheered off the field at the half-time interval and then again at the finish, as an enthusiastic and delighted crowd of 11,000

saluted their attacking prowess. For the first time that season, Fazackerley had failed to get his name among the Tigers' scorers, although he did have one disallowed. It was a very minor disappointment on a day of triumph for his fellow forwards. But the day belonged to Stevens. Having had to endure barracking, and suffering a bad lack of confidence in previous games, he had struggled to make an impression on a crowd used to goal-scoring forwards. This fed his nervousness in front of goal and stifled his play, as he became increasingly aware of his perceived shortcomings. Before his first goal, his style was described as 'rashing play' but having netted against Leeds his play was transformed. Suddenly, gaining confidence, he started to lay off the ball wide to Gordon Wright or McDonald and take up a position in the centre, which proved to be a major factor in the emphatic victory. Describing the change in Stevens' fortunes, it was reported that:

> "The spectators – that is the noisy spectators – may, I am not afraid to say even the most exclusive of the 'Bob-ites' thought it advisable to change their tone. I heard during the early stages of the game 'What bally rot playing Stevens! The bounder does not know football.' Later I heard the same person shout -actually shout! – 'Give Stevens the ball!'

Stevens (shown right) netted again in the 2-0 home win over Bury on November 16th, but this victory was followed by a disastrous run of five defeats, and only in the fifth loss did City manage to score again. This dip in form meant that at the halfway point in the season the Tigers had lost eight out of 19 games. In effect, any chance of promotion was gone. The promising unbeaten start to the season (which had lasted 8 games) seemed a distant memory as the goals rapidly dried up. All that was left, in the league at least, was to

JACK FROST: You can run away home if you ain't brought your skates.

Ern Shaw's take on the City versus Barnsley postponement

avoid getting drawn into the re-election zone at the foot of the table, and with it, the risk of being voted out of the league. For the first time, the club were looking down the table rather than up. At least there was the welcome distraction of the greatest cup competition in the world. A good draw would fill the coffers and re-ignite the season. The English Cup draw once again sent the Tigers to the capital, this time to Fulham. As usual for cup games in the South, the club selected Worthing as its training base.

Training consisted of 'gallops' in the morning followed by a stroll before dinner. Thursday evening was given over to a billiard match against their hosts Worthing Athletic, which the Tigers won handsomely. The next morning the players left their hotel and went by bus to a meet of the hounds. They followed that up with some gentle exercise – nothing strenuous – before leaving for London on the 7.20. Also departing for the game were special trains leaving Hull late on Friday night, carrying City supporters to the capital through snow-covered countryside.

The game at Craven Cottage was played in incessant rain and a tight struggle developed, with Fulham having slightly the better of it. City were forced to defend deep, the old campaigners McQuillan and Nevins both having to work hard to keep the Fulham wingers at bay. They frequently kicked the ball into touch, much to the annoyance of the home fans, but if they did allow Fulham to infiltrate the flanks there was always goalkeeper Nick Hendry on hand to deal calmly with any danger. The pitch was becoming increasingly sodden as both sides sought to assert control of the game. City's training at Worthing seemed to be paying dividends as the game wore on, their stamina and relative freshness becoming evident in the struggle. Having weathered the storm for 15 minutes of the second half, City began to probe with more purpose. Gordon Wright had been relatively subdued but he received a

Nichol or Nick Hendry sketched top right by Ern Shaw, became first choice goalkeeper for the Tigers at the start of the season and went on to play in every game. His masterly display at Glossop on September 14th prompted the cartoon tribute by R.W. Lawson, bottom right.

neat pass and as usual headed for the corner, drawing Grey – the Fulham full-back – into a tussle for the ball. Leaving his opponent in his wake, Wright then advanced on goal and lobbed a precise pass to Fazackerley who had the simple task of converting. Three minutes later Sammy Stevens won a duel with Fulham's full-backs and shot well clear of the Fulham goalkeeper to increase the lead. The margin flattered the Tigers given Fulham's attacking efforts, but City's win was founded on hard work, perseverance and ruthless opportunism. It was the club's first away win proper in the Cup, and the latest in a string of impressive displays in the capital. Sturdy individual performances abounded all over the pitch; O'Connell, unfussy, efficient and simple; Gordon, by now the longest-serving player at the club, as mobile as he had even been throughout his career and exuding youthful happiness at the end; and Tim Wright, the speedy half-back, who repeatedly retrieved lost possession, as City soaked up the pressure.

The draw for the next round was extremely favourable for the Tigers. The winners of the Newcastle United-Bradford City tie would face a trip to Anlaby Road. Both these First Division teams had won the competition in the previous three seasons and would therefore guarantee a large crowd to pack out the cramped Anlaby Road enclosure. Newcastle duly eliminated the West Yorkshire side and the city prepared itself for its biggest game yet.

Hendry, The Tigers' Custodian.

W. HENDRY,
Goalkeeper, Hull City F.C.

HENDRY (CITY), THE HUMAN OCTOPUS, TO WHOM "SATURN" PAID A TRIBUTE YESTERDAY.

City's win at Craven Cottage was greeted with great enthusiasm in Hull.

Reflecting on the size of the crowd the game would attract, speculation turned to the capacity of the ground. Director Jack Bielby, who was involved in all building work at the ground, asserted that it could hold 23,000. The clash of dates between Hull's first game with Hunslet at the Boulevard and City's cup-tie was unfortunate for both clubs. City, however, did not entertain any concerns about the impact of this counter-attraction, such was the allure of the Cup and the famous visitors. They even raised the admission price to one shilling. Rumours abounded that City had been offered £1,000 to switch the venue by Newcastle, but that City had held firm and declined, thereby depriving themselves of at least £500, as it was reckoned that City – after expenses – would only have £400 clear profit from the tie. But by playing at Anlaby Road, they increased their chances of progress into the next round (and hence further revenue).

The team installed themselves at the Alexandra Hotel in Bridlington to prepare for the game and in their usual style passed the days before the game in relaxed surroundings, spending their time in either training on the grass in front of the hotel or in light-hearted seaside pastimes. On the Monday, a keen frost and blue skies greeted the players. The sea was flat and unusually calm, and manager Ambrose Langley suggested a fishing expedition to general enthusiasm. After breakfast the players donned their greatcoats and headed for the harbour. Rows of cod were arranged on the pier and Tommy Nevins expressed the view that a larger boat would provide a more comfortable experience. As the players tentatively stepped on board, Davy Gordon jokingly exclaimed: 'Tell the wife I died like a Britisher'. Once on board, Fazackerley and Nevins seized the fishing tackle with gusto but others appeared less enthusiastic at the rocking of the boat. It was deceptively cold and the apparently calm sea possessed a definite swell, causing the boat to rise and fall alarmingly in the water.

The cold turned noses red and fingers blue, as the hooks were baited and the tackle made ready, but the fish appeared uninterested. Tommy Nevins was the first to announce that all was not well, and he promptly hung over the side of the boat with his head down. Sympathy was in short supply as Nevins' plight was briefly the butt of the players' humour. But there were a few who were suspiciously quiet and before long, Goode joined Nevins at the boat side. Taylor, Fazackerley, McDonald, Stevens, O'Connell and Hendry soon succumbed. Manager Langley with McQuillan, Gordon and Boyton weathered the storm, and Stevens, despite his sickness, managed to keep spirits up singing: 'Everybody's doing it, do-(pause)-doing it. Everybody's-(long rest)-doing it-(oh, dear)-now.' In the meantime, there was no sign of any fish. 'How can you expect the fish to bother with old mussels after such a good feed?', asked one of the players. As the boat headed back to the harbour and the lines were hauled in, it was found that Stan Fazackerley's line had a fish at the end of it, much to the amazement of the gathering. Their jubilation was tempered by the realisation that the forward had thus won the sweep.

Once back on dry land, the players somewhat sheepishly made their way back to the hotel for a very light lunch followed by a sharp walk on the sands, and appetites were soon restored for teatime. The next day the normal training routine was resumed: sprinting in the morning on the beach, walks in the afternoon. If the tide was high in the morning the regime was reversed.

A billiard tournament was started to while away the evenings and maintain a competitive edge among the players. Poor weather restricted outdoor activities and as the week passed, the players continued their sprints, following them with hot saltwater baths.

His Masterpiece.

The drawing by the Tiger of Newcastle or Bradford City is looked upon as the best of its career.

Local cartoonist Ern Shaw depicts the players preparing at the seaside.

Another walk towards Flamborough was undertaken when the weather relented, but nothing too strenuous which might risk the players getting a cold. Interest in the tie in Bridlington was such that a special train was arranged from the resort, local football matches being cancelled to enable players to travel to see the game. The Tigers themselves travelled back to Hull on the 12.17, which was due to arrive into Paragon at 1.31 just as the turnstiles opened at the ground. The one-shilling admission fee (the game was not all-ticket) would allow the spectators into the east and north stands. It was reported that:

> "The admission to the east stand will be two shillings, and the centre portion, reserved, five shillings. The entrance to the two shillings and five shillings seats is through the Cricket Ground."

The day of the game saw frenzied scenes with thousands of people thronging the city centre as at least five special trains from Newcastle arrived, adding to the crush of people seeking to board an 'A' tram up Anlaby Road to the ground. As part of their extensive coverage of the match, the Hull Daily's 'Nimrod' submitted an article capturing the manic excitement and bustling energy in the city on the day of the long-awaited game. His enthusiasm and skill in conveying the electricity of the occasion formed a valuable supplement to the more prosaic factual reporting of the game itself:

> "All roads led to Anlaby-rd this afternoon. What with the struggle for the English Cup on the one side, and the duel for the Hospital Cup on the other, there was toothsome fare for the most confirmed of epicures. Callous brutes pushed their elbows into your optics and crushed your favourite corns as you fought your way into the tram marked 'A'. There was no time for apology, and if there had been I don't suppose it would have been offered. It was every man for himself and the devil take the hindmost. It was a triumph of might over right. There was only one way for the little 'un, and that was to squeeze between the legs of the mighty. Once you got in, there was no risk of falling out. You were wedged in too tightly for that.
>
> Everybody has got it real bad – the most malignant form of it. The epidemic ravaged all ranks from the hysterical schoolboy to the gray-bearded revered seigneurs. Enthusiastic juniors have had such a virulent attack of the fever that they suffered the strangest lapses and incurred the risk of receiving premature notice of dismissal, by addressing heads of departments as Mr Fazackerley, Mr Nevins etc., or substituting 'Dear Mac,' 'Dear Hendry,' etc. for the time honoured 'Dear Sir'. There has been a slump in the 'Deadwood Dick' Library, which has not had an 'earthly' with 'Saturn's' thrilling accounts of

the training operations. The remarkable fortitude displayed by the Tigers when suffering from the pangs of mal-de-mer, has now become a landmark in history, while the denizen of the sea captured by Fazackerley, has now developed into a whale, if not an ichthyosaurus. I did hear that the reason the local militants did not smash windows in the city was because they were too 'wropt up' in the Cup-tie and could think of nothing else, no, not even the ill-fated Franchise Bill.

What a pity some antidote for this epidemic cannot be put on the market. If it could, a fellow might get a chance of a bit of dinner. As it is, he's got to rise betimes in the morning, rush through his work at breakneck speed, and on top of this, make one mad dart Westward ho! Sheer Yankee hustle isn't in it! If he has time to call at

Newspaper shots of the scenes outside the ground before the Cup-tie. Ladies in bonnets, young lads selling souvenirs, and a bit of a scramble for the 'A' tram.

Hohenrein's and speculate in the succulent saveloy or the savoury pork pie, he is lucky. But there was little chance for the luxury of a well-filled 'bread-basket' to-day. 'Gates open at one-thirty' was the official announcement, and my word, if you were not off, the gates were likely to be shut on you. Everybody knew the full significance of the proclamation 'First come first served'.

You'd got to take what the gods gave you if you hadn't invested to the extent of one solid dollar. Comfort and corrugated iron for the early birds; exposure and leaden canopy of heaven for the hindmost. Not table d'hotes to-day. Anything, even a dog biscuit, with a pen'north of 'all 'ots' by way of dessert, was good enough. Talk about the sacrifices of the ancients! What have they to show compared to today? Would they have sacrificed a five-course dinner, have braved the vagaries of an English climate to see a gladiatorial display? Not much.

Of course it had all been cut and dried. My barber vouched for it, and there was no getting away from it. What he doesn't know about football isn't worth knowing, He is the confidant of the directors. He doesn't attend the matches, because, as he gets his information direct from headquarters, there is really no necessity, and it would be a waste of valuable time. 'It's going to be a draw, one-one,' he observed. 'It's all been arranged.' "How d'ye know?' inquired an unkempt and unshaven youth who had dispensed with his services for a month at least. 'Never mind you mind how I knows. I knows, and that's enough. I keep my eyes and my ears open. I have gents come in 'ere wot knows summat. Besides your own commonsense oughter tell you that the clubs are not going to throw away the chance of getting another thousand quid. Not likely.' That settled it. You can't argue with a walking encyclopaedia like that. You must take what he says for granted.

Oh, that 'Robert!' How it stuck in the gills of the proletariat! Fourpence for Lloyd George, an extra sixpence for football, and bang goes four pints of nut-brown nectar! Why can't football clubs base the fee for admission on the amount of income? Why should the unemployed, who earn nothing at all, be debarred from their precious football, the only ray of sunshine in their lives? What if barriers did give way and stands collapse? What if every mother's son was made most confoundedly uncomfortable? What odds if there were a few broken limbs? What if no football match could be played at all? What did it matter? It was the same for one as it was for another.

Besides, look at the 'Geordies' coming all the way from Newcastle having to pay twice over at least on top of the railway fare.

Spies direct from the camp of the enemy had reported that the Tigers were considered 'no class.' Prior to the signing of the treaty, there was an impression to that effect in this district. But since then there has been a change for the better, and the Tigers had been proving that they were their old selves again. They had been very hard to beat, a fact which Preston, Fulham and Clapton would doubtless testify to if called upon. Look how comfortably they disposed of last week, and you all know, what tough customers they have been. Let only our half-backs keep up the fine form they had shown during the month and the 'Geordie' would see whether they were 'no class' or not.

We have heard the same disparagement before. It was applied to the Tigers when they played Tottenham, but all the same the latter had to make three attempts before they could settle the bets. And they might not have done it then if they hadn't had the advantage of being at home. The same censure came again when the Tigers were required to tackle Woolwich at home, but they nevertheless made a draw, and they didn't half scalp the 'Reds' in the replay on the Anlaby-road ground. A mauling of the animal by Aston Villa was in the nature of a confirmation of the indictment, but displays in Cup-ties against Chelsea, Oldham Athletic and Fulham showed that the censure was undeserved. The optimists were cheered by the remembrance of the gallant struggle the Tigers made at Newcastle when the Novocastrians were at the zenith of their fame, and that they had succumbed to several teams of moderate standing in the 'sudden death' competition. Bolton Wanderers, Bury, Southampton, Crystal Palace, Wolverhampton Wanderers, Derby County, and last, but not least, our dear friends Grimsby, have all at times been their undoing. Remembering these, there was hope for the Tigers in the levelling-up contest this season.

The general expectation with regard to the crowd was quite realised. Half-an-hour before the time for the kick off it all was calculated that the attendance did not fall far short of 20,000. A friend of mine from the North reported the inward traffic as being very considerable, five heavily-laden specials having preceded him. The struggle for the trams in the Square was a sight for the cinema operator. Talk about fighting for a place. It was a fight and no error. In fact, a resort to Shanks's pony would have saved a considerable amount of time and energy.

The crowd was wonderfully restrained. Quite decorous they were, and those little pleasantries which beguile the tedium of waiting were hardly noticeable. Perhaps the charms of rag time discoursed by the band soothed the savage breasts, or perhaps it was that their voices could not compete with 'Alexander's ragtime band'. At ten minutes to three the band had had enough. They had expended their wind to the public satisfaction, and they received a round of applause when they gracefully retired.

Punctually at eight minutes to the appointed hour a big roar signalled the appearance of the Tigers, who at once proceeded to experiment with Hendry. Three minutes later the 'Geordies' had the opportunity of cheering their men on, and they made no mistake about it. It was evident that the visitors would not suffer for want of encouragement."

After such eager anticipation locally, the game itself proved to be something of an anticlimax both in quality and in excitement. Perhaps the best chance of the game fell to Newcastle's Wilson in the very first minute as he flashed a left-foot drive past Hendry's far post. The visitors started

Gordon Wright welcomes Newcastle captain and future City manager Bill McCracken to Anlaby Road.

the game full of confidence and their accomplished fluent football left the Tigers chasing shadows or seemingly standing back in admiration at times. Newcastle were guilty of over-elaborate play on the soft and sticky Anlaby Road pitch, and City usually managed to snuff out the danger before the visitors were able to create a genuine chance. As with the Fulham tie, City seemed content to let their opponents take the initiative as long as their goal was not threatened. City successfully continued this tactic until the interval, after which they played a much more expansive game, swinging the ball out to the wings with some attractive passing. Now it was Newcastle's turn to surrender the initiative, as the Tigers stamina and conditioning came to the fore. The visitors withdrew deeper and deeper towards their own goal, packing their own area and seemingly content to hang on for a replay. The Tigers' again had successfully executed their 'defend first half – attack second half' strategy, and their second half dominance outshone their opponents' efforts in the first half.

Nevins as usual defended robustly in his familiar 'bustling' way, partnered by McQuillan whose more considered and constructive style formed an effective rearguard, as well as providing cover for his team-mate on the rare occasions when he was caught out of position. Davy Gordon put in another tireless performance, easily subduing Newcastle's renowned Jack Rutherford. Perhaps the pick of the Tigers was Patsy O'Connell, who faced Newcastle's top-class forwards, reputed to be among the cleverest and most inventive in the land, and came out comfortably on top. He was reportedly:

> "... beaten on occasions, and at times was bluffed, but these occasions were rare, whilst the number of times he came out on top were very numerous. Not only did he take the ball from the Newcastle forwards, but he also gave his own forwards possession, whenever he had the opportunity. 'Patsy' had a rather bad week at Bridlington. He was awfully sick on Monday, and was badly trounced in the billiard handicaps, but he would get his full satisfaction on Saturday. O'Connell is quite on the crown of his form at present, and should again be selected for Ireland."

Gordon Wright found the going tough against the redoubtable Bill McCracken who kept him firmly in check, and on the rare occasions Wright was able to evade him, he was unable to take advantage of the openings. As a Corinthian winger, Wright played the game in keeping with that Amateur club's philosophy and in this game he spurned an inviting chance, since selfishly shooting for goal or keeping possession by going it alone were alien to that club's ethos. Wright saw himself as creator of chances for others, his role being to receive the ball from his inside forwards, go round the opposing fullback and provide inviting crosses or passes to the onrushing forwards. Up front, Fazackerley and Stevens provided a constant threat especially in the second half and Newcastle goalkeeper Lawrence was glad to clear his lines on a number of occasions, as the pair challenged menacingly for through-balls.

A goal-less draw was a more than satisfactory result for both teams, both on the pitch and financially, as the lucrative replay would bring in even more money. The receipts from the tie were £1,061 15s. It was reckoned that the ground could still accommodate more spectators and that Jack Bielby's estimates of some 23,000 paying fans as a maximum capacity was probably an accurate one.

The Spion Kop was not full and other parts of the ground also appeared to have room for more. As had been the case with the Chelsea tie in 1909, the economics and convenient financial benefits of a draw were not lost on the more cynical observers. A local paper reflected on City's gritty performance and their tenacious character against their more sophisticated and renowned opponents, observing:

> "The Tigers, on their part have done all that was expected of them. They have maintained the high Cup-tie traditions of the club – these traditions that seem to be handed down intact from team to team almost as some qualities are handed down from father to son. There is a sort of 'hereditary big-heartedness' about the Tigers in the Cup-Ties."

Reflecting on the draw after the game, Gordon Wright declared that: 'There was not the slightest weak spot about our defence, which I repeat here, is the finest we have ever had in the history of the club.'

City fans wishing to attend the replay at St James' Park were catered for by a 'fast excursion' costing 5s 3d, leaving Paragon at 9.30 arriving in Newcastle at 12.25, the players themselves also travelling on this service after a few days' preparation on the coast, this time Hornsea being the preferred location.

It was reckoned that City's best chance of beating Newcastle had been in the second half at Anlaby Road. City established a firm grip on the game, but they had failed to make the superiority count and the balance of power swung back in favour of the First Division side, who would be playing on their home ground in front of a large partisan crowd. Unfortunately for City, the F.A. Council had ruled that Sunderland had to replay their tie with Manchester City on the same afternoon, and although Newcastle were only charging sixpence against Sunderland's shilling, many spectators from outlying areas had been attracted to Roker Park, thus lowering the gate receipts at Newcastle by a figure estimated to be in the region of £300-£400. City's fruitful recruiting and scouting methods in the North East meant that their team contained more Tyneside players than the expensively-assembled home side, and their fans in the crowd numbered roughly the equivalent of the Newcastle fans at the Anlaby Road game.

Given the disparity in talent between the two sides, City seemingly had no alternative but to employ the same strategy again and seek to 'hustle' their opponents, preventing them settling into their polished 'combination play' on a pitch almost without grass, which resembled a newly-rolled ploughed field. The Tigers started very brightly indeed and took the game to Newcastle who were unable to match the visitors' endeavour. Only a combination of poor finishing and good goal-keeping kept City out in the first ten minutes.

The Tigers pictured at their Bridlington hotel
before the Newcastle replay.

After 12 minutes Nick Hendry dropped a Wilson corner in front of Hibbert who converted. Worse was to follow two minutes later when O'Connell brought down a Newcastle attacker, allowing Hudspeth to convert the penalty. Two-nil down against the run of play with 14 minutes gone against one of the country's top sides, meant that City needed something extraordinary to be able to rescue the situation. Newcastle in the meantime finally played with a hitherto-absent swagger and fluidity. Rutherford added a third after 50 minutes and put the result beyond doubt, and despite their most determined efforts, City were unable to breach the defence so excellently co-ordinated by the shrewd Bill McCracken, who regularly caught Gordon Wright offside.

Contrasted with a few days earlier, City's forward line lacked sparkle and energy, and the Tigers could have no complaints on the day, putting in a good performance against a Newcastle side who (eventually) played in keeping with a side possessing some of the best footballers in the land before a 32, 278 crowd paying £1,061 2s 6d.

In February chairman Alwyn Smith, vice-chairman Kenneth Wilson and secretary Jack Haller resigned from the board in what was – at least publicly – an amicable and controversy-free move. Increasing business commitments were cited as the reason, and generous tributes were paid to the trio for the dedication, energy and time expended on furthering the club's progress since 1905. The club's mediocre season may have had some bearing on these resignations – whether a sense of failure or even an indirect invitation to others to take the club forward were the underlying motives is not recorded. Certainly it may have been felt in

some quarters that it was the turn of others to take up the baton, as the momentum of a few years earlier had seemingly vanished.

Smith was presented with a gold medal inscribed 'Hull City A.F.C. A.D. Smith, Esq., chairman 1905-1913. This token gives the freedom of the home of Hull City A.F.C.' and a handsomely-illuminated address on vellum signed by the directors, which read:

> "At the time Mr Alwyn Dudley Smith joined the Hull City AFC Company Ltd., the club was only in its infancy, endeavouring to introduce Association football to the public of Hull. The club had no standing in any competition, neither had it a home. Mr Smith, however, retired from the chairmanship at the end of eight years, with the club in possession of a well-appointed ground, a sound footing in two competitions, and, what no doubt he would appreciate better than anything else, an established reputation for sport."

Wilson also received a medal giving him the 'freedom of the home of Hull City A.F.C.', which he was to receive upon his return from the South of France. Smith made way for Councillor James Spring, a board member who had served as long as Smith, and a member of the firm A. Spring and Co. Ltd, the Hull trawler owners. Spring served in South Newington ward for Hull Corporation, as well as being president of the Hull Fish Merchants' Association and president of the Hull Bowling Club.

Jack Haller, meanwhile, agreed to continue as secretary until such time as his replacement was appointed. He was instrumental in City's election to the Second League in the summer of 1905, having put forward the case for the club in front of the assembled members of the other clubs. His arrival at the club a year earlier was as a consequence of his long-term involvement in local football in the previous 13 years with Albany F.C. and then the East Riding F.A, for whom he had been committee man, honorary secretary, vice-president and finally honorary auditor. He was also City's representative in the Midland League (in which the club's reserve team played).

The team continued to misfire, winning as many games as they lost and failing to eliminate the worry of a possible re-election battle. Speaking to a local journalist on the Fish Dock shortly after becoming the new chairman, Spring spoke quickly to damp down any talk of re-election saying:

> "We are in no way getting into a panic ...
> We are going to rectify our position, and feel certain that we shall get a little higher ...
> There is no fear of us getting in the bottom two ...
> We shall end a long way above the danger zone."

Speaking of the relationship between the club and the supporters, Spring spoke bluntly:

> "The public hardly gives the support it should do when it especially requires it. They leave a team at a time when it requires most support, and I am afraid they do not take into consideration the adversities that have been encountered in one season ... What club could be more unfortunate than to lose three first team forwards injured – Temple, Best and Chapman – all in one season?"

James Spring.

... he said, referring to the serious long-term injuries which all three had sustained. Addressing the future direction of the club under his chairmanship, Spring said:

> "At any rate we are bent upon building up a creditable team, but we are not going to do anything with a rush or get into a panic, for, as I have indicated, we have nothing to be afraid of."

While the injuries to the forwards had hampered the attack, the goal-scoring prowess of Stevens and Fazackerley had nevertheless made City a potent threat to many defences in the division. Fazackerley had rapidly established himself as a sophisticated and clever player, adjusting to league football as quickly as Tommy Browell had in his first full season. Like Tommy 'Boy' Browell before him, Stan Fazackerley was a young prolific goal-scorer sold off by the Tigers for a substantial fee to balance the books. His record of 19 goals in 29 games – in less than 12 months between April 1912 and March 1913 – had alerted First Division clubs to his raw talent. In his final game for City he scored a hat-trick as Grimsby Town were thrashed 5-0 on 15th March. Sheffield United had a representative at that game and with a transfer deadline swiftly approaching, offered the City directors £1,000 for his services. Given that the club had paid £50 for him 12 months earlier, this seemed excellent business. The fee received would now pay the players' wages for the summer and stabilise the club's finances. From the fans' point of view, this was further proof of the club's lack of ambition and readiness to trade their prize assets, rather than keep them so as to attempt promotion to the First.

'Fazzy' had quickly become a firm favourite at Anlaby Road and was considered to be 'a good height for a forward, and has a nice command of the ball' by local journalist C.E. Sutcliffe. One of the Football League officials present at the Grimsby game, wrote in 'The Umpire':

Stan Fazackerley

£500

STANLEY FAZACKERLEY

WORTH HIS WEIGHT IN BRONZE.

Stan Fazackerley sketched above by R W Lawson, after his hat-trick against Grimsby. It was to be his last City game in black and amber.

Fans make their feelings known in the local papers about the sale of Fazackerley (right), and 'Fazzy' in action (above).

SUPPORTER'S OPINION.

TO THE EDITOR OF THE "DAILY MAIL."

SIR,—Yet another "bomb" has exploded at Anlaby-road. As one of the supporters of Hull City, I do not think that the transfer of Stanley Fazackerley will be hailed with any great delight.

This great player has brought City to many victories this season, and without his help I think I can safely say City would have been a jolly sight nearer the bottom of the table than they are at present.

If it is more money the City directors require, this is not the right way to go about it. If City were a First Division club, the gate would certainly be bigger and that would mean more money. I am confident that the Hull football enthusiasts would willingly support a First Division club could we get one.

How on earth do we expect to get in the First Division with a depleted team such as it is now? All our best players have gradually gone to First Division clubs, and are making a name for themselves, and the club which has given them their "birth" is struggling to escape re-election!

Yet the directors can afford to transfer players of talent such as Leafe, Toward, Browell, and now Fazackerley. Would it not be better to get some ready-made players?—I am, Sir, etc.,

A STAUNCH SUPPORTER.

March 17th, 1913.

Bradford threaten the City goal on 12th April 1913.

"I should much prefer Fazackerley at inside right, for he commands the ball in clever style. He is far from an ideal centre, notwithstanding his three goals. He is a Buchan in the raw, and if he is content to be modest, will make a great player."

'Tim' Wright reflected towards the end of his career, when assessing the best players who had played alongside him: 'I consider Stan Fazackerley probably the greatest player I ever played with.' Given the longevity of Wright's career either side of the Great War and the number of players who lined up in the City team with him in all of those games, it was an accolade indeed. Thankfully the sale of Fazackerley, accompanied by an

immediate slump in form and league-placing as the Tigers went five games without a win, did not have a lasting impact. The Tigers then won their final four games to finish the season in twelfth place – their lowest-ever final placing, but still a better one than had seemed likely only a few weeks earlier. Their form throughout had been utterly unpredictable as they searched for an elusive consistency.

It was not only the directorate which witnessed departures. Club captain Gordon Wright's association with the club was coming to an end some seven years after he first took the field in a black and amber jersey. Manager Ambrose Langley, too, was leaving for a post at his old club Sheffield Wednesday, who enjoyed the First Division status that he had endeavoured to secure for the Tigers.

Hull's Imperial Hotel hosted a dinner on April 25th 1913, as the club held a farewell function to honour Wright, who was leaving England to pursue an engineering career in South Africa, and also departing manager Ambrose Langley, who received a smoker's cabinet from the club. One of his early signings, Harry Simmon, made the presentation and stated that the greatest pleasure an old player could have were thoughts of the past. A contemporary account of proceedings sets the scene:

Eventual champions Preston drew 2-2 at Anlaby Road on Easter Monday.

"The chair was occupied by the Hull City goalkeeper, E. Roughley, who, in calling upon D. Gordon to make the presentation, said both recipients had rendered good services to the clan and it was a great pleasure for the players to offer some token of esteem to Mr. Wright on his departure.

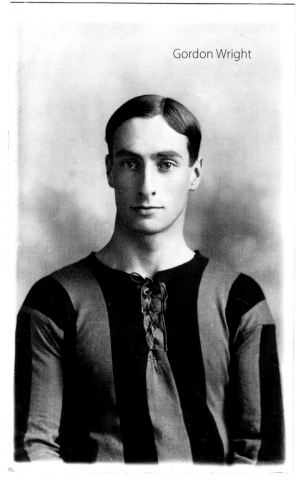

Gordon Wright

Mr Wright's interest in the Hull City team had been great during the past eight years, and many admirers went to the ground specially to see him. They regretted his leaving, but were sure all the directors, players and followers of the Hull City Club would join with him in wishing him success when he reached the other side. Thanking the players for their gift, Mr Wright said he valued more the spirit that had prompted the members to make it. He could assure them that he would value the present as one of his most cherished possessions. He felt very much that he was leaving them all, because he had

BECOME ATTACHED TO THE CLUB,

players, ground, and everything connected with it. No one was more sorry to leave than himself. The one thing he valued during his stay and the time he had played with the club, was that even though he was an amateur, the players always treated him as one of themselves. That was the one thing he wanted more than anything. They had

Gordon Wright in full-flight on the wing at Anlaby Road.

always asked him to join with them in their social functions, and they had never treated him in a 'standoffish' manner. He was proud to recognise every player as a personal friend, for he had not made a single enemy. He had been seven seasons with the club, and his heart had always been with it. He had never wished to play with any other club because he had always been made at home. He thanked them for the personal kindness shown to him not only as a player, but as a man (applause)."

Davy Gordon, in making the presentation to Gordon Wright, which comprised a diamond scarf pin, and gold cuff links, said the gift had been subscribed to by the players. Mr Wright had been connected with the team for eight seasons, and had always played as an amateur. He (the speaker) had been playing with the club all the time, and in every match Mr Wright had played in, his heart had been in the right place and he had done his best in the interests of the club (applause). Off the field, Mr Wright had always been the same as on the field –

A TRUE SPORTSMAN

(hear, hear). On one or two occasions, Mr Wright had done what few would not have thought of, and that showed his sportsmanship when playing Fulham the Hull club were given a corner kick, and Mr Wright somehow missed the kick, as he did not agree with the decision, thinking Hull were not entitled to it. This was one instance of his true sporting spirit. He (the speaker) was a bit of a sportsman, but he did not think he would have done that.

With the season over, City once again crossed the North Sea to play against Continental opposition – this time to Belgium to play Racing Club Brussels in the De Decker Cup (which they had won on two previous occasions) on May 11th. City duly triumphed 6-0 with new signing, Bill Halligan, scoring four goals. 'Looker On' sailed with the group and reported back the highlights of the trip to readers back in Hull:

"We arrived here safely on Saturday night after a crowded ride in the train. The weather was simply awful, and we were told that it had been raining here for twenty-four hours. In the evening we went to a music hall. Yesterday the Tigers were early astir, the weather then being simply glorious, and very hot. Brussels was very busy yesterday, it being the holidays, and the people began to pour into the city at a very early hour. After lunch we took the tramcar to the football ground. I do not want my readers to think that it is a similar ride to that in Hull, as the ground is about halfway to the famous battleground of Waterloo and it took us about three-quarters of an hour to get there. The ground of the Racing Club is very beautifully situated. There are also tennis courts and cricket pitches adjoining."

As to the game itself:

"Our match was originally arranged with the Daring Club, but the authorities here decided to alter things, and we played a picked team from the Brussels club and Bruges. The kick off was at 5 p.m., and the weather was very hot and not a breath of wind."

City kicked off facing a very bright sun and went a goal up in the first half as Halligan received a pass from Gordon just into the Racing half. Heading the ball over the centre-half, he beat the fullbacks before converting. With the sun at their backs in the second half, City quickly gained total control of the game with a long low drive from Tim Wright. Davy Gordon 'nearly broke the net' from a Tim Wright corner and Halligan scored a further three. In the last 20 minutes McConnell and the team eased off, and were content to pass the ball around in an aimless but pretty fashion.

Despite this, Davy Gordon was very magnanimous as he received the trophy. He thanked the Belgians for their hospitality, and remarked that although the better team won, he considered the Belgians the best team that City had ever met on the Continent, adding that the day was not far distant when such a team as they had played would hold their own against good-class English football. Summing up the season in the Hull Daily Mail, the journalist 'Saturn' once again adopted a questioning stance as he considered the events of recent months:

"The end of the season which has not been one which the Tigers can look upon with any feelings of gratification and joy, has arrived with the Tigers in a better position than at one time appeared possible. By winning their last four League matches the Tigers have surprised their most staunch supporters, and have in a matter of 15 days secured as many points as the previous three months yielded. This is an excellent sign that the Tigers have succeeded in getting together a useful set of players, who next season will give a good account of themselves. Mr Harry Chapman is decidedly optimistic, and asserts that the Tigers have got together a team which will prove above the average merit. The Chairman has given out that the Tigers are going to adopt a more progressive policy and intend to make a bold bid for the First Division.

This, I may say, is the first occasion on which a chairman of the City Club has publicly advocated a progressive policy, and undoubtedly the present marks the beginning of a new era for the City Club.

The past season has not produced as many promising young players as usual. McDonald and Stevens have improved wonderfully, and Fenwick has shown that knows the way to the net, whilst in Hendry the Tigers have discovered a first-class goalie. McQuillan and O'Connell have shown consistent good form, and Gordon and Tim Wright have assisted in keeping up the reputation of the half back line. The forwards, however, have not proved successful, and, except on rare occasions, have been disappointing. I understand that before another season opens the Tigers are hoping to secure one or two forwards who are expected to strengthen this department.

Financially the season has been far from a success. The cup-ties, thanks to the Newcastle matches, panned out very well, and the transfer of Fazackerley also brought in a goodly sum, but the 'gates' have been most disappointing, and when the gates open next September it is expected that the club will be £2,000 in arrears.

The cause of the decrease in the attendance is the fault of the moderate form shown by the team as the public of Hull, as elsewhere, refuse to support a losing team. Furthermore, the public prefer a more progressive policy than the club have shown in the past, but the official announcement that the future policy is to be more to the liking of supporters will doubtless see the interest in the Tigers as lively as ever. The chairman is of the opinion that Hull could and would support a First Division team, a statement with which we quite agree."

In his weekly Saturday newspaper column on May 3rd, Gordon Wright said his goodbyes to the sporting public of Hull in an article titled 'Last Adieu'. As well as the obligatory expressions of gratitude and rueful regret he – like his chairman had done a few months earlier – made telling reference to the perceived fickle nature of a section of the local support:

"The season has ended, and despite the fact that it is the worst we have ever experienced, the finish does not make such bad reading, after all. The last four League matches have been won, with the result that we scored ten goals, while our opponents have been unable to penetrate our defence. Nevertheless, we are only one point behind our previous worst. From many personal considerations, I am more than sorry that we have not done better. I should dearly have liked to have seen us attain promotion before I severed my connection with the club, but it is not to be, and I am afraid I shall have to gaze in future from afar and watch the struggle of the City club to arrive at the summit of their ambition.

I have played now for seven seasons with the club, and seven times have I been disappointed at the end of April, and now all that remains for me is to wish the City club and the Soccer-loving Hull public the very best of luck in the future. I can assure them, one and all, that when that time does come, and Hull can boast of a First Division team, no one will be more pleased and proud than I shall be. I believe that it will come, but never until the club receives better support. As the team is supported at present, the City could never hope to keep their place in the First Division should they succeed in getting there. The financial strain would be too great.

I have already expressed the deep regret which I feel on leaving the City club, which has grown very dear to me in many ways. Many happy times I have had in various parts of England while playing with them, times which I shall always look back to with pleasantest memories. One and all – public, players, press, and directors – have always treated me with the greatest kindness and consideration, and I can never forget it.

In conjunction with my fellow players during seven seasons, I have always had one thing in view, and that was Promotion. It has often made me smile when I have read or heard complaints that we never intended to get promotion, or that the directors did not wish for a place in the First Division. I have never met a single solitary player of ours to whom it ever occurred that he was not asked for his best. Promotion has ever been the one aim and object of the team and the directors since the club was founded, and I believe it will always so be.

Personally, it has always been the goal of my ambition, or else I would have given up playing for the club long ago. We nearly got it once, being just beaten on goal average, and some day I know I shall receive a Sports Express' in some far-off part of the world to tell me how Hull City attained their ambition at last. On that day my only regret will be that I had not a hand, or rather, I should say, a foot, in that achievement.

The policy of the City directors is a wise one, to get young, keen, players, and train them up in the way in which they should go. When the public support them better, there will be no need then to sell these men when they have made their mark, and they can be retained to form a team capable of reaching the first or second place in the Second Division.

In conclusion, let me once again thank the Hull public, through the columns of the 'Sports Express,' for the kindly consideration and invariable courtesy which they have always extended to me, both on and off the field. I can assure them that I shall never forget, or regret my stay in Hull, and so I bid my readers, one and all, good-bye!"

At the AGM on June 5th at the Grosvenor Hotel a loss of £322 6s 11d on the year's working was revealed. James Spring put these losses down to increased expenses, bad weather and injuries to players, amongst other things. Clearly the resignations of board members and their financial support had not helped matters. Three new replacements were revealed. George Neale, a supporter since 1904 and formerly a Stoke director, and Heinrich Bremer, a partner in Kirkebye and Bremer fruit merchants in the city, and a resident of Westbourne Avenue (it was felt that he was a timely appointment as the club sought to ensure a good spread of trades and influences locally, and hitherto this area had not been represented). Harry Chapman, whose career had effectively been terminated by a broken kneecap sustained in a reserve game at Anlaby Road against Gainsbrough the previous September, was appointed as the replacement for Jack Haller.

Examining the balance sheet in detail, Spring noted that gate receipts had topped £5,000, thanks in no small part to the FA cup-ties with Newcastle, but wages were up by more than a third to £3, 832 due to new signings and only one player leaving (Fazackerley).

Spring also drew comparisons between the gates for the games against Barnsley, Glossop, Leicester, Wolves, Bristol City and Huddersfield, and the corresponding games the previous seasons and noted that receipts were down, principally due to the bad weather on the match-days concerned.

Turning to the team's performances, he highlighted the serious injuries to Best, Chapman and Temple, and how they had affected the side's attacking capabilities. He revealed that all three players were paid their full wages of £4 per week throughout the season, which strained the club's resources to sign replacements.

In looking forward, Spring sounded a predictably optimistic note, and not for the first time the plea for public support at the turnstile was made and was linked to the club's ability to progress towards the First Division.

The departure of Gordon Wright was marked with a resolution in tribute to the player for his services and sociable disposition, and the presentation of an illuminated address to that effect. One member of the assembly, William 'Pusher' Yiend, was said to be a personal friend of the Tigers' captain, and got up to speak of Wright's sportsmanlike qualities. Yiend was a former sportsman himself – he had been an England rugby international in the late Victorian era, a powerfully-built player and a formidable opponent. He was an original Barbarian and lately a railway traffic agent or chief canvasser for the Midland Railway, based in an office in King Edward Street. As well as excelling at rugby, he also played cricket for Hull CC. His unsolicited warm words for the departing winger typified the widespread respect that Wright generated. The motion was adopted.

At the Annual Meeting of the Club on June 6th 1913 it was unanimously decided

"That the best thanks of the shareholders of the Hull City Association Football Club Co., Ltd. be tendered to

Mr. Edward Gordon Dundas Wright,

for the valuable services he has rendered to the Club for upwards of seven seasons, especially in his capacity as Captain of the team, with the sincere wish for the future welfare in his business career and the hope that at some future time we may again have the pleasure of his services as a player, and that this Resolution take the form of an Illuminated Address to be signed by the officials of the Club and presented to Mr. Wright."

The illuminated address that was presented to Gordon Wright.

HULL CITY A.F.C 1913-14   COPYRIGHT

"If we have a chance of gaining promotion, we are not going to be stopped for money. If we have not sufficient, we shall apply to our supporters to come to our assistance."

Councillor James Spring, Chairman Hull City A.F.C. September 1913.

Manager Ambrose Langley might have gone but his place – and boater – had been taken by Harry Chapman (at the right of the middle row), who James Spring described as 'the finest judge of a footballer I know'. Also shown in this year's team photograph are: Back row (left to right): Davy Gordon, James McIntosh, Jack Lee, James Briggs, Sammy Stevens and Henry McCorry. Standing: Harry Taylor (trainer), Austin Fenwick, Joe Edelston, Patsy O'Connell, Nick Hendry, Ted Roughley, Arthur Temple, John Pattison and Harry Chapman (manager). Seated: Tim Wright, John Boyton, Billy McDonald, Billy Halligan, Tommy Nevins, Jack McQuillan and Joe Potts. Seated on the grass: Bob Hewitson, Douglas Morgan, Sam Lyon and Andy Byrne.

The farewell dinner in April, after Gordon Wright's last game for the Tigers, was not his final appearance for the club. Some five months later, with the team engaged in pre-season training, a series of cricket games were arranged against local opposition, with Wright captaining the Tigers XI. Teams from Willerby (comprised of asylum attendants), Langwith Colliery and a local Fruit Trade XI provided the opposition on the 14th August, plus another formed by Licensed Victuallers.

On the 18th August, in the large dining hall at the Grosvenor Hotel, another event was held in Wright's honour. On this occasion the shareholders thanked him for his efforts on the club's behalf. An hour and a half of speeches presided over by Mr J. Spring the chairman, included contributions from Davy Gordon (again), Teddy Roughley, the goalkeeper, and Patsy O'Connell. A presentation followed, consisting of a case of mining instruments, a set of books relating to mining work and a handsomely bound album containing the following illuminated address:

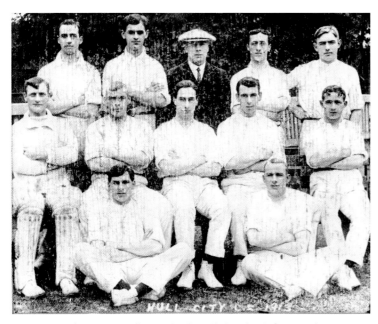

The 1913 Hull City Cricket Club, which featured
Gordon Wright for the last time.

"Presented by the Hull City Association Football Club Limited to Edward Gordon Dundas Wright, B.A., A.R.S.M., D.I.C., on his retirement from the captaincy of seasons 1906-1913. At the annual meeting of the club on June 6th 1913, it was unanimously decided That the best thanks of the shareholders of the Hull City Association Football Club Co Ltd be tendered to Mr E. G. D. Wright for the invaluable services he has rendered to the club for upwards of seven seasons, especially in his capacity as captain of the team, with the sincere wish for his future welfare in his business career, and the hope that, at some future time, we may again have the pleasure of his services as a player , and that this resolution take the form of an illuminated address, to be signed by the officials of the club, and presented to Mr. Wright. We further desire to place on record the fact that during the seasons he assisted Hull City he took part in no fewer than 280 League matches and English Cup-ties, and in doing so often sacrificed, quite voluntarily, much valuable time which he might reasonably have been expected to devote to his own private requirements and studies.

Moreover, owing to living away from Hull, he travelled many thousands of miles in the exercise of his captaincy, which we recognise as proof indeed of his whole-hearted desire for the club's success. The fact of his being a Cambridge Blue when he joined us was greatly in our favour and his captaincy undoubtedly was a dominant factor on the morale of the team with whom he was universally popular.

We congratulate him on being the possessor of twenty Amateur caps, one International, and the South African Badge and Gold Medal. During the same period we were honoured as a club by his selection in many international matches, not only in the United Kingdom, but also in France, Denmark, Belgium, Holland, Sweden, Germany, Switzerland and South Africa. During part of the time he also toured with the Corinthians in Germany, Holland, South Africa, the United States and Canada. We now desire, therefore, to wish him the utmost success in the future, and that it may always have as happy associations for him as his as his career has with us in the past is the sincerest wish of (signed) James Spring (chairman),

A Bulay Glossop (vice chairman)
James Barraclough
J.H. Bielby
H. Bremer
J.A. Dickenson
H.S. Holden
Geo. W.Lilley
J.W. Locking
Ernest Morison
E.H. Mungall
Geo. A. Neale
T.W. Shaw
Alf E. Spring
F.G. Stringer
Henry Chapman (secretary)

Some interesting details emerged of Wright's time with the Tigers, as his close friend Alfred Bulay Glossop recounted how the Corinthian signed on with City in 1905 at Newcastle, and how he had been offered a place in the Irish eleven only to decline it because he wished to appear for his university. Six London clubs had tried to entice him to play for them but he had always declined them to give preference to the Tigers, for whom he had travelled thousands of miles in order to play.

Other directors paid generous and heartfelt tribute to the departing player. Alf Spring, an ex-president of the East Riding Football Association, said he had always regarded Wright one of the pillars of amateur football (applause). Jack Bielby described Wright as "a thorough sport" and hoped that he would have the same amount of success as he had with local football (applause).

Jack Haller added that the club would have a great deal of difficulty in getting Mr Wright's equal. He was a player who had given prestige to the club. The success of the club was very largely due to the example and help he had so willingly given. Their wishes went with him for his future success (applause).

After the speeches by various directors, the local journalist, Harry Comley (alias 'Veritas'), the players Davy Gordon, Teddy Roughley and Patsy O'Connell, it was the turn of Wright himself to speak. On rising he was greeted with the singing of "For he's a jolly good fellow". He said he felt it very deeply having to leave Hull. He thanked them all very much for the kind things they had said about him, and it was exceedingly kind of them to make him such handsome presents, which would so benefit him in future life. He felt it was a great personal kindness that prompted them to do so. The directors, players, press and public had always treated him as a friend and in a kindly spirit. It was with great regret he was severing his connection with Hull City, and he would always follow their movements. They knew it was a regret of his that Hull City were not in the First Division, but it would take away a good deal of the regret if they did it next season – (applause). He would still continue to say 'we' when referring to Hull City – (hear, hear) – and it was with the greatest possible regret he was going away from them – (applause).

As the players reported back for pre-season training in the hot August sunshine, new manager Harry Chapman was moved to comment that he had never seen a set of players report back so fit and yet so anxious to train, and neither could he recall a club where such a good feeling existed among the men. The previous season the Tigers had only 17 players but this time round they had 24 at their disposition – proof, in deed not just in word – that the club meant business and were determined to mount a serious attempt at promotion. Every position in the side was duplicated with a couple of players spare. The effect of long-term injuries suffered by Best, Temple and Chapman himself, which had so hampered the club the previous season, had been addressed. Chapman had retired as a result of his injury, so too had Charlie Best. Arthur Temple had had a cartilage removed at Newcastle Infirmary in the close season, and his effectiveness was still unknown.

Jack Houghton left the club to play for Fulham, Herbert Goode left to play for Wrexham, and Gordon Wright had departed for South Africa to begin his career as a mining engineer. Wright left a gap not only in terms of wing-play but also in leadership and sportsmanship. The Tigers' options appeared limited. Edwin Neve, the ideal replacement for Wright, had left for Derby County, frustrated at being unable to secure regular first team football. Fred Shaw, another Wright understudy, had departed to Portsmouth to further his prospects.

Andy Byrne, reputedly 'the smartest outside-left in Irish football' was recruited from Shelbourne, allegedly in the face of stiff competition from other English clubs. Small, fast and tricky, much was expected of him. He faced competition for that position from Jack Lee, signed in March from South Yorkshire amateur football and much taller than Byrne.

Twenty-two year old prospect Douglas Morgan was signed from Scottish club Inverkeithing United, to play in the left-back position that Jack McQuillan had come to regard as his own.

HALLIGAN, THE ARTIST, WITH THE BALL (with apologies).

"Halligan is more tricky in his methods, and appears to be an artist with the ball, which he manipulates with the cleverness of a conjuror." — "Saturn."

A caricature of Billy Halligan.

The best-known recruit was Billy Halligan who arrived from Wolves for £600 to replace Stan Fazackerley (sold for £1,000 to Sheffield United). Ulsterman Halligan came with an impressive reputation as a clever goal-scoring forward who relied on intelligence and anticipation rather than strength and athleticism. The fee was the biggest yet paid by City. Joe Edelston ('the most promising half-back in the country' according to Ambrose Langley) came from non-league football in St Helens (a fertile recruitment area for the Tigers) to complete the list of newcomers.

Long standing vice-captain Davy Gordon appeared to be heading towards reserve team football and thus, with Gordon Wright gone, captaincy of the Tigers was an unresolved matter on the eve of the new season. As well as grappling with this problem, secretary-manager Chapman also had as part of his job the role of selling season passes (along with appointed agents of the club) and these could be had for the following prices: Reserved portion £1 1s (ladies and boys 15s), Best Stand 15s (ladies and boys 8s 6d), East Stand 10s, ground 7s 6d, youths (15 and under) 4s, schoolboys 3s. Pass sales were reportedly greatly improved on the previous year, which would have been an immense relief to the directors, concerned about their financial obligations to cover an increased number of players.

The expected starting line-up was to be: Hendry, with Nevins and McQuillan as fullbacks; a halfback line of Edelston, O'Connell and McIntosh, with the five forwards consisting of Fenwick, Halligan, Stevens, McDonald and Byrne. This experimental line-up was based on pre-season form and previous seasons' displays. 'Prodigal', writing in the Daily News of the prospects for the forthcoming season – and mindful of the problems experienced the previous season – believed that:

"... the present forces will be sufficient for the day, as it is believed the way to promotion this season will not be a very difficult matter, as there seems to be no exceptionally strong opponents in the Second League at the present time".

The Hull Daily Mail's 'Saturn' identified the increased air of expectancy surrounding the club, stating that:

"The time has arrived when the club, having become firmly established, must make progress, and incidentally they are not going to be left behind by successful and progressive rivals. The public, in emphatic terms, have demanded the best, and the club is making praiseworthy efforts to cater for this demand."

Chapman introduced new training methods unlike those seen under Ambrose Langley. The so-called Swedish system was adopted, comprising a full course of physical drills, massage and ball-punching, amongst other activities. Running and skipping still formed the main part of the training but a more scientific approach was adopted than in previous years. Davy Gordon was prone to putting on weight in the summer break and for him training was arduous. But his determination and professionalism ensured that he needed little supervision or encouragement to get back into condition as he toiled in a thick woollen sweater in the August sun, reeling off lap after lap of the Anlaby Road pitch.

HULL FOOTBALLERS AT PRACTICE.

City players going through their paces in traditional pre-season fashion.

Chapman did not intervene in training too much, allowing the players to gauge exactly what was needed. His astute man-management encouraged personal responsibility rather than passive obedience – 'one volunteer is worth three pressed men'.

The optimistic mood moved one supporter to pen the following verses on Billy Halligan:

"THE 'FOUND' LINE (With apologies to the 'Lost Chord')

Seated one day on the grand stand,
Where the Tigers are at ease,
I saw twenty-two young fellows,
All of them bare at the knees.
I knew well what they were playing,
And I saw one of the "Bhoys"
Who stood out alone from the kick-off,
A disturber of goalie's joys.

He came here from Wolverhampton,
Where we once lost eight to nil,
And if my own opinion's worth aught,
He'll help us to top the bill.
His passes to either wing man
Were splendid to behold,
Yet when the game demanded,
He treasured the ball like gold.

His shooting from every position,
His trapping and tapping all through,
His clean, yet robust, charging
Are worthy of review.
Our weak spot for many a season
At last I'm sure has gone,
And our line, with Halligan centre,
Should land us in League One!

A GOULD, 10, Ella-street, Hull.

Following the final practice game 'Saturn' observed an important change in the style of football being played by City, as he noted that:

"... the Tigers did not appear to play the game which has been their characteristic since they were formed. They have ever been a mad-headed, bustling side. but judging by what we saw on Saturday, they have now adopted a more attractive and probably a more effective style. To see the ball in the air was a rarity on Saturday, yet in the past ballooning it has been a great fault with the Tigers."

In early September chairman James Spring gave a frank interview in which he expressed the traditional positive sentiments associated with any football club at the start of a season. This openness extended to revealing that he had been an ardent Hull FC fan at the time City were formed, and furthermore he had been ever since the former's Holderness Road days – pre-1895. It was Alwyn Smith who recruited him to the City board, spotting his interest in the newly-formed football club, and when

Smith retired from the board, the progressive and energetic Spring was deemed the best man to replace him. Spring reiterated the ambition of all the directors to get promotion, his faith in the present squad of players and his belief that the Hull public would back the club in terms of support. He believed that a £300 gate would adequately maintain a Division One team in the city, and that this figure would be exceeded for some attractive games. He also drew attention to the recent record crowd at the reserve team's Midland League fixture which he took to signify a growing interest and appreciation of that team's talents. He was not blind to the fact that fans in Hull more than most cities wanted to follow a winning team, and that with the city possessing three, it caused a certain level of competition to attract the less partisan follower. Fortunately the clubs were on very good terms and the competition was healthy now that any old bitterness had disappeared. Turning his attention back to the players, he eulogized the good spirit among them and paid tribute to their footballing qualities. He also reminded the readers that the wage bill this season was correspondingly high – indeed the highest ever. Halligan was the most expensive and the best signing in their history – a view shared by all of his fellow directors. Every position was duplicated by a good man, unlike the previous season when the squad was threadbare in places. When asked if the club would transfer any players, Spring, mindful of the contentious nature of the question, responded:

"We have no intention of transferring any players, in fact we are willing and anxious to further strengthen the team if the right men are found. Whether we transfer players later in the season depends entirely upon the support given by the public. If we are £2,000 or £3,000 down at the end of the year, it is only likely that we shall take steps to reduce the deficit. But I do not anticipate having any necessity to consider the question of transfers."

Clearly, the sale of Browell and Fazackerley amongst others had induced a degree of cynicism and suspicion in the minds of supporters, who had voiced their disapproval of such policies. The club, whilst always defending its decisions to sell, were no doubt aware of the damaging impact such transfers had on the relationship between itself and the fans. In other words, this disillusionment expressed itself in dwindling attendances and lack of gate receipts, which in turn led to more pressure to sell players.

As regards the supporters, Spring singled out the newly-identified increased presence of female fans and the 'elevating' effect it had. He complimented their knowledge of the game and enthusiasm, contrasting it with the disparaging remarks often heard by the players and referee at games. Barracking had a very negative effect on the players

Hull City beat Notts Forest by 1 goal, the only goal scored in the match, at Anlaby-road, on Saturday. The photographs show:—1 and 2. Hanna falling in saving hot shots from the City men. 3. Head work in midfield. :. City clearing.—"News" photographs.

Photograph taken at the Hull City ground on Saturday. The photos of those "ringed" are entitled to 2s 6d each if they will make personal application at the "News" Office.

An early newspaper competition involving photos of fans at the Nottingham Forest game. Hull beat Nottingham 1-0 in the first home game on September 13th.

Nick Hendry in action at the Woolwich – Arsenal game in London on September 22nd.

as it 'upset their tempers'. The development, or improvement of, the Best Stand by the construction of turnstiles to the rear, and an increasing in seating, had been shelved as all surplus funds were invested in team-building.

A forceful and detailed statement of intent, tempered with references to the role of the supporters set the tone for the Tigers' latest promotion attempt. In truth, despite the new chairman and his determined message, some fans may have started to wonder if they had not heard similar sentiments form the outgoing chairman Alwyn Smith.

Davy Gordon was now very much an elder statesman of the club and recognised as such by people outside the immediate confines of the club. No longer guaranteed a starting place in the team and still respected as an experienced leader associated with wholehearted endeavour, he would have a wealth of knowledge to pass on to younger players and aspiring amateurs. With this in mind, and accompanied by long time team mates and fullbacks Jack McQuillan and Tommy Nevins, on September 22nd Gordon went to Gilberdyke at the invitation of the Reverend S.C. Allderidge, the vicar of Newport, to give a talk to young local footballers on his experiences, advice and ideas. Some 40 or so aspiring footballers turned up to hear his address, in the hope of gleaning some insight from one of City's most respected and longest-serving players, and by doing so improve their own game:

"Gentlemen,
Having been asked to come here today and give a few points on the Association game, and also a few hints as to the best method of training, I willingly responded to the call. My capabilities of lecturing are not of a very high scale, but being very anxious to help in any little the advancement of the game in Hull and district, I thought I would 'take the bull by the horns,' so to speak, and give it a trial. It is one thing to advise and coach a lad on a football field and another thing to address a meeting on the subject of how to do this and how to do that on a football field, and I hope you will excuse me if I happen not to make a very grand orator.

In the first place I consider football one of the most manly games in the country. It is a game in winter-time that is very popular with the public.

I consider there are two ways of playing football – the right way and the wrong way. Of course there should only be one way, and that the right way. What I mean is this: As I said before, it is a manly sport if it is played in the right, fair and sportsmanlike manner. The game of football is really a small item which contrasts greatly with the great game of life.

The man who goes through life playing the straight and fair game is the man that is always appreciated more in the end. You get many knock down blows, as it were, but you always have the satisfaction of knowing you are doing the right thing, and it always pulls you through in the end.

My advice to everyone to-day who has any intentions of succeeding on the football field is to play the game fair and square, and if you have the ability to succeed at the game that is the right spirit to pull you through and fetch you out on the top of the tree. Always try your best to keep your temper on the field. My experience has taught me that it is a very difficult thing to do; but if you only think for a minute you will see that to lose your temper on the field is to help in your own undoing. Say, for instance, if the referee appears to give a decision against you which you don't appreciate, you, in the heat of the moment, might turn and pass some remark which, later, after careful though, you will say to yourself, was a mistake.

In this way the referee gives his decision, and if he is a man with a mind of his own he sticks to that decision. You accept it as right and the game goes on, and you feel a lot better for it; but if you resent his decision once, then perhaps the next time you do the same thing. Well, you have lost your head and nothing goes right for you.

I am talking from experience; I've been in the same boat myself a few times in my career. The result is that you go through the game prejudiced against the referee's decisions and you go clean off your game and you know it. Accept the ruling of the gentleman in charge and play the game. You finish the match a lot more satisfied. You have done your best, and although you might be beaten, accept your defeat in a sportsmanlike manner. My advice is to keep your temper if possible and try to assist the official in charge by playing the game.

Another thing I would like to mention to young lads with the ambition to succeed in football, is to always take the advice of an older player if it is given in the right spirit. Say, for instance, a young lad has a fair good idea of the game; he gets into a fairly good club, and perhaps the paper gives him a very good name for his play. Now don't let that little bit of play spoil you. For once that disease goes into your head then it is all up with you. You may have a little weakness in your play which, if remedied, will improve you greatly if an older and more experienced player points it out to you. Take notice, and try and remedy that weakness for your own good, and also for the good of the club you are assisting. Don't turn round and say you know as much as he does; that's the wrong spirit, and a spirit which will always keep you from succeeding.

Davy Gordon on a Baines card,
again wrongly described as G. Browell.

Well, when a man gets fit in the month of August and starts to play in September, and looks after himself, the match on the Saturday takes so much out of him that you don't really need a great deal of hard training. Talking from my own point of view, since I came to Hull we have always had a rest from training on Monday after a Saturday match. On the Tuesday we have the ball out, kicking in, kicking in, or doing a few passing bouts just to break a good sweat on you, and also giving you a chance to carry out any little idea perhaps that has occurred to you. Then after kicking we have a good warm bath and a cold shower, which generally makes us feel very fit.

On the Wednesday, Thursday, and Friday we put in some nice useful sprints, some about 50 yards – not starting away slowly and then breaking into a dash, but starting at the first and going the whole 50 yards at a good pace. The main thing on a football field is to get off your mark quickly. Doing some smart sprints is the thing that you want for that. Then you want to get your wind good. Well, you say run a good fast quarter-mile after you have done your sprinting, and after that if you fancy a bit of ball-punching, Indian clubs, or skipping ropes, they are all beneficial exercises, both for the wind and for development. Then there is nothing better than a good fast walk on the road – I think walking is one of the best exercises that one can go in for.

This season we are going in for a course of Swedish drill, which is also a very good exercise for developing the body. Don't forget, lads, what I said before – always play the game straight and you will succeed if it is in you, and try and help a referee on the field, as a referee's job is a very hard one."

Now as to the game itself: it is one thing to lecture how to do this and how to do that, and another thing to do it. Your intention, when you go on is always to do great things, but, of course, they don't always come off. You might find a man a bit too clever for you, or a man a bit too fast for you; but keep plodding away, and your chance may come the next week. The best of players have their off days, and don't let one bad game dishearten you, as there is a full season's results to go by. That's why I say it is a difficult job to preach about what to do before a game, as you generally do as much as you can – or, as the saying goes, as much as the man opposed to you will let you do.

Of course, a talk between the players before a match, if it is carried out on the field is bound to be a great help – and never forget, lads, that it always takes eleven men to take a team at Association football.

On the subject of training, a man that is leading a quiet and a healthy life and has not had the bad luck to put on flesh, doesn't really need a great deal of strenuous training. Training for football, is a different thing to training for, perhaps say, a big sprint handicap or a big fight. For a sprint or a fight you train for that particular event, and when the time comes you have to be as hard as nails, but for football you have eight months' strenuous play.

Despite the abundance of optimism, the Tigers started the campaign modestly. Drawn games and a shortage of goals hampered the team, as the new manager and the new players struggled to find the best deployment of their resources. Billy Halligan played in only three of the first ten games, scoring just once. His possible partnership with Sammy Stevens would take time to bear fruit. However, once the two started to play alongside each other in November, the goals and the victories started to arrive with reliable regularity. In the second quarter of the season, the Tigers embarked on a sequence of results that included seven wins, one draw and one defeat. Stevens scored ten goals in nine games and Halligan weighed in with eight, including four in one game against Wolverhampton at Anlaby Road on December 6th.

Sometime early in the 1913/14 season, City adopted a new style of jersey. The collarless lace-up version of previous seasons made way for a new jersey, with a black round-neck, as the team picture opposite illustrates. The photograph was taken by famous ex-Aston Villa footballer-turned-

1913   HULL CITY FOOTBALL CLUB.   1914

Copyright Photo.   A. Wilkes, ⌀, Legge St., West Bromwich.

TAYLOR   McDONALD.   O'CONNELL.   EDELSTON.   HENDRY.   LEE.   MacINTOSH.   LYON.
(Trainer)
        FENWICK.   NEVINS.   MacQUILLAN.   MacCORREY.   STEVENS.

THE NEWSPAPER THAT SCORES—"THE DAILY CITIZEN."

Ern Shaw's view of the Wolves victory
and Billy Halligan's role in it.

photographer Albert Wilkes, at Birmingham City's St. Andrews ground on October 4th – before the Tigers' 1-1 draw there. It was given away as a free supplement by the Daily Citizen and is one of the earliest examples of a non-local team photograph of the Tigers. Jack McQuillan, after several years' steady service, is now a senior player and is captain. Trainer Harry Taylor flanks the team on the back row, and City's goal-scorer on the day – Sammy Stevens – sits to the extreme right on the front row.

Whether it was the Swedish drill training – or the new players – didn't matter, the Tigers were climbing the league table and heading towards the summit. The old full-back pairing of Nevins and McQuillan had been replaced by Pattison and Morgan, and Patsy O'Connell skilfully marshalled the defence to lend it a durable solidity. Not that it was tested very often, as City's potent attack racked up the goals that decided the matches. Harry Chapman's inaugural season as manager had breathed new life into the team, and in this second quarter he was able to select a core of important players who served him well in every game. Healthy home attendances of around 10,000 were now the norm and a sense of growing momentum prevailed coming up to the New Year period. City were as well-placed as any other team at the halfway point of

the season, with just three defeats in the first 19 games. The festive period would have been a particularly satisfying one for all associated with the Tigers, and as if to capitalise on this spirit, a get-together was organised to reinforce the spirit that had stood them in good stead thus far. In a report by 'Glad-eye' in the Hull Daily Mail, the club's seasonal social event is described in detail, right down to the musical pieces performed and the artistes who sang them:

"City held their Christmas Dinner at the Grosvenor Hotel in the happy position of being at the head of the Second Division, after a run of eight games in which they gained six wins and two draws (both at home). The festive occasion would definitely have been enhanced by this immensely satisfying situation. A healthy goal difference added to the optimism.

Secretary-Manager Harry Chapman's recent illness prevented him from attending, but a full complement of players were present as well as chairman J. Spring, vice chairman A.B. Glossop, and directors Messrs Holden, Morison, Barraclough, A. Spring, F.G. Stringer, Bremer, J. Bielby, J.W. Locking, Shaw, Neal, J. Dickinson, Mungall, and club doctor Dr. Lilley.

Chairman Spring proposed the toast "Prosperity to the Hull City Club" in his speech and said it was rather like asking them to drink a toast to themselves but he gave it with a great amount of pleasure, inasmuch as at the beginning of the season they had said they were out for promotion, and right royally had the players assisted, and intended getting into the First Division.(Hear, hear)

Spring continued by saying that during the last week, and the season, every man belonging to the club had done everything in his power to bring them to their richly-deserved position. They had been struggling for several years, and it was now time that the city had a First Division club. He believed that in the second half of the season, the players would do equally well as in the first half. Every man could not be in the first team, but he thought that all those players not in the first team were imbued with the same idea, and would do all in their power to help to attain their object, and be ready to take their place in the first team when required (hear, hear). No favour was shown in picking the team, they had to do their best for the club and the public.

Closing his address, Spring commented that the gathering spoke well of the happy relationship between the directors and players, and he hoped it would be fostered and continued until they were in the First Division. It could be done if they put their shoulders to the wheel, always remembering that they must play the game.
Nothing would give the citizens more pleasure than to see Hull City attain promotion. The town would ring at their achievement, and he hoped their efforts would be crowned with success deserved.

One of the directors of a musical bent had arranged a musical programme to follow the meal and speeches. Mr 'Billy' Richardson was to the fore with his humorous songs which included 'The matrimonial handicap', 'The night I fought Jack Johnson', 'How are you?' and 'The Spaniard that blighted my life'. Other artistes included the baritone E.E. Draper who performed 'Because' and as an encore 'Happy moments day by day' to warm applause. The tenor Mr William Lely then sang 'Thora' and 'Come into the garden, Maud', before being asked to return with 'Until' as an encore.

Lastly, duets were sung by Messrs Lely and Draper: 'Watchman, what of the night?' (Sergeant) and 'Still as the night' (Gotze)."

City's surge of form had not gone unnoticed further afield, and various periodicals published articles speculating on the likely successful teams at the end of the season. A wide range of opinions was naturally reflected and City's promotion credentials were scrutinised, not always positively, by sporting journalists from as far afield as Leeds, Manchester and London.

WE ARE THE PEOPLE.

THE BIRD: Don't know him, do you?
THE TIGER: Scarcely; he's almost a perfect stranger to me.

We Are The People – the Tiger and the Airlie Bird saunter past Defeat.

The Daily Express:

"The great rise in the Second Division has been that of Hull City; the great fall that of Notts Forest. A year ago the City were thirteenth in the list; to-day they are at the top, and, moreover, are playing so strongly that they must be considered almost first favourites for promotion ... Most of the players are young, and their pluck is as pronounced on foreign soil as at Anlaby-road."

The Daily Chronicle:

"Hull City in many seasons have looked likely to win a place in the First League, but then prospects at the half-season have seldom looked so bright as they do now."

The Sporting Life:

"Hull City have secure the leadership for the first time this season, Notts County having fallen down two rungs. Leeds City, however, are favourably placed, having a match in hand, and being only point behind the leaders. Thus present indications point to one of the Northern clubs securing promotion."

The Leeds Mercury:

"Hull City are now worthy leaders of the Second Division of the League. It is to be feared that they will not continue their success."

The Yorkshire Observer:

"Hull City had no difficulty winning at Nottingham, but in spite of their goal average they do not strike one as being a potential First Division side."

City drew renowned Cup-fighters and fellow Second League club Bury at home in the F A Cup. Opting to stay in Hull to prepare for the game, the Tigers trained using their 'Swedish drill' methods which had served them well so far this season. The day of the game arrived with appalling weather in Hull, which rendered the playing surface very difficult and drastically reduced the expected gate to a mere 12,000. On a muddy pitch, the teams laboured to a scoreless draw, with Bury adapting better to the poor conditions by playing a simpler, less ambitious game. They sought to play the ball wide to their wingers on the better parts of the pitch. One of these wingers was old Tigers favourite Stanley Smith, who displayed his talents to no avail, as his crosses were easily dealt with by the City defence. At the other end, Bury successfully stifled Stevens and Halligan by constant close attention, showing that City did not always have the guile to break down a well-marshalled defence. The Tigers for that reason may well have fancied their chances more at Bury where the onus would be on the home side to attack. City displayed their priorities by seeking to get the game played on Tuesday, to give them an extra day to prepare for the top-of-the-table game with Woolwich Arsenal. Bury, in turn, displaying their own priorities, wanted an extra day to prepare, to give themselves the best chance of progressing.

Both City and Bury headed to Blackpool to prepare for the replay, City making the Victoria Hotel on the Central Promenade their base. Manager Harry Chapman had been sent to his family home at Kiveton, Sheffield to convalesce, after a bad bout of pneumonia worsened after the Saturday game, and versatile secretary Jack Haller temporarily took over his role for the replay.

If the game at Anlaby Road had been played in an exemplary sporting spirit, the replay was just the opposite. Within the first five minutes, and with City playing into a stiff drizzle-laden wind, Bury served notice of their intentions with a series of dubious challenges. The weak refereeing of Mr Shallcross of Leek (who replaced the referee from the first game), seemingly oblivious to the skulduggery going on around him, exacerbated the situation, allowing an ugly mood to prevail among the players. The official finally took decisive action by dismissing Billy Halligan (a player with a hitherto unblemished disciplinary record) for

SECOND LEAGUE,

POSITIONS UP TO DATE

	P.	W.	L.	D.	Goals. F.	Goals. A.	Pts.
Hull City	19	11	3	5	38	14	27
Woolwich Arsenal	19	11	3	5	29	19	27
Leeds City	18	12	4	2	42	19	26
Notts County	21	10	5	5	39	22	26
Bradford	19	12	7	0	33	27	24
Bury	19	8	6	5	24	21	21
Wolverhampton W	19	8	6	5	20	22	21
Grimsby Town	19	8	6	5	25	28	21
Fulham	19	8	7	4	26	20	20
Clapton Orient	18	6	5	7	18	16	19
Barnsley	18	7	6	5	23	23	19
Birmingham	19	7	9	3	25	32	17
Leicester Fosse	20	8	11	1	28	31	17
Stockport County	19	4	7	8	23	29	16
Bristol City	19	6	8	5	28	28	15
Blackpool	19	4	8	7	16	25	15
Glossop	18	5	11	2	19	35	12
Huddersfield Town	19	3	10	6	17	26	12
Lincoln City	19	4	11	4	15	29	12
Nottingham Forest	20	3	12	5	20	42	11

The Second Division at Christmas 1913

allegedly retaliating, after being fouled twice in quick succession by different Bury players. The players of both sides reportedly looked on in amazement. Bury's Smith told the City players that he was to blame but the referee would not listen. The same player also went into the referee's room after the game to repeat his confession. Halligan was upset and declared after the game: "I do not care about losing my wages if I am suspended. It is the disgrace which is worrying me. I never thought I should ever get ordered off a football field."

Cartoonist Ern Shaw depicts a threatening Tiger confronting the Bury Shaker, who turned out to be tougher than expected.

The damage had been done. City's influential forward – their attacking reference point – had gone, leaving four younger and less experienced players to formulate a means of breaking down Bury's doughty defence. Worse was to come. With City already one goal down, Bury's Smith (who had provoked Halligan into retaliating) punched Sammy Stevens in the eye and was dismissed in what the Hull Daily Mail described as: 'the foulest thing I have seen in football.' 'Veritas' in the Hull Daily News called it: 'as cowardly an assault on an opponent in deliberately striking Stevens in the face with his closed fist as I have seen on a football field.'

Despite the numbers being level, City (including the dazed Stevens, sporting a swollen eye) went further behind. The wind and the rain had stopped, and the Tigers had to haul themselves back into the game unaided, which they duly did with a goal from Jack Lee. Despite belatedly gaining control of the game, the visitors were unable to level the scores

and left the field bruised and aggrieved, with the sympathy of many onlookers including Tommy Browell and the next round's opponents Blackburn Rovers. Bury's cynical tactics, combined with weak refereeing, left City's players feeling rankled by a defeat at the hands of what they considered an inferior side. City received £835 from the two games, a modest sum compared to previous years but were able to reflect philosophically that this was all for the best, given their leadership of the division and desire to remain free from potentially disruptive injuries.

The game the following Saturday saw Woolwich Arsenal at Anlaby Road. The London club were separated from City by inferior goal difference. The old fullback pairing of Nevins and McQuillan was recalled for this game, following modest performances by Pattison and Morgan at Bury. In front of 12,000 fans City capitulated to their rivals 2-1 to cede their place at the top of the table.

These two cards together form a panoramic view of the crowd as it gathers for the game, on the open terrace to the east side of the Anlaby Road ground. Like most similar cards of the era, it displays a wide range of headwear and smart clothing. The cards probably date from the 1913/14 season, and the one directly above has actually been postally-used, having been franked in Hull on 26th January 1914. The sender of the card ('Will') thanks the recipient for recent hospitality offered in Grimsby (City had won there two days earlier on 24th January) and describes a 'tottering' journey back on the Humber ferry. He concludes with: "You may be able to find Alder and myself" in the crowd. Two spectators on the far left of the photograph have been marked with an 'x' – presumably Will and Alder. There is no indication, either by Duncan or the sender, of at which game the picture was taken. None of the spectators are wearing gloves or overcoats, suggesting a game played early in the season.

Other curiosities include the spectator with the pipe, the light coloured suit, the bow-tie and the boater – who also appears in the crowd postcard 228 above (presumably next in the series at the same game) and the bowler-hatted gentlemen behind him to the right, who is apparently overcome with shyness in front of the camera. To the left of the picture, the edge of the less crowded covered section of the east stand near the halfway line can be seen. In the card above, numbered 228, the crowd further toward the Anlaby Road end of the stand is shown. The same dapper pipe-smoking spectator has found his way to the right of the picture. Another cross section of spectators is seen awaiting the start of the game, reading the match programme, standing good-naturedly for the camera, or making their way towards the halfway line along the top of the terrace. In the centre a uniformed tram driver can be seen. The usual schoolboys are congregated along the wooden picket fencing.

The trip to Grimsby was a happy one and is described in detail by the Hull Daily Mail's 'Saturn':

"I was one of the many who went to support the Tigers on Saturday. In fact, the occasion reminded me of the days when the Hull club used to take an army of followers with them on their West Riding excursions. Fortunately, I made the journey in the early morning, along with the team, and so missed the experiences of the large party who journeyed later in the day, 16 and 17 in a carriage, with the guard's van packed. Unfortunately, the pickpockets were busy, the unseemly rush to and from the boat giving them an ideal opportunity to indulge in their nefarious practices. Judging from what I heard, they had a busy and profitable time. I was in Grimsby when the Hull crowd arrived, and I could not but help comparing them with the football crowds of some years ago. There we had a well-dressed, respectable lot of fellows, amongst whom I noted some of our leading citizens. Only a small proportion wore favours, and tin whistles, rattles, and other instruments of torture were conspicuous by their absence.

There was not a lack of enthusiasm, however but it was not a noisy enthusiasm, the City supporters being, as a whole, an anxious body, who recognised the seriousness of the occasion. The information first announced in the 'Mail' that the Tigers had found a difficulty in fixing up a forward line had a disquieting effect, and whilst enthusiasm was high, optimism was not pronounced. The topics of conversation were the disastrous effect defeats would have on the Tigers' chances of promotion, and the fear that the rivalry between the teams might lead to dangerous tactics and further injuries to players. I do not know how many of the Tigers' supporters made the journey, but I do know that there was a large number on the Blundell Park ground, and out of the 10,000 present, fully 4,000 must have been 'in sympathy with' the Tigers. There are a large number of Hull natives residing in Grimsby and district, and they rolled up in brave numbers to encourage their favourites. On the whole it was a good-natured assembly, and one quite appreciated the cross chaff indulged in by the rival supporters. The Grimsby folk were more than confident, and it was rather annoying for us to hear the condescending remarks of our Grimsby friends 'Sorry you could not bring your full side, so as to make it a decent game'."

Following City's unexpectedly comfortable 3-1 win, the same journalist concluded his article:

"The Grimsby supporters willingly gave the Tigers the palm, and even wished them good luck. The journey home was performed by a happy party, Councillors, merchants, clerks, labourers were a happy and fraternal lot – and if anyone had dared to suggest another season in the Second Division he would have been pitched overboard."

AN UNEXPECTED SHOCK FOR THE MARINER.
The Grimsby Mariner hoped to take advantage of the Tigers' inability to field a full team, but was rudely disappointed.

City's triumph in adversity in the Humber Derby at Grimsby caught the popular imagination.

Grimsby had had an unbeaten home record with a miserly defence, and the Tigers' weakened side had gone there and upset the predictions with a superb performance, which must have even surprised many of the travelling fans. The emergence of a new goal-scoring forward the season after the sale of Fazackerly would have been a source of satisfaction (and relief) to the directors, lessening the impact of their decision to sell.

In a profile written in January 1914 – when Stevens was scoring with almost monotonous regularity to keep City's strong promotion push going – he is described thus:

"SAM" STEVENS AND HIS TRIPLETS
(Goals against Stockport County last Saturday.)

"STEVENS – THE 'CENTRE FORWARD.'

When Hull City transferred Tom Browell, his brother Andrew, and 'Stanley' Smith – you've heard of Joe? – to Everton, there was weeping and wailing and gnashing of teeth Anlaby-Rd way, and letter writers with pens loaded with vitriol were not slow to denounce the management as 'moneygrabbers'. But the passing of Time has changed all this, and I venture to think that those in authority, also the crowd – particularly that section of it which was the most indignant – would not exchange the present leader of the forward line, one, to wit, Samuel Stevens, for 'Boy' Browell at his best.

The Cradley Heath boy is a youth with the greed for goals flush in his veins, as witness his record to date of top scorer in the Second Division.

When he first came to Hull the boy was raw, a 'rough diamond,'

but they know talent when they see it up at 'The Lair', my masters, and the newcomer was, with the patience of Job, persevered with. That waiting policy is now being rewarded, as the 'goals for' column denotes. Stevens has practised the art of shooting, and on one occasion, I remember, at the recent Hull Fair, I was walking round the ground on a tour of inspection.

It was night, and the festival was in full swing. Passing a saloon where hungry-looking people and people not hungry looking, were devouring hot peas and the like with rapidity alarming. I came upon the subject of this sketch slamming a leather ball with his right foot past an astonished goalkeeper at one of the football side shows. After scoring the 'hat trick' innumerable times 'Samuel' went his way, and I had a chat with the somewhat amazed goalkeeper. When I informed him who the deadly marksman was he said – well, I won't tell you what he said! Centre forwards are scarce in this country, if they aren't in Scotland, yet the appellation of 'centre forward' to the name of Stevens is no misnomer. He slings the ball to the wings with judicious freedom, feeds his inside confreres with tact, and is ever ready, a' la Shepherd, for a dash between the backs, culminating in a shot of the "hot" description.

'Sometime-somewhere-someday' as the panto song says, Samuel Stevens will done the white shirt and blue knickers for England, as leader of the attack. Conjecture? Yes. 'But we shall see ---' etc."

Davy Gordon was also profiled in the same way by 'CWR' of the Hull Daily Mail. At this late stage of his career, he would still have been a very familiar sporting figure to the people of Hull:

"Hoots, Mon!

It has been asserted that when Duckworth, the right half of Manchester United, stepped on the field he only saw one man of his own side. From the kick-off to the final whistle, Duckworth's passes were all for Meredith. His one mission in life was to feed the great Welshman at every opportunity, and he was entirely oblivious to the claims of any other member of the team.

This is largely true. Certainly, the Duckworth-Meredith combination was something to marvel at; and, in a lesser degree, that indictment could be levelled against David Gordon, the subject of this 'portrait'.

When Gordon Wright, Hull City's – and England's – outside left, was such a scintillating figure at Anlaby-rd, 'Davy' Gordon used to play behind the great amateur, and those long sweeping passes of his were mostly for Hull City's captain. But the end justified the means.

Davy Gordon

side down at Ashton Gate, you can take it from me it won't be good old 'Davy'. I'll let you into a secret but don't tell anyone. It is this. David Gordon's one ambition is to see Hull City in the First Division, and, moreover to help them there THIS SEASON. Somehow, I think he'll succeed, – but what think you? CWR."

A more recent recruit to the Tigers' ranks was Patrick O'Connell, who had joined City in the Spring of 1912 from First Division Sheffield Wednesday. He had failed to establish himself there, making just 21 appearances in three years. Whether O'Connell became frustrated at Sheffield – or the South Yorkshire club decided to allow him to leave – did not matter to City, who made him a first team regular, wearing the number five shirt almost immediately. He very quickly found his feet at the heart of City's defence with his solid and skilful displays, and soon amassed more appearances for City than he had done in three years at Sheffield. His commanding performances for the Tigers did not escape the attentions of the Ireland selectors whilst he was at Sheffield, and he had been twice chosen to play for his country. In the Spring of 1914 the same selectors made him part of the victorious Irish team that won the Home Championship tournament outright for the first time, choosing him to play in all three games (against Wales, Scotland and England). Ireland's 3-0 victory against England at Middlesbrough was a celebrated achievement, and McConnell no doubt marshalled his defence against the home forwards. Written shortly after the England victory, this local newspaper profile of him pays tribute to his playing qualities as an attacking centre-half, and to City's good fortune in having acquired so talented a player for such a modest outlay:

"PATSY O'CONNELL OF IRELAND

In these days of huge, exorbitant transfer fees, when the condescending individual who performs the multifarious duties of secretary-manager, groundsman, gatekeeper, and trainer all rolled into one of the small village club informs you with an airy wave of the hand that 'Brown can be had for the paltry sum of £800,' or 'Jones is on the transfer list for a beggarly £1,000 – a mere nothing!' I often wonder, if he were assessed at his real value in lieu of present-day prices what Hull City would have to pay Sheffield Wednesday for O'Connell instead of the small sum of £250, which was the actual cost of the great Irishman when he was transferred from Hillsborough (then Owlerton) some time ago to Anlaby-rd.

As an attacking centre-half Patsy O'Connell has, I consider, no superior in England to-day. Those long, sweeping passes of his to the wings, or those short gliding tips to the inside forwards – all of them are gems of art; and when O'Connell has the ball at his feet it reminds me somewhat of clay in the potter's hands. His control is such that

As a club half, Gordon, who, as you might have probably guessed is a Scotchman, had few superiors in his prime, and during his long connection with the Tigers I can't remember him playing a really bad game. Although now the veteran of the team, 'Davy' is as enthusiastic as ever, kicking an old tin about on a piece of waste ground, as some players experience in an hour and a half's 'class' football.

His heart's in the game, you see. There was some talk, two seasons, of 'Davy' retiring, but across the Humber they are prepared to take a lease of his life, in a football sense, because at Blundell Park a week or two ago, Gordon exhibited all his old skill and ardour, and he was no mean factor in Hull City's success.

He has been coaching the Reserves a lot this season, but on Saturday he will doubtless journey to Bristol in the Second League match there, because O'Connell will be at Middlesboro', putting a check on the ambitions of Elliott, Shea and Co., I hope; and if any man lets the

Patsy O'Connell

you would verily think he had the leather sphere tied to his boot with a piece of string, and his wizardry makes a music hall conjuror or magician look sick in comparison.

Like all Hibernians, 'Patsy' is never at a loss for a word in an argument, or a witty retort at banter, but you will never see his friends indulging in chaff at O'Connell's expense, because they know he is bound to have the laugh at the finish. In the art of bluffing an opponent the Hull City centre-half has learned all there is to be taught, and in the words of our friends across the 'herring pond', he's 'all wool and a yard wide.'

On his day, O'Connell can make the finest centre-forward in Britain look foolish, he possesses the knack of putting a crowd in a good humour, and if your mind and thoughts are wandering from the field of play, and you hear a roar of laughter from the crowded banks, well, you can stake your bottom dollar that O'Connell has been 'giving the dummy again' because his humorous antics, like his Irish grin, are infectious.

On Saturday night, at Middlesbrough, Patsy O'Connell was the happiest man in all England, because for the second time in the history of International football 'the distressful Isle' had beaten England on her merits by three clear goals. The victorious side has defeated Wales but has yet to meet Scotland in the tournament, and O'Connell, as captain of the Irish eleven, very much hopes that the Championship will go to Ireland this year, and like the little boy in the Pears' Soap advertisement 'he won't be happy till he gets it.'

CWR."

P. O'CONNELL,
Centre Half, Hull City F.C.

O'Connell: "Who cares for Home Rule, says I, so long as I am sound again, says I."

"So happy did Patsy look that I really thought he had found a sixpence, but O'Connell contradicted this daring flight of imagination. The cause was far more important, and I feel assured my readers will join in O'Connell's jubilation. During a short chat, he informed me that, for the first time for some three seasons, he is quite sound."—"Saturn."

At the end of the season, O'Connell would leave the Tigers, and his house at 188 Perth Street, for Manchester, as United paid City £1,000 for his services. Little did Patsy know what the future held in store for him as he left West Hull – he would spend almost 30 years in Spain, managing no less than five clubs: Racing Santander (twice), Real Oviedo, Real Betis (twice) Barcelona and Sevilla. His association with Barcelona from 1935 to 1940 included a tour of North America in 1937 (when the Civil War raged in Spain and caused the suspension of La Liga). This provided sufficient funds to save the club, as it was paid a handsome sum to appear in friendly exhibition games at a time of anarchy and economic chaos in Spain. For this role in removing the players from their troubled homeland and securing some $15,000 in North America, O'Connell is seen by some to have safeguarded the existence of the club.

City's home game with Leeds City on February 21st assumed an immense importance as their erratic League form had reduced their advantage over some of the chasing teams, and raised new doubts about their promotion credentials. The Grimsby win had been followed by a home draw with Birmingham and an away defeat at Bristol City.

The brothers Harry and Herbert Chapman are the respective managers of the Hull City and Leeds City Football Clubs

The game against Leeds brought the Chapman brothers together, as respective managers of City (Harry) and the visitors (Herbert).

The captains meet at kick-off.

Other promotion hopefuls were also faltering. To counter this inconsistency and shore up their squad, City had signed Bury forward, Billy Cameron for £600, and Bradford City reserve forward Tommy Murray for £500. The outlay for these two players alone was more than the total outlay for signings in any other season. As well as providing cover, the hope was that these players would bolster the team and restore their wavering fortunes. It was also a statement of intent by the directors to the fans that they were deadly serious in their promotion ambitions, as many fans believed the club needed to spend freely to increase its chances of going up. The club was in effect challenging its local critics to respond at the turnstiles, as it was reputed that the fans would only turn up to watch a winning team or one that was backed financially by the directors.

The Leeds game drew some 20,000 to Anlaby Road – 8,000 up on the previous game. The attendance was approximate but was reckoned to be a record for the ground. The attraction of a Yorkshire Derby against a promotion rival captured the public imagination in West Yorkshire as well as locally, and the visitors were backed by a large number of travelling supporters. Spectators flocked into Hull

New signing Tommy Murray.   A cartoon of Billy Cameron.

from 'all parts of the East Riding, North Lincolnshire and even Grimsby' to provide receipts of £530 (more than the cost of Murray's transfer). They were not to be disappointed. A close game between two very evenly-matched sides ensued. Both showed enough quality and strength to suggest that they would not be out of place in the First Division. Cameron and Murray made a good impression, with the former playing a prominent attacking role whilst the latter was more peripheral and daintily skilful. The main City threat came from the left flank occupied by Halligan, who combined often and well with Cameron to provide a constant threat. The only goal of the game was scored by Sammy Stevens in his usual storming fashion – his 21st in 26 league games.

Leeds pressed hard for an equaliser in the final 15 minutes, laying siege to the City goal. Not for the first time Nick Hendry in goal was City's outstanding player as he kept the Peacocks' forwards at bay with a series of saves of every description. City were deemed slightly fortunate, on the balance of play, to have prevailed, but Hendry's defiance and Stevens' opportunism in the face of suffocating marking were no fluke. Leeds sportingly recognised this as such and their captain Spiers sought out Hendry at the end to shake his hand, as both sides went off to loud applause and cheers.

Pre-match optimism from Ern Shaw the cartoonist.

The Hull public had demonstrated that they would turn out in large numbers if the occasion warranted it. "Tradition counts, and Hull City are not a Club, as constituted, to put up with a 'hopeless' team", as the Hull Daily Mail put it when discussing the supporters' response at the turnstiles for the game. Their reporter 'Saturn' concluded his match report:

> "The result of the match, combined with Woolwich's defeat at Lincoln, places the Tigers in a strong position but the least slip will let in Woolwich, Leeds or Bradford. With our present side, however, I expect to see First Division on the Anlaby-rd ground next season."

Renowned national cartoonist Tom Webster's view of the Clapton game

Bob Hewitson

Struggling Glossop were then defeated 3-0 at Anlaby Road, with Sammy Stevens scoring a couple and new signing Billy Cameron getting off the mark. Outside-left Bob Hewitson (shown left) made his debut for the Tigers in this game. More injuries, more changes, more unfamiliar colleagues away to Lincoln in midweek as Halligan was injured. 'Tim' Wright was recalled for his first game since Boxing Day to be deployed on the right flank as City laboured to a draw at rejuvenated Lincoln. The draw obtained took City up to second place in the table.

The rapidly-faltering promotion charge took a further blow at Stockport on the following Saturday with a 2-1 defeat. The third defeat in four away games and only one point out of eight secured. The once formidable away record was becoming almost ordinary. The defeat put City in third place below Arsenal again and new signing Cameron was starting to be found wanting under press scrutiny. His impact had been negligible in his six games, With just one goal, he was also judged to lack sharpness and pace. His experience was not up for discussion, but his goal-scoring abilities were, as he was thought guilty of missing a host of point-gaining chances.

The bubble of optimism was soon punctured the following Saturday at Clapton. Like Grimsby, Clapton had an unbeaten home record; the 3-0 defeat they inflicted on the Tigers was the heaviest of the season and – worryingly – it was totally merited. Clapton seemed fitter, faster and more forceful than City, who went behind after only five minutes. The second consecutive away defeat was proof that injury, fatigue and inexperience were taking their toll. The new fullback pairing of Pattison and Morgan again appeared to be a weakness in the team.

For the following game the stale Morgan was dropped, and his partner Pattison's troublesome knee also kept him out. Expensive new signing Murray also aggravated an old injury, and after just two games would play no further part in the season – a disastrous investment from the club's viewpoint. Back came Davy Gordon, Jack McQuillan and the injury-prone Jack Lee, who had been out since the Woolwich Arsenal game.

Spoiling the Poor Tiger's Chance.
Bradford: "There, I've spoiled your chance! I'll bet she won't look at you now!"

The Tiger's advances thwarted by Bradford

On March 21st City hosted Bradford (Park Avenue) who spent a few days at Withernsea to prepare for the game. The West Yorkshire side had been steadily climbing the table to feature amongst the leading pack. Their momentum – aided by East Yorkshire ozone – was enough to see off a sorry City at a rain-soaked and muddy Anlaby Road. Although only the second home defeat of the season, the collapse of City's away form just as other clubs around them were raising their own, meant that their promotion bid was now virtually over. Irrespective of points, City yet again were clearly second best on the pitch to a rival who had taken the lead after only five minutes. Stevens scored a consolation goal as Bradford netted three. The defeat meant that City had now taken only eight points from the last ten games, and dropped five points in the last five at home. Mid-table form at best, and it meant that City lost touch with the leaders.

Indeed City's very next match was with 'top-of-the-table' Notts County. A boisterous contingent travelled by train from Hull as the fixture had been selected for the annual away outing for supporters, and they were determined to make the most of it. Unfortunately the home side were in no mood to enter the party spirit and the Tigers suffered a 4-1 defeat, which by all accounts flattered the hosts. Cameron again was unimpressive as Stevens was kept under strict surveillance, and City seemed to offer no real threat to the goal. With the spirited home forwards shooting at every opportunity, Hendry was beaten four times despite playing his usual excellent game in front of the travelling onlookers. "The Hull excursionists, if very quiet during the second half, had a good day. They were favoured with ideal weather, and painted Nottingham red. These Hull boys are a noisy lot when away from home."

Writing in the Hull Daily Mail the day after the Bury defeat, 'Saturn' penned perhaps the harshest article yet published on the club and its players, questioning their honesty and integrity as well as challenging them to provide some form of explanation for the abject surrender and dismal lack of effort shown the day before. Titling the article 'An Explanation Required – Hull City's Terrible Debacle – Supporters Disgusted', he wrote:

"Just so! Still one cannot make such statements in the Press. We may make moderate criticism, but the comments of many of Hull City's supporters were altogether 'too much' to appear in print. I can quite understand the frame of mind of the Tigers' supporters. To be buoyed up by false hopes often leads to shipwreck, and this is the experience of the loyal supporters of the Tigers. Before going further, let us consider the figures which the matches since the re-play in the Cup-tie at Bury have to offer

P	W	L	D	F	A	Pts
15	3	9	3	12	21	9

This is the record of a team which was first favourite for promotion! Even worse are the figures for the last eight matches:

P	W	D	L	F	A	Pts
8	0	6	2	3	13	2

Can one wonder that the loyal public, who pay their pass money, or who contribute to the 'gate" require an explanation. Last evening I heard many so-called "explanations,' but these were invariably merely abuse, which at any time is a very poor apology for argument or reason. Having had the so-called privilege of seeing the Tigers on so many occasions, I am asked to provide the required explanation, but unfortunately, I find myself quite as hopeless and helpless as the enquirers.

Prior to the cup-ties, the Tigers were a side worthy of promotion. Then followed a period when they were certainly the victims of circumstances, when injuries to players accounted for the loss of points. This particular period has long since expired, but we have failed to note any revival. Why and wherefore the best side in the Second Division should suddenly become most impotent side is one of the mysteries of fate as inscrutable as the 'Man in the Iron Mask.' I had a gleam of hope at Wolverhampton, where the players showed quite decent form, and where we were unfortunate in not sharing the points. Evidently that was a false alarm, and judging from yesterday's display, I must say that the Tigers are a hopeless case.

It is not necessary for me to give a complete review of the Bury match. The proceedings did not deserve special notice. It was too apparent that a goodly proportion of the team were playing for their own bat, and the side and the club were a secondary consideration. Thus it was that men who were desirous of being and were satisfied with being units in the eleven were the victims, and had to stand by and see their efforts spoiled by players who were attempting to glorify themselves.

The results were disastrous, and I for one absolutely refuse to make comments on individuals who were playing so selfishly. I cannot blame the players when I do not know the official position, but where I join with my readers is in asking – 'What is the explanation'?"

The new manager saw his team get off to a fair start before consolidating mid-season into genuine promotion prospects, but a poor last quarter of the season saw City fade badly, winning only one of their last ten games and scoring only one goal in their final six games to finish in seventh place, some eight points behind the second placed team. New inside forward Bill Halligan was unable to keep up with Sammy Stevens in the scoring stakes. Had he done so, City would almost certainly have gone up.

As the season neared an anticlimactic finish, worse was to come. At around midnight on the evening of Easter Monday (when City had lost at home to Bury), a fire was started in the Best Stand, which quickly spread and destroyed the entire western part of the stadium. No one was killed or injured, but many valuable items relating to the club and its early history were lost forever. Contemporary reports recount how suspicions fell on suffragettes, passing sparks from railway engines, disgruntled supporters, or even a mystery letter-writer with some grudge against the club. Most of the club's important items ('books, records, documents and valuables') were stored in a fireproof safe which 'fell asunder under the terrific heat, and its contents were reduced to ashes'. Chairman James Spring, speaking to the Hull Daily Mail, said:

"It's a difficult job, but we shall get over it. We have lost absolutely all our books and records which had been removed to these offices, and this will make it very awkward for us. We however, thought our important documents would be safe in the safe. How the fire originated we have not the slightest idea".

"You have an oil stove in the directors' room" – said the Mail. "Yes, – but it had nothing to do with it, for the stove was out hours before the fire. It is a fortunate thing we are nearly at the end of the season – we have only one more Second League match at home, that with Barnsley, on April 25th, and that with Sheffield United Reserves in the Midland League the previous Saturday. For these engagements we shall have to manage without the best stand, and we shall be able to clear the debris off the ground and erect some railings for the next match. We are covered by insurance ... and the re-erecting of a new stand will be considered at an early meeting of the directors."

THE "LAST STRAW" FOR THE POOR TIGERS.

After three successive defeats at Easter, Hull City's cup of sorrow was filled to the brim by the destruction by fire of the Grand Stand last night. Sympathy must be expressed with the hard-working Club officials, who have had such a heart-breaking termination to the season's working. Incendiarism is suspected, but the loss is covered by insurance.

The Daily News.
Hull Daily News, Hull Express, Grimsby Express, Hull Morning Telegraph and Evening News.

TELEPHONES: CENTRAL 4000 (4 lines)   TUESDAY, APRIL 14, 1914.   REGISTERED AT THE G.P.O. AS A NEWSPAPER

HULL CITY FOOTBALL CLUB GRANDSTAND BURNT DOWN.

(1) Showing the ruins of the main part of the stand. (2) The safe which was burnt out. (3) General view of the wreckage.—("News")

HULL CITY'S GRAND STAND DESTROYED.

Our photo shows the ruins from end to end of the Grand Stand of the Hull City Football Club, which was burnt down in the early hours of this morning.

Our To-day's Opponents.

Last Season's Results : Home, City 0-1; Away, City 1-2.

BARNSLEY are our very oldest opponents because we played them our first match here on September 2nd, 1905, and it is a matter of particular interest at the moment that practically the only relic we have of our early days is the football used on that day, which is yet in our ex-Secretary's (Mr. Haller's) office, and so was saved from the fate which befell all our other interesting mementoes in the disastrous fire on Easter Monday.

However, away with sentiment ; let's to the game. We defeated the Colliers 4—1 on our opening day, and until last season consistently managed to have the best of matters so far as their visits were concerned. As a matter of hard fact, we accumulated eighteen goals to two before the unexpected happened as above mentioned.

The programme's editorial in the next and final home game made little of the fire. William Duncan's shop at 15 Anlaby Road is a prominent advertiser on the same page.

The City chairman then responded to the journalist's enquiry about the loss of a collection of items in the safe, by saying:

"We have lost all this" ... "Our collection, as you will be aware, included the first sixpence taken at the turnstiles, and we had a fine series of photographs of the team from the commencement. One of the most interesting was a photo group including those early favourites., such as Tom Jones, Spence, and other veterans. Several mascots sent along to the club, including one presented by the Hull Forge, were also devoured."

The fire and the swollen wage bill were becoming an unsustainable financial burden, and the club had to make drastic economies. The consequences of ambitious financing of another failed promotion attempt required immediate action, as James Spring had hinted the previous September.

On the eve of the final home game, the retained list was announced and many familiar faces departed. O'Connell, who had made public his desire to be transferred, was to join Manchester United. Jack McQuillan was another who had come to the end of his time at Anlaby Road, as he refused the terms offered to him. His partner Tommy Nevins had already been informed that his services would no longer be required next season – his recent benefit payment of £175 no doubt sweetening the parting of the ways.

Sentiment was not clouding the vision of the directors, as Davy Gordon was released after acting in a semi-managerial capacity with the reserve team all season. Having rendered such long and loyal service to the club who had paid £60 for him, the club gave him some letters of their appreciation of his services, and a free transfer.

Nor was Arthur Temple retained, after seven years of service as a goal-scoring forward capable of dashing runs. The removal of his cartilage seemed to signal a decline in his effectiveness, and like his colleagues, his undoubted experience and proven ability was deemed not to be worthy of continued employment at Anlaby Road.

Only one first team game remained that season, which was staged in front of the smallest crowd of the season (5,000) as any promotion aspirations had already gone up in smoke like the Best Stand.

What had promised to become a memorable season with a thrilling climax, had not only turned into a major disappointment, but also a minor disaster. The only consolation it seemed, was that the club had the summer to rebuild their grandstand in time for the 1914 season.

This Tigers' team never actually played together, but would have possessed a formidable attacking prowess.

Ted Roughley

Tommy Nevins

Jack McQuillan

Davy Gordon

Tim Wright

E.G.D. Wright

Charlie Best

Bert Goode

Stan Fazackerley

Sammy Stevens

Tommy Browell

O.H.M.S.

Wanted, 1,000 Athletes

and other followers of Sport.

Recruiting Now Proceeding

for the

3rd Hull (Service) Battalion

East Yorkshire Regiment.

If You Mean to
PLAY THE GAME
Join at Once.

CITY HALL

Open Daily 10 to 10.

HULL CITY F.C. NEW STAND.

Building the new grand stand at the Hull City Ground. It is designed and built by Messrs J. H. Carr and Sons —"News."

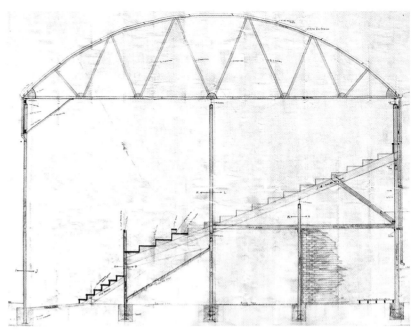

Left – the new stand under construction in August 1914. Above – a section-plan of the new Best Stand. Below – a section of the floor-plan.

Following the fire which had destroyed the Best Stand in April 1914, a replacement was taking shape in time for the start of the new season. J.H. Carr and Sons of nearby Cholmley Street (the contractors for the original stand) had constructed a replacement, which outwardly resembled its predecessor. Nevertheless, it was evidently fit for purpose at the time, and admired enough for its successor to be modelled on it. Note from the plan shown bottom right however, that the away team had less than half the amount of changing room space that Hull City enjoyed; the 'visitors room' is shown on the right of the plans, which Carr & Sons drew in May 1914. As well as the Home dressing room and that of the Visitors, the rear of the stand also housed individual offices for the club Secretary, Directors and a Referee/Linesmen's dressing room. Towards the front of the stand (across the concourse) there was a Groundsman's room, one for the Assistant Secretary and Gatemen, and directly opposite the Home dressing room, a room for the Trainer.

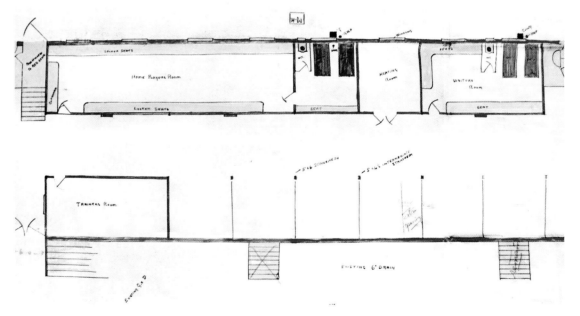

The new stand had a 3,500 seating capacity and room for 1,500 standing spectators. Innovations included 400 tip-up seats in the centre of the stand, which were numbered and reserved. These were flanked on either side by 200 tip-up seats that were not numbered or reserved.

HULL CITY PLAYERS, 1914-15.

Top Row.—H. Taylor, J. Middlehurst, B. Gibson, A. Dagnall T Hodgkiss, and W. Wright.
Middle Row.—Mr F. J Stringer (director), C. Deacy, Lee, S Stevens N Hendry, D. Melville, J. Pattison, A. C. Betts, and D. Menzies (trainer).
Bottom Row —D. Mercer, W. S. Cameron, J. Eddleston, D. Morgan, W Halligan (captain), H. Turner, and C. Best (assistant trainer).

—Photo by Duncan, Hull

This rare image of the 1914-15 squad shows David Menzies as trainer in the absence through illness of manager Harry Chapman, and Fred Stringer representing the directors. Billy Halligan is captain and long-serving Tim Wright is still in the group, joined on the back row by the unfamiliar names of Middlehurst, Gibson, Dagnall and Hodgkiss. With a rapidly-escalating European crisis overshadowing everything else, the public's appetite for football was diminishing on a daily basis and this photograph appeared when many supporters' thoughts were on the events overseas.

Back row: James Middlehurst, B. Gibson, A. Dagnall, T. Hodgkiss and Tim Wright. Middle row: Fred G. Stringer (director), Charles Deacy, Jack Lee, Sammy Stevens, Nick Hendry, David Melville, John Pattison, Arthur Betts, and David Menzies (trainer). Front row: David Mercer, Billy Cameron, Joe Edelston, Douglas Morgan, Billy Halligan (captain), and Henry Turner. Seated on the ground: Charlie Best.

Director Fred Stringer was starting to play a more prominent role in footballing matters and was now closely associated with the players, often in a custodial role alongside the manager. He had been profiled in a

newspaper feature a few months earlier and revealed something of his history in local football, both as a player and administrator, as well as how his commercial activities assisted the club in its foreign trips:

"Besides occupying the position of 'head' of local soccer, Mr Stringer is a director of the City Club to which he acts as guide, philosopher, & friend during its sojourns on the Continent, and is an old player of some repute. His credentials, therefore, are of the highest.

'To go back to the beginning,' said Mr Stringer, 'is like dipping into the realms of antiquity. Twenty-two years ago – that is the extent of my football life so far – five clubs was Hull's contribution to the soccer world. But they were good clubs, as the names St.Paul's, Kingston Amateurs, Albany. East Hull and Dairycoates Loco will prove. East Hull, who afterwards changed their name to Hull Albion, was my first love. I played full-back for them. We had a good side. We once went for a season and a half, without having a goal scored against us at home.

We owed this largely to our goalkeeper, Peter Simpson, whom members of the old St. Paul's club will remember we 'persuaded' to leave them and join us.'
– Trophies?
'Yes; we played for a cup which I begged from the Sunlight Soap people, and which the East Riding Association still possess.'
– Now I should like to hear your experiences in the management of the game:
'Well, I was in at the birth of the East Riding Association. It was I who called the meeting which ultimately decided to form a league. I was made the first secretary of that league. Put it another way, I was the first official of what is now the E.R.C.F.A. In those days we had to affiliate with the Scarborough and District Association. We were not a separate Association. When the time was ripe for that, I was appointed one of the deputation to wait upon the Commission (Messrs Crump, Woolfall, and Wall), who came to Hull to see if we were a properly constituted body, and if we were capable of becoming a fully-fledged County Association.'
– And you have been in harness ever since?
'Yes'."

HULL ALBANY AN ELEVEN 1906-7

Two early Albany team photographs by Frank Overton (top) and R.T. Watson (bottom)

Stringer then went on to discuss the club's end of season trips by boat across the North Sea to play matches in the Low Countries or Scandinavia and the benefits of these visits:

"– Why do you organise these tours? 'My business makes me acquainted with the Continent, and naturally I am interested in it.'
– What benefit do the players get out of it? 'Benefit indeed! Merely a broadening of the mind. Most English people that we are the only pebbles on the beach. The only way to dispel that illusion is for them to go on the Continent. Then they find that the other nations are quite as wide awake and as full of progress as ourselves.'
– And what is the benefit generally? 'I firmly believe that football among the nations will eventually do more to foster and maintain a peaceful spirit among them than all the treaties signed and to be signed'."

Alas such idealistic sentiments were in sharp contrast to events rapidly unfolding in mainland Europe, which obliged most nations to honour treaties of military assistance against aggressive acts by other nations. In this way, treaties and pacts formulated to ensure peace and stability became obligations to join conflicts.

On Saturday September 15th 1914, with recruitment for the war gathering momentum, a meeting was held at the Park Street Artillery Barracks to recruit 'athletes' into a third battalion of Hull Pals, similar to those already recruited for the first ('commercials') and second ('tradesmen'). A powerful and persuasive coalition of military, religious, sporting and civic dignitaries was assembled to address interested men. This group comprised City's Ernest Morison as president, supported by the Lord Lieutenant (Lord Nunburnholme), the Hon. F.S. Jackson (the famous Yorkshire and England cricketer), Cyril C. Lempriere

OVER THE ARSENAL.

The Divers descended on the Gunners at Highbury to-day.

The onset of war brought patriotic and bellic tone to many cartoons. Above, a game at Plumstead against Woolwich Arsenal is an excuse to feature an airship and the south east London munitions centre. Below, another Ern Shaw cartoon depicts the Tiger, the Airlie Bird and the Rover resplendent in their uniforms (of sorts).

MOBILISED !

(the former Hull FC wing three-quarter from the 1890s), Colonel Lambert White, Dr T.C. Jackson (Under Sheriff), the Rev. A.C. England, Major Scaum, Mr. John Watson J.P., Mr. A.J. Boynton J.P., (the Hull FC chairman), Mr. J. Spring (City's chairman), Mr. F.G. Stringer (City director and member of the East Riding County Football Association), and others. The group took it in turns to put their case to the men, appealing to their sporting instincts, their patriotism and their sense of duty, amid enthusiastic cheers from the men themselves.

Local bodies volunteered their facilities; Mr. A.J. Goodinson, secretary of Hull CC offered the use of the Circle and its stands to the military. Mr. Boynton of Hull said (to cheers) that his club would stop playing 'next week' if he thought that their programme of matches was preventing even one young man enlisting, adding that the Boulevard too would be at the disposal of the military and that two of his own sons had enlisted. The City chairman added that his own son, too, had joined up, and was of the opinion that football matches were not the place for young men who were eligible for the army.

Recruiting opened at the City Hall the following Monday and prominent advertisements were taken out in the local press to support this drive, as men were encouraged to present themselves for the cause. 'I want you all' – was the unambiguous recruiting message of Lord Kitchener shown here – 'these are not times for sport and pleasure'. Despite these patriotic calls to arms, a counter opinion existed that life should continue as normal, and that sports events should not be affected. As the war dragged on, more and more men were drawn into the conflict and inevitably – 'business as usual' – was just not possible.

HULL ATHLETES AND THE EMPIRE CALL.

NEW BATTALION FORMED.

Lord Kitchener's Stirring Message.

"I WANT YOU ALL."

Duty must be first! These are not times for sport or pleasure. There is but one game—and that for every able-bodied young man in the country. It is the game of war: the stakes are the honour of our nation and the suppression of military arrogance any tyranny. To arms, then, every man who calls himself British! The country needs every single one of you, and none more than the young athletes of our cities. Aside with playthings; the gun and the sword alone can safeguard that which is dearest and most sacred to us all.

To this clarion call the athletes of Hull have responded most nobly, and on Tuesday the large room at the Grosvenor was densely packed with an eager, ready crowd of sturdy young men ready to sacrifice pleasure to duty. They will form the neuclens of the 8th Battalion of the E.Y. Regiment.

The first men recruited under this campaign – the 'Sportsmen' or 'Athletes' – were shown on the front page of The Daily News of Tuesday September 15th. These men were being drilled on the pitch at the Anlaby Road ground, together with a picture of new adjutant, Major Harrison which is reproduced here.

This photograph appears to be taken at the same time as the postcard shown below it. The position of the camera is more or less identical and some of the men are clearly visible on both pictures. The photographic postcard offers a rare panoramic view of two sides of the Anlaby Road ground, complete with advertising, and the nearby railway sheds behind the covered north stand. The north stand goal posts are still visible on the left of the picture. As for the football ground, apart from the goalposts, there is an expansive view of the covered standing accommodation of this rather basic 'enclosure', adorned with advertisers such as G. F. Hohenrein and Son, one of the dozens of German pork butchers resident in the city. Many of these were later to have their businesses attacked as feelings ran high after German Zeppelin bombing raids had inflicted damage and loss of life on Hull's citizens. The Hull Brewery also advertises its products claiming that 'Win lose or draw, you'll enjoy' its ales.

On the back, someone has written "You will find me the ninth on the front rank, the one in the straw hat" – no address or signature. Neither does the card bear the name of a photographer or issuer. As for the calibre of these new recruits one 2nd Lieutenant B. L. Pearson found that the:

> "... men were generally speaking a sound and very hardy lot, mostly recruited from the Hull Docks area and including some members of a body known as 'The Silver Hatchet Gang', which had made for itself in peacetime quite a reputation for violence in the dockland."

As the men cast shadows towards the east side of the ground, with the sun in the west, it suggests the picture was taken in the late afternoon.

DRILLING THE ATHLETES' BATTALION

Major Harrison, the new adjutant of the Athletes' Battalion; 2. Drilling the battalion on the ground of the Hull City F.C.

HULL CITY A.F.C 1914

DOUGLAS MORGAN (Hull City.)

Captured above in their training kit on a fine October day in front of the pavilion at the Circle, are (left to right): Billy Cameron, David Mercer, Charlie Deacey, Henry Turner, Nick Hendry and Joe Edelston. A bare-footed and grinning John Pattison can be seen behind Mercer and Morgan on a bicycle, which may belong to the man in the suit and straw boater wearing bicycle-clips to the right of Joe Edelston, who is also holding a pipe in his right hand. Some drying laundry items are placed on the benches in front of the pavilion. Flanking the group to the left is another unidentified man in a straw boater. A closer scrutiny of the photo reveals a variety of sporting footwear (as well as bare feet) including spiked running shoes, football boots and plimsolls.

Despite the war the players seem relaxed and happy, perhaps realising that a day spent training on the Circle is preferable to time spent in military uniform.

Shown top-right is Douglas Morgan, left-back for Hull City and a soldier in the Royal Garrison Artillery. Having made his debut in 1913, he was in his second season with the Tigers when the war started. This cartoon portrait from February 1915 depicts a defender who loved to maraud. Morgan was killed in action on New Year's Day in 1917 and is buried in Vlamertinghe Military Cemetery, just outside Ypres in Belgium.

The worsening situation in France and Belgium continued to influence attitudes to the continuation of the football programme. In November the Football Association itself entered the fray with a poster to be displayed at all football grounds. It was headed "An Appeal to Good Sportsmen" with "Football Players and Spectators" as a sub-title, and the wording was:

"The need for more recruits for our army is very urgent. Appeals should not be necessary. Every man must know his duty to himself and his country. There are approximately three millions of men with no family responsibility playing in and watching football matches. I ask these to show they are good sportsmen and to enlist now and help other good sportsmen who are so bravely fighting England's battle against the world's enemy.

F.J. WALL.
(Secy., Football Association)."

The Tigers embarked upon their FA cup campaign in early January at home against First Division side West Bromwich Albion. On a heavy pitch the Midlands team played the more sophisticated football, but the conditions favoured the more simple and robust style of the home side. As a result City carved out more chances in the first half and visiting goalkeeper Pearson was kept fully occupied. A well-taken goal before half time by Sammy Stevens – as he cut in following Mercer's pass a dozen yards from the corner flag – enabled City to lead at half time. The Tigers forward:

> "… forged his way to the goal mouth, and, though he looked like being dispossessed at every stride, he kept control and carried the ball right in front of Pearson, whom he deceived with a flick of the foot, and into the net the ball went, accompanied by tumultuous cheering."

Goalkeeper Nick Hendry was the busiest and best Tigers player, playing with what was described as 'bulldog tenacity, feline perspicacity and unfailing sagacity'. As the game wore on he became busier and busier as City became pinned down, in and around their own penalty area. The last ten minutes was a virtual siege of the Tigers' goal as Hendry repelled all efforts to score, and the final whistle signalled loud cheering by the 13,000 fans – a mixture of jubilation and relief.

A pre-arranged (regardless of result) dinner that night at the Grosvenor Hotel saw the directors entertaining the whole of the playing squad. A predictably convivial and boisterous occasion ensued in view of the victory a few hours earlier. Captain Bill Halligan responded to the directors' toast and struck a cordial note saying "We players are doing

Mr and Mrs Proctor, the new manager and manageress of the Grosvenor Hotel, Hull.

Mine Host Ernest Proctor and his Wife.

all we can for our directors because they are a jolly good lot of employers."

The draw for the second round paired City with Northampton, again at Anlaby Road. If the West Bromwich game saw the Tigers facing more sophisticated opposition, this game was to prove an ugly and scrappy game, often lacking technique or finesse. The ball was frequently up in the air and the visitors played a predictably energetic and vigorous game, in keeping with the cut-and-thrust tradition of the tournament. Sammy Stevens scored five minutes after half-time, displaying fine control and speed, before adding a second after Lee and Halligan had skilfully

The win against West Bromwich allowed Ern Shaw free rein to portray some of the main protagonists, in a series of little vignettes that conveyed his impressions of the tie.

After West Brom, the Cobblers of Northampton were City's next opponents. Ern Shaw invents the latest Tiger guise of a hopeful young customer in a cobbler's shop.

JACK LEE (Hull City.)

Jack Lee was prominent in the
West Bromwich cup game.

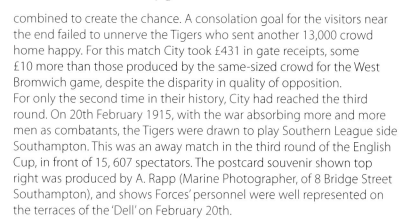

combined to create the chance. A consolation goal for the visitors near
the end failed to unnerve the Tigers who sent another 13,000 crowd
home happy. For this match City took £431 in gate receipts, some
£10 more than those produced by the same-sized crowd for the West
Bromwich game, despite the disparity in quality of opposition.
For only the second time in their history, City had reached the third
round. On 20th February 1915, with the war absorbing more and more
men as combatants, the Tigers were drawn to play Southern League side
Southampton. This was an away match in the third round of the English
Cup, in front of 15, 607 spectators. The postcard souvenir shown top
right was produced by A. Rapp (Marine Photographer, of 8 Bridge Street
Southampton), and shows Forces' personnel were well represented on
the terraces of the 'Dell' on February 20th.

The local newspapers of the day gave admirable coverage to the tie,
sparing the interested reader no detail in the build-up to the game,
informing readers in Hull on the day before the match of the Tigers'
preparations in Worthing, where they had gone, as they usually did
when playing a cup-tie in the south. This was the fifth time in eight years
that City had used the Central Hotel in the Sussex resort as their base.
City director Bob Mungall paid for the club's stay at the hotel himself.
(Mungall's generosity had already manifested itself in the form of a £1,000
loan for the repair and reconstruction of the main stand the previous

summer, and he duly became a director. Having only arrived in the city
in 1909 from Scotland, Mungall quickly became involved in the coal-
exporting activities, which formed an important and lucrative part of the
commercial life of the Third Port; firstly with D.M. Stevenson and Co., Ltd.,
and then in partnership with a Mr. Wadsworth. No doubt he would have
been acquainted with City director James Barraclough and new director
Erik Ohlson, as all three worked in the coal-exporting, timber-importing
and/or shipping sectors.

As the players prepared, they could not have failed to notice the
wounded French and Belgian soldiers who had been evacuated to
the English coast from the Western Front. Injured Indian soldiers were
stationed at Brighton just along the coast and journeyed into Worthing
by car. Slowly but surely the war was becoming impossible to ignore.
Regarding the expected attendance at the game, a local paper opined:

"If the military element were given facilities to be present, there would
doubtless be an enormous attendance, but owing to reasons I am not
at liberty to explain, the majority will be unable to be present It is
the same with the club's supporters in the outside districts. The train
services are so liable to be strung up that it is unsafe to make a journey."

In the same paper on the following Monday after the 2-2 draw, it was reported that the match saw 'a better gate than was anticipated' and that: 'Included amongst the spectators were a lot of soldiers who hailed from the North, and they gave the Tigers every encouragement.'

The Tigers based themselves at Scarborough to prepare for the replay which was to be played in Hull the following Saturday. In the sharp wintry weather at the North Yorkshire resort, amid blue skies and light snow showers, the players enjoyed the picturesque views from the Prince of Wales Hotel on the South Cliff and the steep walks to and from the beach. Again, the generosity of director Mungall paid for the sojourn. Training consisted of 'kicking, sprinting and long walks' on the sands. David Menzies was now acting as Trainer to the team and possessed a level of medical expertise useful in treating injured and recovering players. Director Ernest Morison's advertising agency in Lowgate was selling reserved seat tickets for the game at 2s 6d.

After a goal-less first half, City went ahead in the opening minute of the re-start. Sammy Stevens weighed in with a couple more to put the

Tigers in an unassailable position after 70 minutes. City had finally got the measure of their stubborn opponents by using long balls to the flanks to utilise the pacey Lee and Mercer. The visitors collapsed and a further goal by Lee completed the rout. The fourth round (the last eight) now beckoned.

The following Monday, the players once more packed their bags and journeyed to a coastal resort. The reward for beating Southampton was an away tie at Bolton Wanderers, and the training preparations would take place at Blackpool. This time the players made their base at Cleveley's Hydro. Taking advantage of the brine and other baths on offer, the Tigers group eased away their aches and pains accumulated in the Southampton games in anticipation of the stiff task presented to them by a trip to Burnden Park. Playing for a place in the semi-finals, City succumbed to a vigorous and aggressive Bolton side playing on their own pitch with an inexperienced referee (a Mr. Sephton). Mr. Sephton awarded two disputed penalties against the visitors in as many minutes after half time, effectively ending the Tigers' chances.

AN EXCITING MELEE IN THE VISITORS' GOAL, WITH MERCER, HALLGAN, AND LEE MANŒUVRING FOR POSITION.—(" News.")

Mercer and Halligan threaten the visitors' goal in the third round replay at Anlaby Road on Saturday February 27th.

"Don't Stop Me!"

Don't stop me – Captain Billy Halligan with Wembley in his sights, rushes past Bolton with a spread-eagled Saint in his wake, and a bag of money in his hand.

City had led by two goals after 20 minutes but had subsequently been pegged back to a draw by half time. Bolton's muscular approach seemed to go unnoticed by the official and this may have contributed to the Tigers' lack of composure in front of goal. Even with a two-goal deficit, City continued to carve out chances – and waste them. Their lack of polish in front of goal was the only blemish in an otherwise plucky and resilient display. But four goals conceded told its own story.

With their semi-final hopes ended, the Tigers could turn once again to the league, where their lowly position owed much to their continued involvement in the cup. The backlog of mundane fixtures was duly tackled. First were Lincoln City – hammered 6-1 at Anlaby Road in front of just 3,000 spectators. Glossop were routed 5-0 the next week, on their own ground in front of only 500 people.

Indifferent and unpredictable results were played out in front of rapidly dwindling gates, as the season slowly petered out against the backdrop of a worsening war situation and mass mobilisation of the men who had formed the crowds, and in some cases played in the teams they came to watch. The final three home games against Huddersfield Town, Glossop, and Grimsby Town were watched by crowds of 2,000, 2000 and 3,000 respectively.

The financial implications of this, as well as the heightening sense of national crisis were evident as shareholders convened in late June at the Grosvenor Hotel for the shareholders' AGM. The scheduled start was delayed until a quorum of 20 shareholders was obtained, which no doubt added to the atmosphere of disarray and unease.

Our To-day's Opponents.

LAST SEASON'S RESULTS: CITY, home, 0—0; away, 4—0.

LEICESTER FOSSE have had a most disastrous season and are certain to finish in the bottom pair. This is most regrettable as the Fosse have an honourable record and have figured in the First Division. They only had one season, however,—1907-8—amongst the select company and have had to since be content with Second Division fare. Leicester Fosse are one of the teams who have yet to gain a victory on our ground. They have visited us on eight previous occasions, City winning four, with four drawn games. At Leicester the returns are, City three, Leicester five, draws one. Last season at Leicester our team won in sensational fashion by four clear goals, but this season we had to be content with a solitary point.

CITY CLUB CHATTER.

"A fair field and no favour."

The page above from the programme against Leicester, shows an advertisement for Billy Duncan's studio and the members of the board, who as well as the more established members, now included Erik Ohlsen (sic), the then Sheriff of Hull.

Ohlsen (shown above right) was the son of a farmer from Fellingsbro in Sweden, who had started in business in Hull in 1902 and had steadily risen to commercial and civic prominence through exporting coal, importing timber and shipping. His enthusiasm for sport extended to becoming president of the Exporters Cricket and Football Club. In 1915 he was knighted and created a Baronet of Scarborough five years later in recognition of his efforts to bring Sweden into the War on Britain's side. Other members included (Alderman) George Hall, a former Mayor and J.P.

The Annual General Meeting was presided over by City's chairman James Spring JP, who was supported by the following:

R.H. Mungall (vice chairman)
Sir Erik Ohlsen
J. W. Locking
Mr H. S. Holden
J. H. Bielby
Dr G. W. Lilley JP
T. W. Shaw
and George Neale
– who were all directors.
Plus F. G. Stringer (secretary)
Mr Gosschalk (solicitor)
and Councillor W. Lofthouse (auditor).

Ernest Morison, for so long an active and participating director, had accepted an army commission and the assembled shareholders wished him a safe and successful time in the hope that they would see him again soon. The stark financial reality of the season was then dissected. A loss on the year of £1,687 5s 3d was recorded, and the cause of this adverse balance was no doubt the war. No club had made any profit and none had expected to do so. City's gate receipts were greatly reduced when compared to the preceding season's matches.

ERIK. O. OHLSEN, Esq.
(Sheriff of Hull).

The generosity of director Bob Mungall was recorded and greatly appreciated, with specific regard to his contribution of £1,000 towards the building of a replacement grandstand, and the special training at the coast before the cup-ties. In previous seasons the Board had paid for this but this season they were unable to do so. The club had played with the smallest number of players it had ever had on its books and despite this handicap, the team enjoyed a very successful cup run and satisfactory league-placing. More players might have ensured a higher league position but inflating the wage bill, at a time of declining attendances and receipts, was not a course of action the Board wished to pursue. But the club had no argument with people who did not care to come and watch football and accepted that young men had an overriding duty to their country.

The year's loss of £1,687 5s 3d, when added to the existing debt, made a total of £4, 723 14s 8d.

Fred Stringer told the assembly that the future of organised league football would be debated the coming weekend at Blackpool, as leading representatives of the Football League, the Scottish and Southern met to discuss whether to continue playing next season.

"TOMMIES" AT THE FOOTBALL MATCH.

A SMALL SECTION OF THE CROWD AT THE HULL CITY MATCH WITH PRESTON. A GREAT NUMBER OF THE MEN IN KHAKI WERE AMONG THE SPECTATORS.—"NEWS."

Soldiers at the Birmingham game at Anlaby Road on October 17th 1914 and the Preston match in March 1915.

SOLDIERS AT HULL CITY MATCH

A large number of soldiers in uniform were to be seen among the spectators at the Hull City match

James Spring made the final speech of a reflective meeting as he replied to Fred Stringer's words. He lamented the poor numbers through the gates, and the financial pressure that that had exerted on the directors. At the same time, the very existence of the country was at stake and it was felt that they ought to do everything they could to induce young men to join the army. Football was only a third consideration. It was noted that Hull had done very well as regards recruits and that they compared very favourably with other cities of a similar size. During the coming season, it would be their wish that the Board would strive to provide football matches if they could be played without detriment to the country. He believed the Football Association and the Leagues would devise some scheme whereby they would be enabled to continue playing. Spring noted:

> "If we do – we don't want to see any slackers at our matches. We would rather they stopped away. There are plenty of elderly, men and women who come to our matches, without a lot of young men. Their place is not watching football matches but at the front."

Many of these men who were now being exhorted to enlist were the very people whom the club had battled to attract to the early games in 1904, when as a fledgling organisation, it had sought to sway open-minded sports-enthusiasts to rally to its cause. Now the message was very different; the club was actively encouraging its fans to stay away and do their duty.

The end of the 1914-15 season for City was the ending of a period of optimism, growth and innocence which had started some eleven years earlier. National concerns far greater than football engulfed the club, the game and the country. Footballing activities would be drastically scaled down as travel became problematic under wartime conditions and spectator numbers dwindled. Many of the men who had frequented the Anlaby Road ground on Saturday afternoons never returned, having perished on the Western Front. They would never again enjoy the camaraderie and wit of the Spion Kop, or the warmth and shelter of the Best Stand. Their untroubled pursuit of sporting glory gave way to a grimmer and more desperate wartime life, and unlike the club, their battle to survive the conflict would be lost.

Stringer believed that football would continue – probably with teams playing local friendlies, allowing players to work in support of the war effort during the week. Acting as secretary-manager, Stringer played an increasingly prominent role in the running of the club. He was close enough to the players, having accompanied them on foreign tours, and as a Hull merchant, he had his own produce business. A former player who became a local football administrator, Stringer was to play a pivotal role in the war as unofficial 'caretaker' of the club, ensuring its well-being.

Fred Stringer, assisted by Jack Bielby, would navigate the club through uncharted waters as David Menzies (who had taken over the trainer's role from Harry Taylor in June 1914) became increasingly involved in looking after the players. These men ensured that the club continued to function throughout and after the war, and that the endeavours of the original founders had not been in vain; their ambitions and vision would be preserved, their quest for success, for the time being at least, unfulfilled.

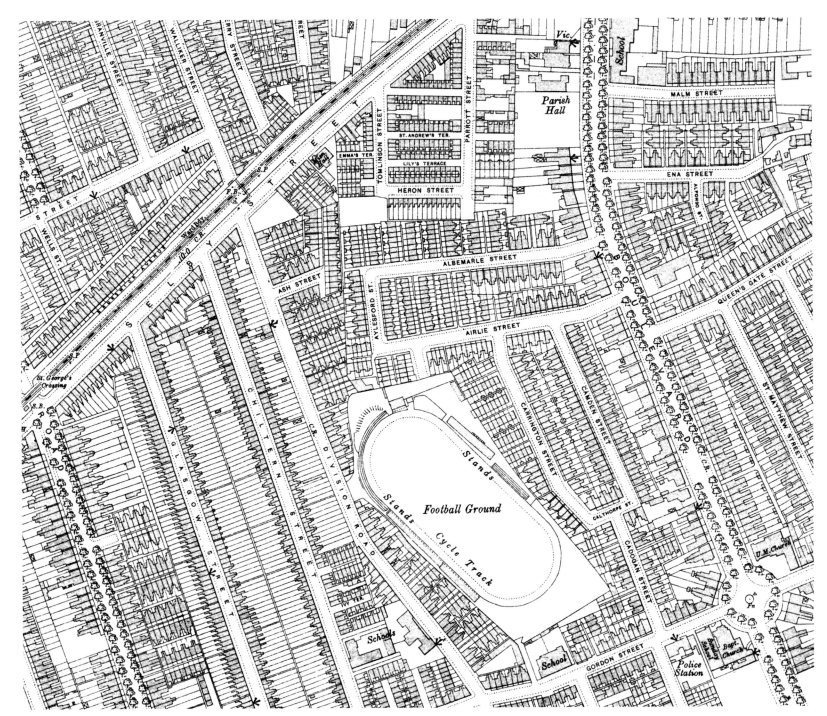

The maps shown on pages 190-191 are adjoining sections, edited from the 1911 Ordnance Survey plans of Hull. Above is an area south of Anlaby Road showing the Boulevard, where Hull City played from 1904 until 1905.

On the following page is the area directly north, where Hull City's later ground can be seen alongside the Hull Cricket Club grounds, to the east of West Park.

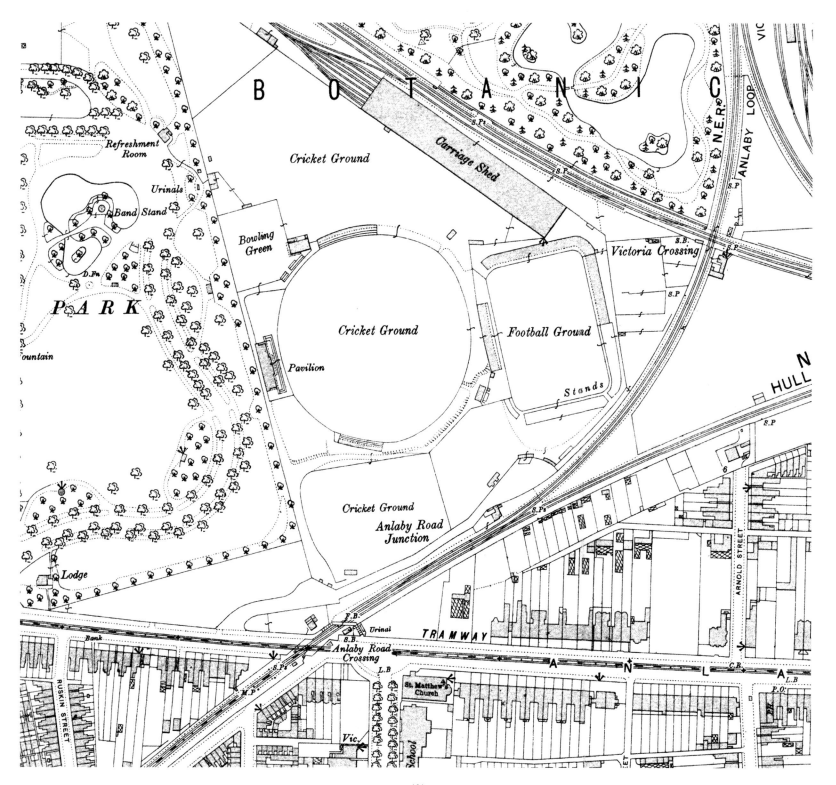

B O T A N I C

PARK

Refreshment Room

Urinals

Band Stand

D.Fn

Fountain

Cricket Ground

Bowling Green

Carriage Shed

S.P.

S.P.

S.P.

N.E.R.

ANLABY LOOP

VIC

S.B.

S.P.

Victoria Crossing

S.P.

Cricket Ground

Pavilion

Football Ground

Stands

HULL

S.P.

Cricket Ground

Anlaby Road Junction

S.P.

6

ARNOLD STREET

Lodge

F.B.

S.B.

Urinal

TRAMWAY

A   N   L   C.R.   A

L.B.

St. Matthew's Church

L.B.

P.O.

Bank

RUSKIN STREET

S.P.

M.P.

Anlaby Road Crossing

L.B.

Vic.

School

Brief Bibliography

Football – the Rugby Union game.
Rev. F. Marshall (Ed), Cassell & Co. 1892.

Men of the City.
J. O'Hara, Hull City & County Printing Company. Hull, 1914.

A Who's Who of Hull City AFC.
C. Elton, Hutton Press. Cherry Burton, 1984.

A Century of City.
M. Peterson, Yore Publications. Harefield, 2005.

Hull Pals; 10th, 11th, 12th and 13th (Service) Battalions of the East Yorkshire Regiment – A History of the 92nd Infantry Brigade, 31st Division, 1914-19.
D. Bilton, Wharncliffe Books. Barnsley, 1999.

Hull and East Yorkshire Trade Directories (various).

The Hull Daily Mail

The Hull Times

The Hull Daily Mail Sports Mail

The Hull Daily News

The Hull Sports Express

Acknowledgments

The edited maps on pages 190-192 are courtesy of the Ordnance Survey.

The edited plans of the new stand on page 178 are courtesy of the Hull History Centre.

The chapter title image on page 25, and the photograph of the cyclists on page 47, are courtesy of Hull Museums.

My thanks go to the staff of the Hull History Centre, and the staff of the British Library Newspaper Archive, Colindale.

Special thanks also go to Paul Gibson, Stuart Quinn and Katherine Reidel.